Representation, Subversion, and Eugenics in Günter Grass's *The Tin Drum*

In receiving the Nobel Prize for Literature in 1999, Günter Grass finally gained recognition as Germany's greatest living author. If there is one book in post-1945 German literature that is known throughout the world, it is Grass's novel *The Tin Drum* (1959), which remains one of the most important works of literature for the construction of postwar German identity. Peter Arnds offers a completely new reading of this novel, analyzing an aspect of Grass's literary treatment of German history that has never been examined in detail: the Nazi ideology of race and eugenics, which resulted in the persecution of so-called asocials (including the physically and mentally handicapped, criminals, homosexuals, and vagabonds) as "life unworthy of life," their extermination in psychiatric institutions in the Third Reich, and their marginalization in the Adenauer period. Arnds shows that in order to represent the Nazi past and subvert bourgeois paradigms of rationalism, Grass revives several facets of popular culture that National Socialism either suppressed or manipulated for its ideology of racism. In structure and content Grass's novel connects the persecution of degenerate art to the persecution and extermination of these "asocials," for whom the persecuted dwarf-protagonist Oskar Matzerath becomes a central metaphor and voice. This comparative study reveals that through intertextuality with the European fairy-tale tradition, the picaresque novels of Rabelais and Grimmelshausen, and through an array of carnivalesque figures Grass creates an irrational counterculture opposed to the rationalism of Nazi science and its obsession with racial hygiene, while simultaneously exposing the continuity of this destructive rationalism in postwar Germany and the absurdity of a *Stunde Null*, that putative tabula rasa of 1945.

Peter O. Arnds is associate professor of German and Italian at Kansas State University.

Studies in German Literature, Linguistics, and Culture

Edited by James Hardin
(*South Carolina*)

Representation, Subversion, and Eugenics in Günter Grass's *The Tin Drum*

Peter Arnds

CAMDEN HOUSE

First published 2004
by Camden House

Camden House is an imprint of Boydell & Brewer Inc.
668 Mt. Hope Avenue, Rochester, NY 14620, USA
www.camden-house.com
and of Boydell & Brewer Limited
PO Box 9, Woodbridge, Suffolk IP12 3DF, UK
www.boydell.co.uk

ISBN: 1–57113–287–2

Library of Congress Cataloging-in-Publication Data

Arnds, Peter O., 1963–
    Representation, subversion, and eugenics in Günter Grass's The Tin
Drum
    p. cm. — (Studies in German literature, linguistics, and culture)
Includes bibliographical references and index.
ISBN 1–57113–287–2 (hardcover: alk. paper)
    1. Grass, Günter, 1927– Blechtrommel.   2. Eugenics in literature.
I. Title. II. Series: Studies in German literature, linguistics, and culture
(Unnumbered).

PT2613.R338B55323 2004
833'.914—dc22

                                                               2004002996

A catalogue record for this title is available from the British Library.

This publication is printed on acid-free paper.
Printed in the United States of America.

Contents

Acknowledgments

INITIALLY, THE IDEA for this book took shape during the summer of 2000 at Washington University, St. Louis, where I was able to conduct research thanks to the DAAD summer grant at the Center for Contemporary German Literature. I wish to thank Professor Paul Michael Lützeler for this opportunity and the generous financial support that accompanied it. I would also like to thank the National Endowment for the Humanities for a summer stipend in 2001, as well as Kansas State University for several faculty development awards that assisted me with travel to conferences as far away as Bergen and Bangkok. I am especially grateful to Robert Corum and Michael Ossar for proofreading the final manuscript, as well as to my good friend and office mate Lucia Garavito for never failing to lend an ear to tales of Tom Thumb when she was trying to work. Finally, I wish to extend my gratitude and love to my dear wife Jerrilynn Romano for staying awake and listening to uncounted wee-hour-in-the-morning ideas about folk culture and Nazi racism.

P.A.
September 2003

Abbreviations

The following abbreviations have been used in the text.

AS Grimmelshausen, Johann Jakob, *Der abenteuerliche Simplicissimus* (Frankfurt am Main: Fischer, 1962).

B Günter Grass, *Die Blechtrommel* (Darmstadt: Luchterhand, 1986).

BK Daniel Wildmann, *Begehrte Körper: Konstruktion und Inszenierung des "arischen" Männerkörpers im "Dritten Reich"* (Würzburg: Königshausen & Neumann, 1998).

D Pär Lagerkvist, *The Dwarf,* trans. Alexandra Dick (New York: Hill and Wang, 1945).

DP Mikhail Bakhtin, *Problems of Dostoevsky's Poetics,* ed. and trans. Caryl Emerson (Minneapolis: U of Minnesota P, 1994).

FSLH Enid Welsford, *The Fool: His Social and Literary History* (New York: Farrar & Rinehart, 1935).

GP François Rabelais, *Gargantua and Pantagruel,* trans. J. M. Cohen (Harmondsworth: Penguin, 1955).

HM Lynne Lawner, *Harlequin on the Moon: Commedia dell'Arte and the Visual Arts* (New York: Harry N. Abrams, 1998).

MC Foucault, *Madness and Civilization,* trans. Richard Howard (New York: Random House, 1988).

NT Klaus Wolbert, *Die Nackten und die Toten des "Dritten Reiches": Folgen einer politischen Geschichte des Körpers in der Plastik des deutschen Faschismus* (Gießen: Anabas Verlag, 1982).

RW Mikhail Bakhtin, *Rabelais and His World,* trans. Hélène Iswolsky (Bloomington: Indiana UP, 1984).

S Grimmelshausen, Johann Jakob, *Simplicissimus,* trans. Mike Mitchell (Sawtry: Dedalus, 1999).

SM Wilhelm Hauff, *Sämtliche Märchen,* ed. Hans-Heino Ewers (Stuttgart: Reclam, 1986).

T Wilhelm Hauff, *Tales,* trans. S. Mendel (Freeport, NY: Books for Library Press, 1970).

TD   Günter Grass, *The Tin Drum,* trans. Ralph Manheim (New York: Vintage, 1990).

TMW   Lewis Hyde, *Trickster Makes this World* (New York: North Point, 1998).

All translations are my own unless otherwise noted.

Introduction

IN GERMAN LITERATURE THERE ARE two texts in which the telling and remembrance of history is accomplished by the use of a drum. One is Heinrich Heine's *Ideen: Das Buch Le Grand* (Ideas: The Book Le Grand, 1826), the other, Nobel Laureate Günter Grass's *Die Blechtrommel* (The Tin Drum, 1959). While the drum of Heine's *tambour-major* Le Grand conveys the spirit of the French revolution and announces Napoleon, Grass's Oskar Matzerath evokes German history in the making and drums for the remembrance of this history. A further connection between these two texts is established through Napoleon's famous words quoted by Heine — "du sublime au ridicule il n'y a qu'un pas" (from the sublime to the ridiculous is only one step) — words that Napoleon uttered upon his return from Russia where almost his entire army of about 600,000 had just been defeated by the Russian winter and the Cossacks.[1] These words have a special significance for Grass's novel. Heine's narrator describes how Aristophanes offers us the most terrible images of human madness through comedy, how Goethe expresses the greatest pain by means of a puppet play, and how Shakespeare puts the deadliest lamentation about the misery of the world into the mouth of a fool.[2] Grass, as this study will demonstrate, approaches the representation of the horror of the Nazi crimes through various aspects of popular culture, and through the spirit of the carnival. In *Die Blechtrommel* it is also often only one step from the sublime to the profane.

The present study offers a new reading of Grass's masterpiece, which to this day remains one of the most important prose works written after the Second World War in which a German author comments on Germany's past. *Die Blechtrommel* accomplishes what many critics could not forgive: it reverberates with laughter where one would normally expect awe and silence. The outrage this novel has met with in various parts of the world from the Allgäu to Oklahoma shows to what extent our European post-Enlightenment society, unlike the Middle Ages and the Renaissance, distrusts jocularity and jesting.[3] The screams of indignation the novel received were directed primarily at its abundance of alleged pornographic and blasphemous scenes, by means of which Grass satirizes the conservative spirit of the bourgeois world, in particular the Christian moralism of the new government. The period from the end of the war well into the sixties was a time when in Grass's view democracy was stifled by the CDU government and its new authoritarian father figures, Konrad Adenauer (1876–1967), the leader of postwar Christian democracy and first chancellor of the Federal Republic of Germany from 1949 to 1963, and Ludwig Erhard (1897–1977), the second chancellor from 1963 to 1966. As Jost Hermand has argued, it was the legacy of fascism during these restorative years as well as the hypocrisy of its conservative values that left-wing liberal authors like Günter Grass attacked through their work.[4] Jeffrey Herf argues that Adenauer's Christian renewal of West Germany was the result of his belief that National Socialism was based on a "pagan and atheistic celebration of secular idols" but that this reaction largely ignores the fact that during the Third Reich the Church silently supported the Nazis' anti-Semitism.[5] Adenauer failed to see that the Church had been in conspiracy with Nazi politics; Grass targets this issue in *Die Blechtrommel* by way of his blasphemous church scenes and the muscular Aryan Jesus on the cross of the Sacred Heart Church. Although Adenauer was strongly supportive of punishing Nazi criminals, he seemed unaware of "how broadly and widely the circle of criminality had expanded," and shut his eyes to the fact that former Nazis and antidemocratic conservatives were joining the CDU.[6] In many of his speeches from the early 1960s, Grass accused Adenauer of this oversight by pointing out, for example, that he installed Hans Globke (1898–1973) as Secretary of State in 1953.[7] Globke was a man with a dubious past. Although he had never formally joined the Nazi party, he had co-authored a comment on the Nuremberg Racial Laws of 1935 that became the basis for the exclusion of Jews from German public life.

As an author Grass has always seen himself as a political and social commentator, "denn der Ort des Schriftstellers ist inmitten der Gesellschaft und nicht über oder abseits der Gesellschaft" (for the place of a writer is in the midst of society and not above or beside it).[8] Literature's political function, Grass argues, especially holds true in times when politicians ask writers to stay away from politics, as was the case with Ludwig Erhard, who called West German left-wing writers "Pinscher" (little yapping dogs). In the late 1950s and early 1960s, Grass saw in the CDU government a continuation of the Nazi past, while he viewed the Social Democrats as the only alternative party, and the one that ought to govern West Germany. In a speech delivered in August 1961, he argued that voting for Adenauer meant voting for war.[9] He held Adenauer's politics of re-armament and his nonrecognition of the Oder-Neisse line as Germany's eastern border responsible for the consolidation of dictatorial power in the German Democratic Republic, for the widening rift between East and West Germany, and consequently for thwarting the possibility of reunification.[10] In connection with the discussion of popular culture and conservative politics in this study of *Die Blechtrommel*, it is particularly striking that Grass compares postwar CDU politics with Hans Christian Andersen's fairy tale *The Emperor's New Clothes*. In this tale two con men dupe an emperor into believing that he has magnificent new clothes on, while he is actually walking stark naked in front of his people, who do not dare to speak up because they are afraid of their authoritarian leader. Grass uses this fairy tale in one of his speeches to describe the political situation in postwar Germany: its unbroken taboos about the German past and Adenauer's and Erhard's keep-your-mouth-shut politics that attempted to stifle under the cloak of newly-gained prosperity any skepticism that might arise in the population regarding affairs of government.[11] To Grass the postwar period was neo-Biedermeier, a restorative time during which the people turned away from politics and comforted themselves with their materialism and prosperity, with Adenauer and Erhard as the fathers of the *Wirtschaftswunder* (the miracle of German economic recovery), turning West Germany into a TV-democracy.[12] He wrote *Die Blechtrommel* not only as a contribution towards fulfilling the Germans' responsibility to come to terms with their Nazi past, an endeavor he likens to that of Sisyphus, but also in the spirit of what in the late 1950s and early 1960s he considered democracy as opposed to postwar CDU politics.[13]

If there is one cultural critic whose work is useful in analyzing *Die Blechtrommel*, it is the literary theorist Mikhail Bakhtin (1895–1975). Just as Bakhtin's focus on the grotesque and on pornography and blasphemy in the work of François Rabelais was a way for him to reveal, criticize, and subvert the Puritanism of Socialist Realism, so for Grass these categories presented the possibility of commenting on the Nazis' cultural politics and breaking postwar taboos. And with this thesis in mind, and, more precisely, by applying the cultural theory of Bakhtin to *Die Blechtrommel*, this study aims to demonstrate Grass's use of different manifestations of popular culture for the purpose of unmasking Germany's dark past at a time when nobody wanted to be reminded of it. Through recourse to the tradition of popular culture, which had been tainted by Nazi ideology, *Die Blechtrommel* portrays the Nazis' persecution of "asocials." This practice was nourished by the concept of "life unworthy of life" and culminated in euthanasia killings that were carried out throughout the twelve years of Nazi rule and were one dimension of Germany's tainted past that was repressed and tabooed in the Adenauer years.

The Nazis' persecution of so-called *Untermenschen* (subhumans) included not only the physically and mentally disabled but also criminals, vagabonds, aimless wanderers, and other social outsiders — in other words, those who could not or did not want to work. Grass's protagonist, Oskar Matzerath, fits into all these rubrics. He embodies the voices of all the victims of the social groups whom the Nazis tried to silence. These persecuted social groups form the basis for Grass's literary representation of euthanasia through different manifestations of popular culture. These manifestations, at the root of which stands the archetype of the mythological trickster, include the dwarf fairy tale, such carnivalesque figures as the clown and the fool, the harlequin of the *commedia dell'arte*, as well as the picaresque novel. At the same time, Grass's use of popular culture is a comment on the Nazi party's ideology concerning such aspects as the body, gender, the mind, and choice of lifestyle, an ideology that targeted the individual's social integration and remained deeply rooted in German life during the postwar era. The Nazis themselves either tampered with some of these cultural manifestations, like the dwarf tale, the tradition of the carnival, or the picaresque novel, which they used for their ideology, or tried to eliminate them if they were too grotesque to reflect adequately the German spirit and folk soul. *Die Blechtrommel* thus cleverly ties the persecution of so-called degenerate life to the suppression of degenerate art. This study analyzes the various groups persecuted under the "life unworthy of life" policy and the respective genres of popular culture used as vehicles of representation. Grass represents the persecution of the physically disabled primarily through the medium of the dwarf fairy tale, he represents the persecution of the mentally disabled through such figures as the trickster, the fool, and the harlequin, and he represents the persecution of thieves, aimless wanderers, vagabonds, and other social outsiders through recourse to the tradition of the picaresque novel.

Oskar Matzerath embodies all of these figures from popular culture: he is the Tom Thumb of the fairy tale, he is the trickster that anthropologists like Paul Radin (1883–1959) and psychologists like C. G. Jung (1875–1961) have identified as a universal human archetype, he is the Janus-faced harlequin that reaches back to the medieval *diableries* and the *commedia dell'arte* of the Renaissance, and he is the picaro of pre-Enlightenment literature, a rootless wanderer outside the pale of society. The boundaries between these manifestations of popular culture are porous. Bakhtinian themes such as the grotesque body, mockery, and banquet images are often common to all of these manifestations: the fairy tales, the trickster myths, the carnival tradition, and the picaresque novel. The chapters on the dwarf, on madness, and on the picaro show to what extent the grotesque images of the carnival and the fairy-tale world are connected. Dwarves often played the fool in order to render themselves useful to society; the trickster is related to all other figures, the fairy tale Tom Thumb, the fool, and the picaro. As a protagonist who combines all these figures of popular culture Oskar stands for those other minorities that are less talked about than the Jews and that the Nazis sterilized, interned in concentration camps, and eliminated in euthanasia institutions.[14] Despite its obviously problematic conflation of the sublime and the profane, this novel's highly artistic representation of the crimes committed against what the Nazis considered subhuman creatures, *Untermenschen,* and low culture is a major achievement in German literature.

The use of the term popular culture in this study goes back to Herder, who distinguished between "popular culture" (*Kultur des Volkes*) and "learned culture" (*Kultur der Gelehrten*).[15] Popular culture implies the oral traditions of the lower social sphere. It is a culture that arises from the poorest in society largely as a result of illiteracy. The boundaries between the various figures that Oskar embodies are indistinct but they all display what

Bakhtin calls the "carnival sense of the world" that pervades the culture of the lower social sphere. It is to a large extent the Tom Thumb folk tale of the Grimm Brothers (Jacob, 1785–1863 and Wilhelm, 1786–1859) and the French collector/author of fairy tales Charles Perrault (1628–1703), as well as the literary dwarf tales by the German author Wilhelm Hauff (1802–27), that share a structure that becomes the foil for historical representation in Grass's novel. Certain elements of this structure — the dwarf's body, the fact that he is ridiculed and ridicules others, that he is exploited for his freakishness, as well as his desire to eat and his fear of being eaten — correspond to the paradigms of the carnival that Bakhtin envisions for the descendants of the Menippean satire,[16] primarily Rabelais's novels *Gargantua* and *Pantagruel* (published from 1532 on): paradigms such as the grotesque body, the principle of mockery, and images of the marketplace and the banquet. The fairy-tale world and Bakhtin's carnival as they resurface in Grass's novel are inseparable, a fact which surprises us little, since both the folk-tales and the carnival reflect the world of the lower classes, their desires and fears. The distinction between popular oral culture and learned written culture is at times also blurred. While folk-tales derive from the oral tradition, they entered written culture at the moment when the Grimm Brothers recorded them, and were "frozen" when they were published, and while the literary fairy tale (*Kunstmärchen*), such as the tales of Hauff, is the result of written learned culture, it often reflects elements that are also found in folk-tales. While the carnival is an event that used to fill the streets of Renaissance Europe, there is also carnivalesque literature, such as the picaresque novel or the romantic literary fairy tale. While the written literary fairy tale became unpopular in the Third Reich, the oral folk-tale experienced a revival, in support of party ideology. The Nazis exploited certain themes of popular culture, such as the Germanic myths behind the folk-tales, for their blood-and-soil ideology, while suppressing others that did not fit into their politics, such as the grotesque. In their persecution of *Untermenschen*, they targeted primarily the *Unterschicht*, the lowest social classes, because it was here that they perceived the greatest danger to the health of the collective body of the people, the *Volkskörper*. Paradoxically, popular culture became part of the official ideology, but at the same time the class from which this culture had originally emerged was increasingly targeted as asocial. As a consequence, popular culture was detached from the people who had originally produced it and was then entirely subordinated to party politics. This was as true for the folk-tale as it was for the carnival (as shown in chapter 1).

The intertextual reading between diverse cultural genres that is undertaken in this study enables one to see the diachronic fabric that holds cultures together and how certain symbols and mythological icons are transported and recycled through time and genre. One also realizes that most often art and politics are connected and that one and the same artistic construct can regenerate itself to represent different historical contexts. The first two chapters of this study serve as a basis that introduces the reader to the two central issues, totalitarianism and popular culture, upon which the ensuing chapters will build. While chapter 1 shows to what extent the historical phenomenon of the persecution of asocial life is reflected in *Die Blechtrommel,* chapter 2 summarizes those texts of popular culture through which this historical phenomenon is represented. Subsequent chapters focus on Grass's individual paradigms of the subversive grotesque that function as satirical attacks on right-wing ideology: the grotesque body of the dwarf (chapter 3), Oskar's dysfunctional family and his cannibalistic fairy-tale mother (chapter 4), his madness, which is that of the fool, trickster and harlequin (chapter 5), and his vagrant lifestyle, in which he resembles the picaro (chapter 6). In each chapter, the grotesque clashes with the Classical, which the Nazis cultivated to the highest degree and to the point that the grotesque was to be eliminated. The grotesque body clashes with the Classical body of antiquity, which became the bedrock of Nazi body politics. Oskar's dysfunctional family, particularly his bulimic mother, clash with the conservative family and gender politics of the Nazis and the postwar period. The chaos of carnival and the madness of such figures as the fool, the harlequin, and the mythological archetype of the trickster clash with bourgeois aspirations towards order and sanity. These carnival figures had been largely eliminated during the Enlightenment with the bourgeoisie on the rise, but they experience a revival in Oskar Matzerath as well as some other works of art after 1945, such as Thomas Mann's *Die Bekenntnisse des Hochstaplers Felix Krull* (The Confessions of Felix Krull, 1954), Arno Schmidt's *Das steinerne Herz* (The Stony Heart, 1956), Heinrich Böll's *Ansichten eines Clowns* (The Clown, 1963), and Edgar Hilsenrath's *Der Nazi und der Friseur* (The Nazi and the Barber, 1971). The same holds true for the genre of the picaresque novel, which clashes with the central genre of the bourgeois age, the Bildungsroman. The grotesque mode of life that Grass's novel offers as a counter-culture to Nazi officialdom and postwar rationalism includes the unconventional body, the unconventional mind, insanity at the individual level but also at the level of the family, as well as the vagrant lifestyle as an act of becoming rather than the closed, static lifestyle of the bourgeoisie with its teleology of *Bildung.* This dichotomy of the Classical versus the grotesque *modus vivendi,* if applied to Nazi Germany, corresponds to the clash between Nazi eugenics and all forms of so-called asocials: the physically and mentally disabled, vagrants, criminals, and those considered lazy (*arbeitsscheu*). My reading of Grass's novel demonstrates to what extent the uses and abuses of popular culture in twentieth-century Germany reflect this country's politics and social history. In particular, Germany's social history of the last two decades (the 1980s and 1990s) and the debates surrounding the question of whether its great wound ought to be kept open, as Martin Walser once put it,[17] necessitates a re-evaluation of this masterpiece, a work that testifies to the role of popular culture in the process of *Vergangen-*

heitsbewältigung, Germany's unceasing attempts to come to terms with her own past. Although the carnivalization of Nazi atrocities that takes place in *Die Blechtrommel* may indeed provoke reactions of outrage, the question of representation with regard to this novel should never lose sight of the subversive intent tied to it. In a representation of German fascism through carnival motifs I detect two functions. The sinister side of carnival can be shown in complicity with the horror of fascism, as for example in Michel Tournier's famous novel *Le Roi des Aulnes* (The Ogre, 1970). On the other hand, by dethroning state authority, carnival offers a moment of relief from historical suffering. This latter function can be illustrated by way of Albert Bloch's painting *March of the Clowns* from 1941. Just as Oskar subverts the official rhythm of the Nazi party in the famous scene in which he sits under a rostrum, Bloch's cartoon characters dethrone Hitler. Bloch's vision of Hitler hanging from the swastika and carried round a circus arena by a clown is a vision of the end of fascism, four years before it actually happened. As the Homeric hymn says about Hermes the trickster, he "moves among the gods, who do not die, and human beings, who must. And though he serves a few, most of the time, when night has fallen, he deceives the race whose time runs out" (*TMW*, 331). The painting illustrates beautifully the two sides of carnival, its jovial and its sinister dimension, thus reflecting what Hannah Arendt famously called the "banality of evil."[18] It alludes to fascism as a sort of short-lived frantic carnival whose end will re-establish a more humane reality, but at the same time it highlights popular culture's main tasks in its friction with official culture: suspension of everyday reality (quite literally suspension here in the hanging of Hitler) and subversion. These functions of popular culture partly explain the astonishing fact that artists have again and again in varying degrees chosen to represent the horrors of the Nazi crimes through humor. Examples that come to mind are Primo Levi's *Survival in Auschwitz* (1958), the novels of the German-Jewish writer Edgar Hilsenrath, Art Spiegelman's *Maus* (two volumes, 1986 and 1991), Jurek Becker's *Jakob der Lügner* (Jakob the Liar, 1969), and Roberto Benigni's film *Life is Beautiful* (1998). Undoubtedly, the fictionalization of such a largely unrepresentable historical event as the Holocaust is problematic and Napoleon's famous words "du sublime au ridicule il n'y a qu'un pas" have their validity for a film like Benigni's *Life is Beautiful*, in which the grim reality of the Holocaust is turned into a jocular game between a father and his little son. If writing poetry after Auschwitz is barbaric, as Adorno says, what is art that employs popular culture, the fairy tale and the carnival, in the context of the Third Reich and the Holocaust? This study, like numerous earlier studies, cannot succeed in providing answers that give closure to this discussion. For victims such as the Italian author Primo Levi and the German-Jewish writer Edgar Hilsenrath, Holocaust humor was undoubtedly a means of survival and of coming to terms with their past. If nothing else, humor is the last weapon left to man when facing an indomitable force of evil.

Notes

[1] Heinrich Heine, *Werke,* vol. 3 (Berlin/Weimar: Aufbau, 1986), 43.

[2] Heine, *Werke,* vol. 3, 43.

[3] After the appearance of Grass's book, a judge attempted to ban the book in a conservative town in the Allgäu. Cf. Otto von Loewenstern, "Der Blechtrommler in der Käsestadt: Wie ein Vollstreckungsrichter die Bekanntschaft von Oskar Matzerath machte," in: *Die Zeit* 23 (7 June 1963). Due to its alleged content of child pornography, Schlöndorff's movie version became an eyesore in the conservative state of Oklahoma in June 1997, when police seized tapes from local video outlets as well as from private homes; cf. for example, Michael Feingold, "A different drummer," in *Village Voice* 42.32 (1997): 83: ". . . an amusing incident took place in Oklahoma City.[. . .] A gullible old man, believing himself to be a Christian, heard a radio talk-show host attacking a film for its obscenity. A real Christian might have muttered, 'Judge not, lest ye be judged'; and gone about his business. But being gullible and pseudo-Christian in the traditional American mode wherein Christianity means judging everything and meddling in everyone else's business, and never mind what Jesus said, the old man immediately set about trying to ban the film. He enlisted the help of the Oklahoma City Police Department, which applied to a local district court judge for a ruling on the film's obscenity. The judge viewed the film, allowed how in his opinion it was obscene, a judgment he later asserted was merely advisory and without legal force, and went back about his business. The police, feeling empowered by this judicial view, went to the local video stores, where they rounded up all the cassette copies of the film available in Oklahoma City, except for two, which were in the hands of rental customers. Though the police had no warrant, one video store obligingly supplied the customers' names and addresses; still without a warrant, the police went to the two homes and demanded the videocassettes, which were duly surrendered after some discussion. . . . The film was Volker Schlöndorff's 'The Tin Drum.'"

[4] Hans Adler and Jost Hermand, eds., *Günter Grass: Ästhetik des Engagements* (New York: Peter Lang, 1996), 1–8.

[5] Jeffrey Herf, "Multiple Restorations: German Political Traditions and the Interpretation of Nazism, 1945–1946," in *Central European History* 26.1 (1993): 43.

[6] Herf, "Multiple Restorations," 45.

[7] Günter Grass, *Essays und Reden* 1 (Göttingen: Steidl, 1997), 143.

[8] Grass, *Essays und Reden,* 124.

[9] Grass, *Essays und Reden,* "Teufel und Beelzebub," 43: "Wer Adenauer wählt, wählt den Krieg!"

[10] Grass, *Essays und Reden,* 112–13: "Der Bundesregierung ist es spätestens ab 1955, als der Deutschlandvertrag unterzeichnet wurde, und bis in unsere Mauerbauzeiten hinein gelungen, die Teilung des restlichen Deutschlands, zum kurzfristigen Nutzen der Bundesrepublik, zum andauernden Schaden der Landsleute in der DDR, zu zementieren." (The federal government has succeeded, at least from 1955 when the "Contract of Germany" was signed, and up to the present time and the building of the Berlin Wall, in cementing the partition of Germany, for the temporary benefit of the Federal Republic but with permanent damage to our compatriots in the GDR.)

[11] Grass, *Essays und Reden,* "Des Kaisers neue Kleider," 121–36.

[12] Grass, *Essays und Reden,* 101.

[13] Günter Grass, Harro Zimmermann, *Vom Abenteuer der Aufklärung* (Göttingen: Steidl, 1999), 46: In an interview with Harro Zimmermann, Grass insists that the past cannot be mastered; he uses the image of Sisyphus rolling the rock up the hill and then having to start all over again for Germany's unending task to work through its own past.

[14] The question of *Die Blechtrommel*'s addressing this persecution of minorities both in the Third Reich and in the Federal Republic has never been thoroughly examined. Although in *The Language of Silence: West German Literature and the Holocaust* (New York: Routledge, 1999) Ernestine Schlant argues that West German literature has largely remained silent about the topic of the Holocaust, I would argue that this silence, which filled primarily the years from the end of the war until the late 1960s, is observed less and less often in German works of art, for example in textual representations of Nazi atrocities that make use of fairy tales, like Ingo Schramm's novel *Fitchers Blau* (Fitcher's Blue, 1996), or in the Holocaust paintings of Anselm Kiefer (born 1945). Although Schlant briefly discusses *Die Blechtrommel* (on pages 69–71), she ignores the fact that a close reading reveals it as a text in which there is definitely no silence about Nazi atrocities. These are represented through an elaborate intertextual fabric. Although it is true that the persecution of Jews and their elimination in concentration camps is not a central theme in this novel, the persecution of other minority groups that the Nazis considered *artfremd,* alien to their own kind, definitely is.

[15] Cf. Peter Burke, *Popular Culture in Early Modern Europe* (New York: New York UP, 1978), 8.

[16] The Menippean satire was founded by Menippos of Gadara (third century B.C.) and became a favorite genre, primarily with Lucian, Varro, Horace, and Seneca. Its main theme was human folly, which was depicted through serious dialogue in a mixture of prose and verse.

[17] Martin Walser, *Über Deutschland reden* (Frankfurt: Suhrkamp, 1988), 89.

[18] Cf. Hannah Arendt, *Eichmann in Jerusalem: A Report on the Banality of Evil* (New York: Viking, 1963).

1: Representing Euthanasia; Reclaiming Popular Culture

Historical Context

B EFORE ELABORATING ON Grass's strategies in his use of popular culture, this study must address a pivotal question: to what extent does Oskar become a victim of Nazi persecution? The novel has two temporal levels that converge at the end: the period from 1952 to 1954, during which Oskar Matzerath is an inmate of a mental asylum, from where he narrates his story, and the retrospective account of his life, which starts in 1899 and ends with his thirtieth birthday in September 1954. The central historical periods are the Third Reich and the postwar years. Oskar witnesses this time from the perspective of a dwarf who vacillates between resistance to and involvement in Nazi activities. In 1935 Oskar's drumming breaks up a Nazi party rally; in the winter of 1936–37 his voice destroys the shop windows in Gdansk, a prelude to the "night of broken glass" of November 1938.[1] The novel describes the beginning of the Second World War: Oskar in a Polish post office, the Russian invasion; and it shows Oskar as a Nazi entertainer on the western front. The end of the war is marked by his physical transformation. He grows a few inches and develops a hump as he is escaping to West Germany with his mistress/stepmother Maria and his son Kurt. The next phase shows Oskar trying to become fully integrated into West German society, an attempt that ultimately fails. He is seen discussing the phenomenon of collective guilt with Protestants and Catholics, becomes a stonemason's apprentice, and just as he once performed for the Nazis, now he is trying to assimilate into the new society that is becoming increasingly prosperous. More and more, however, he is drifting into the isolation of the mental institution. His attempt to marry Maria, the book's chief representative of the new rapacious bourgeoisie, likewise fails. Once again he performs for this society, this time as a jazz musician in the "Onion Cellar," a chapter that addresses what the Mitscherlichs later came to describe as Germany's inability to mourn.[2] Guilt, be it his father's, his own, or that of Germans in general, remains a leitmotif throughout the novel.

It has been argued that Grass's attempts at commenting on the Holocaust, particularly Kristallnacht and the death of the Jewish toy store owner Sigismund Markus, are muted and reveal no true mourning but instead resort to a language of silence, to metaphor, irony, and parody as well as a stereotypical rendering of a Jewish character.[3] The Holocaust looms large, however, in other parts of the book, not only in the third book, on the postwar years and German guilt, but primarily in such chapters as "Glaube Hoffnung Liebe" (Faith, Hope, Love), "Desinfektionsmittel" (Disinfectant), and "Wachstum im Güterwagen" (Growth in a Freight Car).

In the chapter "Glaube Hoffnung Liebe" Oskar first has an intimation of the hard times that lie ahead of him. Following the ransacking of Sigismund Markus's shop and his death, Oskar's suspicion that hard times lie ahead for gnome-like drummers like him contains a certain ambiguity. Although Oskar will experience hard times because he can no longer rely on a regular supply of tin drums, behind this minor problem looms the Nazi euthanasia program that threatens gnomes like him. This sort of ambiguity conflating seemingly irrelevant childish concerns with the larger historical context does not invalidate the threat of euthanasia but makes it even more ominous. The painter Anselm Kiefer once played with the same trilogy of terms from chapter 13, verse 13 of the First Epistle to the Corinthians — faith, hope, love — in a painting from 1976 that bears the same title. Like Grass, Kiefer questions the validity of these concepts after Auschwitz. By merging religious icons and images of Christmas such as Santa Claus, the Savior, and the Holy Ghost with the process of gassing, Grass blasphemously equates faith in Christianity with faith in the *Führer* and the Nazis' gassing of Jews, the disabled, and other groups. That Santa Claus was really the gasman is a detail that Volker Schlöndorff considered important enough to take verbatim from the novel and incorporate in his film version. These passages in the "Glaube Hoffnung Liebe" chapter doubtlessly contain much cynicism and blasphemy, and as such they may not reflect a language of mourning, but neither is this a language of silence.

Two images of the Holocaust stand out in *Die Blechtrommel*. One is that of Mariusz Fajngold disinfecting the barracks, shower rooms, cremating furnaces, and the victims' clothes in the chapter "Desinfektionsmittel" (Disinfectant). The other image is that of Oskar and his family traveling west in the type of freight car that was used for deportations to the death camps. In the chapter "Wachstum im Güterwagen" Grass inverts the positions of *Übermensch* and *Untermensch* (subhuman), in that the Germans are now inside the train cars and are being bossed around by the Poles. One of the travelers demands *special treatment* because he claims that during the war he was a Social Democrat and not a Nazi, a macabre reference to the Nazis' use of the term *Sonderbehandlung,* which after 1939 became the Gestapo's official word for execution.[4] *Sonderbehandlung* is a central concept in Grass's novel, not so much within the context of the persecution of Jews, but primarily as applied to Oskar himself.

As Leni Yahil pointed out, during the Third Reich *Sterbehilfe*, euthanasia in the sense of helping incurably ill people die, became *Vernichtung lebens-unwerten Lebens*, the destruction of unworthy life, whose continuance was considered socially undesirable.[5] While euthanasia aims at alleviating the suffering of the individual, "racial eugenics was to develop and improve the human race and, in light of this seemingly noble aim, the individual and his suffering became insignificant. . . . People who were no longer useful to the state were perceived as monsters in contrast to true human beings."[6] They were described as *geistig tot* (mentally dead) and placed on a level lower than animals. It is only a short step from this concept to the denial of the right to exist. Yahil goes on to describe the implementation of the euthanasia program in Nazi Germany. She explains how the *Sonderbehandlung*, that is, the gassing and subsequent burning of undesirable *Ballastexistenzen* (ballast life) originated as the central operation of the euthanasia program in 1940 before it was used in concentration camps. After public protest against these practices the Nazis halted the euthanasia operation and the gassing was officially stopped. The euthanasia practice continued, however, in secret, and came to be called wild euthanasia, killing in special institutions through injection, sleeping pills, or starvation. In the case of child victims the doctors often deceived the parents by informing them that their children had to be moved for special treatment to special institutions, from which they never returned.[7] Other than employing a language of silence in *Die Blechtrommel*, Grass explicitly addresses these concepts of a) *Sonderbehandlung*, b) *Ballastexistenz*, c) the perception of the handicapped as monsters at a lower level than animals, d) their perception as mentally dead, and e) their consequent institutionalization. Oskar's friend, the dwarf Bebra, refers to the concept of *Sonderbehandlung* when he says:

> "Unsereins darf nie zu den Zuschauern gehören. Unsereins muß auf die Bühne, in die Arena. Unsereins muß vorspielen und die Handlung bestimmen, sonst wird unsereins von denen da *behandelt* [my italics]. Und jene spielen uns allzu gerne übel mit!" Mir fast ins Ohr kriechend, flüsterte er und machte uralte Augen: "Sie kommen! Sie werden die Festplätze besetzen! Sie werden Fackelzüge veranstalten! Sie werden Tribünen bauen, Tribünen bevölkern und von Tribünen herunter unseren Untergang predigen. Geben Sie acht, junger Freund, was sich auf den Tribünen ereignen wird! Versuchen Sie, immer auf der Tribüne zu sitzen und niemals vor der Tribüne zu stehen."(*B*, 92–93)

> ["Our kind has no place in the audience. We must perform, we must run the show. If we don't, it's the others that run us. And they don't do it with kid gloves." His eyes became as old as the hills and he almost crawled into my ear. "They are coming," he whispered. "They will take over the meadows where we pitch our tents. They will organize torchlight parades. They will build rostrums and fill them, and down from

the rostrums they will preach our destruction. Take care young man. Always take care to be sitting on the rostrum and never to be standing out in front of it." (*TD*, 114)]

Oskar later joins Bebra in performing for the Nazis in France. The lives of both dwarves would be greatly imperiled if it were not for their usefulness as entertainers, for as long as they entertain the Nazis they can escape from being classified as *Ballastexistenzen,* ballast life. Oskar survives thanks to his voice, his miracle weapon that enables him to scream glass to pieces. By destroying glass he also becomes an accomplice to the Nazis in the sense that this activity is associated with Kristallnacht. Despite his miracle weapon, Oskar is a prime victim for Nazi euthanasia for a number of reasons. His physical handicap, the ugliness of his dwarfish body, his alleged mental inadequacy, his schizophrenia, his aimless wandering, and his criminal nature all combine to mark him as useless in the eyes of society, a parasite on the margins of society.

What started in the form of sterilization laws in the early thirties soon became a vicious death machine. As the war carried on, the Nazis would kill not only those who were beyond hope of recovery but also war veterans and the old, who were no longer considered useful to society.[8] That thousands died was the result largely of a superficial bureaucratic procedure that involved doctors in central positions of power deciding over the death or extension of patients' lives based not on personal contact with these patients but relying entirely on registration forms filled out by doctors and hospitals all over the country. Due to this anonymous handling, the patients were often killed not because they were incurably ill but because the documentation of their background and disease was superficial or faulty. In cases of doubt as to whether or not a patient should die, the doctors' decision was usually not in favor of the patient. Especially during the war years, the "euthanasia" of patients increasingly resembled the work of a conveyor belt. While in the early years of the Nazi reign the purification of the German race was the dominant reason for sterilization, during the war the primary criterion for killing patients was that they were no longer able to perform productive and useful work. As Ulrike Schulz pointed out, after 1939 the motivation to kill someone was no longer a result of racial hygiene but the elimination of as many *nutzlose Esser* (useless mouths to feed) as possible.[9] There was, however, little consensus as to what type of work was considered useful. This fact too led to random decision making on the part of the doctors. Therefore what started as an ideal to clean German society of its undesirables became an increasingly more practical solution as food and money became scarce during the war years. Klee expresses this thought quite succinctly: in order to make room, not only the mentally disabled, but also people with arteriosclerosis, tuberculosis, cancer, and other diseases were killed.[10] Oskar's persecution falls into this time towards the end of the war when in order to make room even old people were killed because they could no longer work.[11]

Euthanasia in Poland began right after its occupation, even before Hitler signed the letter that empowered institutions to perform the killings. After his return from France, Oskar is in great danger of being taken to a killing institution, when one day a man from the Ministry of Public Health turns up at Matzerath's father's apartment and asks him to sign a letter that requires Oskar's institutionalization. Although Matzerath refuses to give his signature, he receives official letters from the Board of Health every two weeks. In the following chapter, "Die Stäuber" (The Dusters), this letter is mentioned once again and this time it is only "der Schatten meiner armen Mama, der dem Matzerath lähmend auf die Finger fiel, wenn er ein vom Reichsgesundheitsministerium verfaßtes Schreiben unterzeichnen wollte, [der] verhinderte . . ., daß ich, der Verlassene, diese Welt verließ" (*B*, 299; "it was only the shadow of my poor mama, falling across Matzerath's fingers and paralyzing them whenever he thought of signing the authorization form drawn up by the Ministry of Public Health, that kept me alive": *TD*, 362). Although Matzerath's position as putative father is a weak one, he has a healthy reaction to the letter by exclaiming that he cannot send his own son away, that the doctors can say what they like and that they probably have no children of their own.

It is Maria, Oskar's first love and later stepmother, who is not as sure about keeping Oskar at home. She would not mind seeing him disappear in an institution. Her vacillation already becomes evident upon Oskar's return from France. Her reception is a lot less emotional than that of Oskar's father, and is accompanied by the comment that he has given them plenty of trouble. Although she claims that she hopes that they will not put him in an institution, she adds that he would no doubt deserve it. She shows the same kind of indifference towards Oskar's life when the letter is mentioned a second time. In response to Matzerath's healthy reaction that he cannot send his own son away, she cautions him to take it easy. "Du tust grad so, als würd mir das nuscht ausmachen. Aber wenn se sagen, das macht man heut so, denn weiß ich nich, was nu richtig is" (*B*, 298; "You talk as if I didn't care. But when they say it's the modern way to do, I don't know what to think": *TD*, 361–62). The "modern way to do" this, as the English translation reads, is, of course, to kill the likes of Oskar. Despite the apparent ambivalence of Maria's reaction, she tries to exert some pressure on Alfred and push him into signing the letter, quite possibly not so much to get rid of Oskar as to get rid of the trouble he causes them. Matzerath seems shocked at her willingness to get rid of Oskar and he exclaims that Oskar's real mother Agnes would never have allowed it. Maria's reaction expresses an idea with which we are familiar from the fairy-tale world: "Na is verständlich, weil se de Mutter war und immer jehofft hat, dasses besser mecht werden mit ihm. Aber siehst ja: is nich jeworden, wird überall nur rumjestoßen und *weiß nich zu leben und weiß nich zu sterben* [my italics]!" (*B*, 298; "Of course not, she was his mother, she kept hoping he'd get better. But you see how it is: nothing has happened, he's always being pushed around, he don't know how to live and he don't know how to die": *TD*, 362). This is undoubtedly the evil fairy-tale stepmother wanting to get rid of the real mother's child[ren]. But in this very comment the fairy-tale world also collides with the historical reality of euthanasia. Apart from the fact that she is wrong, because Oskar knows very well how to live — has he not just returned from a voyage like Ulysses with whom he likes to compare himself — she adopts the Nazi party's own reasoning that because there is no visible physical growth, a cripple like Oskar has no life inside and should therefore be put out of his misery. This is the very idea implied by the euthanasia program, under which the disabled were considered mentally dead.

Ernst Klee's work on Nazi euthanasia has uncovered many historical documents that reflect such attitudes. He quotes, for example, from the book by Karl Binding and Alfred Hoche *Die Freigabe der Vernichtung lebensunwerten Lebens: Ihr Maß und ihre Form* (1920), who said of the disabled precisely what Maria says about Oskar:

> *Sie haben weder den Willen zu leben, noch zu sterben* [my italics]. So gibt es ihrerseits keine beachtliche Einwilligung in die Tötung, andererseits stößt diese auf keinen Lebenswillen, der gebrochen werden müßte. Ihr Leben ist absolut zwecklos, aber sie empfinden es nicht als unerträglich. Für ihre Angehörigen wie für die Gesellschaft bilden sie eine furchtbar schwere Belastung. Ihr Tod reißt nicht die geringste Lücke — außer vielleicht im Gefühl der Mutter. . . . Wieder finde ich weder vom rechtlichen, noch vom sozialen, noch vom sittlichen, noch vom religiösen Standpunkt keinen Grund, die Tötung dieser Menschen, die das furchtbare Gegenbild echter Menschen bilden und fast in jedem Entsetzen erwecken, der ihnen begegnet, freizugeben.

> [They have the will neither to live nor to die. Therefore they do not agree to their own killing, nor does their killing conflict with their will to live, which would have to be broken. Their life is absolutely useless, but they do not find it unbearable. For their relatives as well as society they are an awfully heavy burden. Their death does not cause anyone grief — except perhaps to the feelings of the mother. I cannot think of any legal, social, moral, or religious reason to stop the killing of these humans, who are the terrible counterimage of real humans and who cause feelings of horror in almost everyone who encounters them.][12]

Euthanatos, the good death (a macabre cynicism if one considers the fact that the use of carbon monoxide made it a rather slow and painful death), was in store for those who were considered marginal existences between life and death, neither quite alive because they were seen as mentally dead nor quite dead because physically they were still alive. The Nazis were actually surprised that the mentally disabled showed signs of distress just before they died and that they fought to stay alive in the gas chambers, which were equipped with peep holes so that their agony could be observed. Oskar, whom Maria considers mentally dead, asserts his existence in opposition to her words by taking refuge in his two gifts, the drum and his voice, "mir jedoch war Oskars Stimme über der Trommel ein ewig frischer Beweis meiner Existenz; denn solange ich Glas zersang, existierte ich" (*B*, 299; "but to me Oskar's voice, even more than his drum, was proof of my existence . . . for as long as I sang glass to pieces I existed": *TD*, 362). These words are, of course, also a reference to his earlier usefulness to the Nazis at the front, because Oskar has survived this long solely because of his strange gift of screaming glass to pieces. Oskar's screaming is itself an act of protest against such atrocities as Kristallnacht and euthanasia. His blacking out of attic windows that have not been properly blacked out, while he is running with the street gang called the *Stäuber* (Dusters), conjures up two images at the same time, the breaking glass during Kristallnacht and the blacked-over bus windows behind which the disabled were gassed.

Maria's disparaging words have a strong impact on Oskar. They disillusion him about her, which becomes clear from his vision of the clinic, through which Grass alludes to the Nazi euthanasia institutions:

> [er] sieht sogar heute noch, sobald ihm Maria unter die Augen kommt, eine wunderschöne, in bester Gebirgsluft liegende Klinik, in dieser Klinik einen lichten, modern freundlichen Operationssaal, sieht wie vor dessen gepolsterter Tür die schüchterne, doch vertrauensvoll lächelnde Maria mich erstklassigen Ärzten übergibt, die gleichfalls und Vertrauen erweckend lächeln, während sie hinter ihren weißen, keimfreien Schürzen erstklassige, Vertrauen erweckende, sofort wirkende Spritzen halten. (*B*, 299)

> [Whenever he lays eyes on Maria, he beholds a vision of a beautiful clinic situated in the mountain air, of a light, airy, friendly, and modern operating room; outside its padded door, Maria, shy but smiling, hands me over confidently, to a group of first-class physicians, who are smiling too and ever so confidence-inspiring and holding first-class, confidence-inspiring and immediately effective syringes behind their white, sterile aprons. (*TD*, 362)]

The Nazis' methods of camouflaging their activities as well as using injections are both addressed in this passage.[13] The neglect that Oskar experiences from his stepmother Maria nearly causes his death, were it not for the good angel of his mother and Matzerath's persistent reluctance to sign. Finally, however, after Oskar's trial following his and the Dusters' desecration of the Church of the Sacred Heart, Matzerath signs the letter that would put his son into a killing institution. Luckily for Oskar, the city of Danzig is attacked just in time to prevent the mail from being delivered. The end of the war saves his life.

It may not surprise the reader that Maria, who almost causes Oskar's premature death, becomes the chief representative of the postwar affluent bourgeoisie. Although Oskar proposes to her, their marriage seems out of the question. In a moment of rage she reduces him to the kind of *monster* of which Binding and Hoche spoke when they defined people like Oskar as creatures who are the terrifying counterpart of real humans and stir disgust in everyone who encounters them.[14] Maria calls Oskar:

> eine verfluchte Drecksau, einen Giftzwerg, einen übergeschnappten Gnom, den man in die Klappsmühle stecken müsse. Dann packte sie mich, klatschte meinen Hinterkopf, beschimpfte meine arme Mama, die einen Balg wie mich in die Welt gesetzt habe und stopfte mir, als ich schreien wollte, es auf alles Glas im Wohnzimmer und in der ganzen Welt abgesehen hatte, den Mund mit jenem Frottierhandtuch, das, wenn man hineinbiß, zäher als Rindfleisch war. (*B*, 238)

> [a loathsome pig, a vicious midget, a crazy gnome, that ought to be chucked in the nuthouse. She grabbed hold of me, slapped the back of my head, and reviled my poor mama for having brought a brat like me into the world. When I prepared to scream, having declared war on all the glass in the living room and in the whole world, she stuffed the towel in my mouth; I bit into it and it was tougher than tough boiled beef. (*TD*, 290)]

Maria's use of a towel in order to gag Oskar reflects one of the subtexts of this novel, the Grimm Brothers' tale of Tom Thumb, who is chased by his Master's wife with a rag. The rag in the fairy tale and the perception of the physically handicapped as monstrous are, as we shall see, also linked to Oskar's perception of Goethe. Although Maria fails to see Oskar institutionalized during the Third Reich, she witnesses how this is finally accomplished in the Federal Republic, thus finding her theory confirmed that he is a crazy gnome who ought to be chucked into the nuthouse. By calling him a gnome she reduces him to a fairy-tale creature, an otherworldly being, stripping him of his humanity, in line with the Nazis who regarded the disabled and the Jews as lower than animals. We need merely think of the transportation methods to the camps, for example, and the fact that the deported had less space in the train cars than was accorded to cattle. Art Spiegelman's *Maus* series may also come to mind, particularly the caption at the beginning of the book, Hitler's words that "the Jews are undoubtedly a race but they are not human." This view applied to both the Jews and the disabled, who were primarily considered a health hazard and thus fell victims to the politics of racial hygiene.

The Cultural Politics of Socialist Realism and National Socialism

The historical context of Grass's novel has revealed Oskar as a potential victim of Nazi euthanasia. The Nazis' elimination of degenerate art and degenerate life forms a sinister background in this text. As Grass centralizes Oskar's grotesque body and his insanity, his criminal nature, and his vagrant life style, he centralizes grotesque art forms like the dwarf fairy tale or the picaresque novel. In its dual functionality of representing history while salvaging popular culture from its ideological pollution, *Die Blechtrommel* displays an abundance of intertextual allusions. Intertextuality is a problematic phenomenon, since each text is part of a universe of texts. And yet Grass's novel communicates with a tightly woven fabric of texts and displays a variety of genres, something that Bakhtin analyzed under the term *heteroglossia* for the comical novel. Among this variety of texts and genres, Grass's novel harks back to François Rabelais's *Gargantua* and *Pantagruel,* which inspired him while he was working on his manuscript in Paris.[15] *Die Blechtrommel* reflects the paradigms of the carnival that Bakhtin outlines in his monumental study *Rabelais and His World* (1965), images of the grotesque body (versus the classical body), the marketplace, and the banquet. All three books are literary reactions to oppressive regimes in different times: the rule of Charles V in Rabelais, Stalinist Russia in Bakhtin, and the Third Reich in Grass. For Rabelais, Bakhtin, and Grass, the spirit of carnival, with its emphasis on the grotesque, signifies the symbolic destruction of authority and official culture and the assertion of popular renewal. An intriguing parallel between Bakhtin and Grass, which makes it impossible to read *Die Blechtrommel* without thinking of the Russian critic, is that both writers critique the ideology of a regime that appropriates popular culture to support its oppressive politics and the rejection and killing of undesirable individuals. While Bakhtin, however, did so contemporaneously, Grass is temporally well removed from the totalitarian regime he targets.

Stalin's Socialist Realism of the 1930s radically politicized the function of literature by demanding that it draw from folklore. *Narodnost* was Socialist Realism's concern with peasant culture and corresponded to Herder's concept of the *Volksgeist.*[16] The centrality of popular culture had the purpose of making the people aware that they had won the class struggle.[17] Gorky announced at the First Writers' Congress in 1934 that any literature to be written ought to model itself on the folkloric tradition, that in the history of literature there was a moment when the simpletons of folklore became smarter than their feudal masters whom they had the courage to mock. As examples Gorky mentioned Sancho Panza, Simplicissimus and Eulenspiegel, and he emphasized the influence of oral folklore on the creation of such major works of literature as *Faust, Baron Münchhausen's Adventures, Gar-*

gantua and Pantagruel, and *Till Eulenspiegel.*[18] Certain aspects of popular culture, however, had to be avoided, such as bodily functions, which in Socialist Realism were euphemistically called *naturalism* or *zoologism.*[19] This puritanism of the Stalinist era went hand in hand with a purification of the people, a purging of undesirable elements, very much in parallel to what the Nazis attempted. While under Stalin Rabelais's works were officially praised for their proximity to the revolutionary spirit, in which the lower orders finally mustered up the courage to ridicule their superiors, Bakhtin's interpretation of Rabelais, with its primary focus on the grotesque body, on the lower bodily stratum and its related principle of mockery of any serious officialdom, is a hidden attack on Stalinism's official denial of the human body, which no doubt contributed to the purges in the late 1930s. Whereas Socialist Realism manipulated popular culture in the interest of its own political ideology, Bakhtin's book interprets the Rabelaisian carnival as a celebration of heterogeneity directed against any form of official ideology.[20] Bakhtin hence does with regard to Stalinism what Grass does in reaction to the Third Reich and the neo-conservative period in which *Die Blechtrommel* was written. Both try to liberate popular culture from the narrow definitions of their times. Arguably, reactions to both authors' obsession with the grotesque body and its functions differ in intensity. Since Grass wrote his book at a time when in West Germany democracy and liberalism were on the rise, he never experienced the kind of censorship that Bakhtin did. *Rabelais and His World* was not published until 1965, although Bakhtin wrote it in the late 1930s and early 1940s as a comment on the purges of 1936 to 1938.

Socialist Realism's strategies of manipulating popular culture did not differ significantly from those of the Nazis. Both regimes tampered with the fairy tales and the carnival. In politicizing their national popular cultures, both governments attempted to establish more national unity by ideologically elevating peasant culture, by distancing themselves from those social groups who were seen as not belonging to this peasant culture — in Germany primarily the Jews, in Russia the bourgeois class — and also by exploiting the peasant way of life in the interest of labor and productivity. Fairy tales and the *bylina,* the epic song, were exploited as weapons for class struggle, primarily for their inherent optimism and their heroic characters. Gorky called the attention of his comrades to the fact that folklore reflected the unwritten compositions of toiling man, and that it had created vivid and artistically perfect heroes in the struggle for the renovation of life, by which he was referring to the construction of communism. In folklore the new hero was the one who worked, as opposed to the *superfluous man.* Just as the Nazis' exploited popular culture for its active heroes and hard-working peasants in order to fight against the lazy, the *Arbeitsscheuen,* there was in Russia the attempt to destroy a national malaise, the typical lethargy described in the famous nineteenth-century novel *Oblomov* (1859) by Ivan Goncharov (1812–91). Pessimism, Gorky goes on to explain, would be entirely foreign to folklore.[21] The optimism reflected in such Russian folklore heroes as Ivan the Fool and Petrushka, who overcomes the priest, the policeman, the devil, and death, corresponds to the Faustian quest of the folk-tale hero that the Nazis detected in this genre, and is opposed to any romantic sensitivities.[22] While Socialist Realism condemned "bourgeois" romanticism as escapist,[23] the Nazis decried the psychological subtleties of the Romantic literary fairy tale as unrealistic and not applicable to the idea of optimism and the Faustian quest. One consequence of this renewed concern with folklore in Stalinist Russia was an obsession with collecting old folklore, while another result was the creation of so-called pseudofolk: prose narratives in which some of the best-known tellers of the traditional folk-tale celebrated not only Lenin and Stalin but also outstanding Soviet workers, from collective farmers to border guards, aviators, and even Arctic explorers.[24]

Socialist Realism was thus a period of renewal and inversion, a period in which what the bourgeois age used to see as low culture became the official culture. Stalinism even co-opted carnival techniques of inversion for its political ideology. In the Stakhanovite movement, for example, workers on the lowest social level were raised to the level of superheroes, the *Übermenschen* of Stalinism, so to speak. This movement was named after Alexander Stakhanov (1905–77), a miner, who had managed in six hours to bring up fourteen times as much coal as was the norm and whom Stalinism consequently turned into a superhero other workers were encouraged to emulate. As a rule, the Stakhanovites were unskilled workers singled out by the party for their superb achievement in over-fulfilling production norms, although the party tended to exaggerate these workers' exploits in staged public performances. Such public celebrations of these workers' successes, during which their superiors had to undergo mock humiliations that lowered them to a level beneath their workers, made it clear to what extent Stalinism used carnival rituals to illustrate Communism's upheaval of the class system.[25]

The Nazis' manipulation of the carnival and the fairy tale will serve as a backdrop to the ensuing discussion of Grass's own co-option of these categories. The evanescence of the carnival's subversive nature has for many critics been the cause for skepticism towards Bakhtin's theory of the liberating forces of carnival. Rather than subverting the existing order, carnival actually reinforces it: because of its brief life span, it merely functions as a safety valve, allowing the higher order to go back to ruling undisturbed. Although there have been numerous attempts in German history from the seventeenth to the twentieth century to eliminate carnival, it has never simply disappeared. Considering the carnival's blasphemous and physically grotesque nature, one might assume that in the Third Reich, the church and the state became allies in their battle against what Lewis Hyde has called the mercurial imagination (*TMW*, 198): carnival and grotesque art. However, although it holds true that grotesque art was banned during the Third

Reich, the carnival was instead, like that other dimension of popular culture and folk humor, the fairy tale, manipulated and exploited by Nazi ideology. Berthold Hamelmann has pointed out that the carnival was instrumental to the Nazis in their foreign politics, in that it served the purpose of depicting Germans as jovial and harmless in order to distract the world from the horror that reigned within Germany's borders. The Nazis saw in carnival a possibility of presenting National Socialism as a humane (*menschenfreundliches*) system to an international audience. Through carnival, they thought, they could camouflage any nefarious activities at home, such as the persecution of Jews and other minorities.[26] For that purpose the National Socialist regime organized the "First International Carnival Congress" in Munich, the capital of the movement, from 14 to 17 January 1937. Yet the carnival had at least two other functions: it united the different regions and cities in Germany, and it offered joy to a nation whose primary task was productivity: work. Carnival thus became a prime vehicle for the concept of *Kraft durch Freude* (strength through joy), and was therefore still a safety valve for the seriousness of daily life. To make sure that these aims were to be fulfilled, the "Bund Deutscher Karneval" (Federation of the German Carnival) was founded on 16 January 1937. This manipulation of the carnival reflects how different the Nazis' understanding of the event was from Bakhtin's association of carnival with free-wheeling laughter and, above all, its revolutionary spirit. The Nazis attached their aggressive phraseology to the carnival, which certainly deprived it of its joyousness and any liberating effect it might have. The idea that carnival has *conquered* all of Germany, the BDK's tasks to *fight* (*Bekämpfung*) a mentality that sees in carnival nothing but business, and to *prevent* (*Unterbindung*) excesses of all kinds (*Auswüchse aller Art*) in public events are examples of the vocabulary of belligerence and the distorted functions of carnival in the Third Reich.[27] The carnival's usual function of interrupting the seriousness of daily life should, however, not be underestimated for Nazi Germany. What initially was an interruption from the strains of work and a stimulation for more productivity became in 1940 and 1941 a distraction from the strains of war. As in the Middle Ages and the Renaissance, the rulers waging war still needed their fools, if not for the assertion of their own power through juxtaposition with the powerless, then at least for entertainment. Grass's novel addresses this function of carnival during war in the shape of its dwarf fools Oskar, Bebra, and Raguna, who entertain German soldiers at the front in France.

The carnival that Stalinism and the Third Reich ideologically manipulated contrasts sharply with Bakhtin's concept of carnival as the expression of a permanent revolutionary spirit. As Hamelmann points out, one feature of totalitarian regimes is the suppression of free speech. Critical utterances or even skepticism towards official ideology are seen as criminal acts to be punished by prison, concentration camp, or death.[28] He discusses carnival newspapers in the Third Reich that were able to criticize the regime only through satire. However, one of the most well-known satirical attacks of the regime in the *Münchener Nettesten Nachrichten,* a Munich carnival paper, was Ulrich Link's parody of the Grimm fairy tale "Little Red Riding Hood" of 1937.[29] One of the main features of this rewritten folk-tale was that it ridiculed official NS institutions and ideological norms: in this parody the little girl with the red hood is a BDM member (*Bund deutscher Mädchen* [Federation of German Girls]) with an Aryan grandmother. The wolf inspires no fear in Little Red Riding Hood because she knows that all *Volksschädlinge* (those who could harm ordinary people) are sitting in concentration camps. In the end the wolf is shot because of his "un-German snoring," the little girl is promoted to a high-rank position in the BDM and the grandmother is sent on a voyage to Madeira on a KdF [Kraft durch Freude — strength through joy] cruise ship. Although the party may have laughed at this jocular retelling of a fairy tale, one will have to agree with Lutz Röhrich that, as a model for how to attack a totalitarian regime in a humorous way, this sort of oppositional writing required extraordinary courage. It should not surprise us that subsequent to the publication of this tale, the Munich Gestapo became particularly interested in its author.[30] During the Third Reich, satire and carnival humor increasingly became the victims of control and censorship. Carnival's fundamental nature — its temporary liberation from higher authorities and its subversive character — was restricted by police ordinances. In Munich, for example, an ordinance regulated the number of days during which it was possible to celebrate Mardi Gras (*Fasching*) in the streets and public squares and stipulated that "in garment and behavior everything had to be avoided that would break with the moral code; wearing uniforms or any other official clothes was likewise prohibited."[31] The *Münchener Nettesten Nachrichten* spoke of the "standardization of the Munich *Fasching,*" well aware of this contradiction in terms. Its jokes finally led to the paper's disappearance in the late 1930s. Goebbels's announcement in the *Völkische Beobachter* that Germany had better things to do than to be humorous meant the end of all jokes that were critical of the regime. As the war dragged on, such humor was frequently met with capital punishment, due to its alleged corrupting influence on the army (*Wehrkraftzersetzung*).[32]

The Soviets' perception of the fairy tale, resulting in its exploitation for political purposes, had little to do with Vladimir Propp's structural approach in his pioneering study of fairy tales, *Morphology of the Folktale*. To him, according to Svetlana Boym, they were merely tales, with no mission for the construction of a nation.[33] In Germany the politicization of fairy tales started in the years of the Weimar Republic, as progressive writers and conservatives fought over the legacy of the Grimm Brothers' folk-tales.[34] For the Nazis the fairy tales then became a prime vehicle in support of their Aryan policies. Like the carnival, the German fairy tale, particularly the folk-tales of the Grimm Brothers, was used for ideological and political purposes. German folklore studies in the 1930s were engaged primarily in a search for Nordic-Germanic symbols, an undertaking that came to be called the *Nordic Renaissance*.[35] As Christa Kamenetsky convincingly argues in her articles and book on children's literature in the Third Reich, folklore became a political tool in the attempt to unite and bring permanence to the *Volk,* an objective that is reminiscent of the cultural politics of Stalinist Russia.[36] As in Russia, such cultural renewal and striving for cultural unity went hand in hand with defining the nation by the exclusion of all foreign and alien elements in German culture.[37] The word *artfremd* (alien to one's kind) became a key-word in the Nazis' racist policies: "Whatever is alien does not belong physically, and it does not belong spiritually. [It was] the folklorist's first responsibility to weed out all alien elements that had crept into the Nordic-Germanic myths, customs, and rituals, and to select and propagate that folklore which was as purely as possible related to the ancestors."[38] Like Stalinist Russia, Nazi Germany celebrated its peasant way of life, a component of its racially oriented *Blut und Boden* (Blood and Soil) policy. The Nordic peasant was considered strong, healthy, and dynamic, and thus directly opposed to unhealthy city dwellers and, above all, to Jewish intellectualism. German folklore had to mirror this image of the heroic peasant, not only for the sake of productivity at home, but also for the Nazis' eastern expansionist policies. Folklore was to become a weapon primarily for the peasant community of the newly conquered areas in Eastern Europe, where these German peasants were to form a fighting community in order to assert themselves against their alien environment.[39]

As a consequence of the Nazis' abuse of folklore, the entire field of *Volks-kunde* (Folklore Studies) became ideologically polluted far into postwar Germany. In 1945 the Allied Forces even briefly banned the publication of the Grimm tales in Germany, because they associated the horrors expressed in many of them with the violence in the death camps.[40] In reclaiming the fairy tale tradition from the abysses of ideological abuse, Grass recovers a deeply humanitarian aspect of the Romantic Age for postwar German literature. As chapter 3 will reveal, *Die Blechtrommel* is densely intertextual with the European dwarf-tale tradition, with the Tom Thumb tales of the Grimm Brothers, and the dwarf tales by Wilhelm Hauff. Because of the grotesque bodies of their "anti"-heroes and their physiques' blatant irreconcilability with the much-cherished notion of fertility, the dwarf folk-tales and the literary fairy tale featuring dwarves were not popular among *völkische* ideologues, who either did not include them in their anthologies of fairy tales or used them shamelessly for their ideology. As early as 1924 Georg Schott offered a twisted interpretation of the Grimm tale "The Brave Little Tailor," in which the dwarf-like tailor wins a kingdom by cleverly killing several giants. Schott saw Germany's fate inscribed into this David-against-Goliath tale in that the Germanic giants had for centuries been duped by the dwarves, the Jews.[41] At the same time this interpretation already implies a comment on the Jewish versus the Aryan body. While the Nazis perceived in Wilhelm Hauff's literary tales of dwarves products of a diseased mind that had created grotesquely misshapen characters, they could not altogether ignore the German dwarf folk-tale, since it too stemmed from the spirit of the *Volk*. Consequently, it was interpreted in such a way that it would fit Nazi ideology. In 1937 Reinhold Franke compared the German *Däumling* (Tom Thumb), with the French one, *Le Petit Poucet*, by Charles Perrault, and concluded that unlike the French tale the German one reflects the Faustian quest of the Germanic race.[42] In spite of this interpretation, dwarves or dwarf-like figures were not particularly popular among Nazi ideologues, who considered them un-heroic and *artfremd*. It becomes clear that this twisted vision is abstruse if one considers that the Grimm Brothers were very much aware that the folk-tale material they recorded was part of an international pool. They borrowed many fairy tales from Perrault; *Le Petit Poucet*, for example, is typologically related to the German version of *Hänsel und Gretel*.

Bakhtin and Grass react in their writing against the manipulation of literature by a totalitarian regime, Stalinism in one case, Nazism in the other. By resuscitating the spirit of carnival they criticize a view of art that excludes its grotesque elements as degenerate. Both writers' cooption of the carnival and its grotesque images is thus a reaction to narrowly defined views of popular culture, above all to the Puritanism of the extreme left and the extreme right, which seem to converge in their outlook on culture. Bakhtin's and Grass's celebration of the grotesque body corresponds to their defense of a work of art that ultimately helps create in their societies an openness towards its heterogeneous members. In opposition to these politics of the heteroglot novel stand Nazism's and Stalinism's worship of the classical body, the closed work of art with a limited interpretability imposed on it, and the closed society, the *Volkskörper* that is hostile to humans it considers alien to its own kind.

Notes

[1] Hanspeter Brode, *Günter Grass* (Munich: C.H. Beck, 1979), 72.

[2] Alexander Mitscherlich and Margarete Mitscherlich, *The Inability to Mourn*, trans. Beverly R. Placzek (New York: Grove Press, 1975).

[3] For Grass's treatment of Jewish characters in *Die Blechtrommel* see Ernestine Schlant, *The Language of Silence* (New York: Routledge, 1999), 69–71 and Bruce Donahue, "The Alternative to Goethe: Markus and Fajngold in *Die Blechtrommel*," in *The Germanic Review* 58.3 (1983): 115–20.

[4] Ernst Klee, ed., *"Euthanasie" im NS-Staat: Die "Vernichtung unwerten Lebens"* (Frankfurt/Main: Fischer, 1989), 345.

[5] Leni Yahil, *The Holocaust: The Fate of European Jewry* (Oxford: Oxford UP, 1987), 307.

[6] Yahil, *Holocaust,* 307.

[7] Yahil, *Holocaust,* 309.

[8] Ulrike Schulz, *Gene mene muh raus mußt du: Eugenik von der Rassenhygiene zu den Gen- und Reproduktionstechnologien* (Munich: AG SPAK, 1992), 57: The Nazi politics of victimization were so grotesquely vicious that they persecuted even those who were traumatized by war, the *Kriegshysteriker,* but only if they were from the lower social classes; the war neuroses of the socially higher officers were seen as a kind of fatigue that was not persecuted. Like many others this example demonstrates clearly to what extent the difference between living and dying depended entirely upon the linguistic definition of an individual's problem.

[9] Schulz, *Gene mene muh,* 51.

[10] Klee, *"Euthanasie,"* 121–22: "Es soll Platz geschaffen werden. Da kann es nicht verwundern, daß nicht etwa nur Geisteskranke, sondern auch Leute, die Arteriosklerose, Tuberkulose, Krebs und andere Krankheiten haben, beseitigt werden."

[11] Klee, *"Euthanasie,"* 122.

[12] Klee, *"Euthanasie,"* 22.

[13] Schulz, *Gene mene muh,* 47: "[Die Eltern] wurden über die bevorstehende Tötung hinweggetäuscht, indem ihnen eine Zustimmung zur "Gesundung des Kindes" entlockt wurde. Die Kinder wurden durch mehrmalige Verabreichung von Luminal in Tablettenform und einer abschließenden Spritze mit Morphium-Scopolamin ermordet." (The parents were deceived about the impending killing of their child in that they were asked to agree to his/her "health-restoring treatment." The children were then murdered through the repeated treatment with Luminal in the form of tablets and a final injection of morphine-scopolamine.) (My translation.)

[14] Klee, *"Euthanasie,"* 22: "die das furchtbare Gegenbild echter Menschen bilden und fast in jedem Entsetzen erwecken, der ihnen begegnet."

[15] Cf. Günter Grass, Harro Zimmermann, *Vom Abenteuer der Aufklärung: Werkstattgespräche* (Göttingen: Steidl, 1999), 63: Grass states here that while he was working on *Die Blechtrommel* in Paris, it was Paul Celan who alerted him to Rabelais.

[16] Régine Robin, *Socialist Realism: An Impossible Aesthetic* (Stanford: Stanford UP, 1992), 52.

[17] Katerina Clark and Michael Holquist, *Mikhail Bakhtin* (Cambridge, MA: Harvard UP, 1984), 272.

[18] Maxim Gorky, "Doklad A. M. Gor'kogo o sovetskoj literature," *Pervyj s"ezd pisatelej: Stenografičeskij otčet* (Moscow: Ogiz, 1934), 6 and 10, quoted in Clark/Holquist, *Bakhtin,* 272.

[19] Richard M. Berrong, *Rabelais and Bakhtin: Popular culture in* Gargantua and Pantagruel (Lincoln, NE: Nebraska UP, 1986), 106.

[20] Cf. Berrong, *Rabelais and Bakhtin,* 108.

[21] Dana Prescott Howell, *The Development of Soviet Folkloristics* (New York: Garland, 1992), 325.

[22] Frank J. Miller, *Folklore for Stalin: Russian Folklore and Pseudofolklore of the Stalin Era* (New York: M.E. Sharpe, 1990), 8.

[23] Howell, *Soviet Folkloristics*, 325.

[24] Miller, *Folklore for Stalin*, 75.

[25] Cf. Clark and Holquist, *Bakhtin*, 309.

[26] Berthold Hamelmann, *Helau und Heil Hitler: Alltagsgeschichte der Fasnacht 1919–1939 am Beispiel der Stadt Freiburg* (Eggingen: Edition Isele, 1989), 317.

[27] Hamelmann, *Helau und Heil Hitler*, 325.

[28] Hamelmann, *Helau und Heil Hitler*, 334.

[29] Martin Broszat, "Rotkäppchen vor vierzig Jahren: Zur politischen Satire im dritten Reich," in *Süddeutsche Zeitung*, 20 February 1977, 79.

[30] Lutz Röhrich, *Gebärde — Metapher — Parodie: Studien zur Sprache und Volksdichtung* (Düsseldorf: Schwann, 1967), 137.

[31] Broszat, "Rotkäppchen," 79.

[32] Broszat, "Rotkäppchen," 79.

[33] Svetlana Boym, "Paradoxes of Unified Culture: From Stalin's Fairy Tale to Molotov's Lacquer Box," in *The South Atlantic Quarterly* 94.3 (Summer 1995): 826.

[34] For information on the fairy tale of the Weimar Republic, see Jack Zipes, ed. and trans., *Fairy Tales and Fables from Weimar Days* (Hanover and London: UP of New England, 1989), 3–28.

[35] See, for example, Maria Führer, *Nordgermanische Götterüberlieferung und deutsches Volksmärchen: 80 Märchen der Brüder Grimm vom Mythus her beleuchtet* (München: Neuer Filser-Verlag, 1938) and Hannjost Lixfeld, *Folklore and Fascism: The Reich Institute for German Volkskunde*, ed. and trans. James R. Dow (Bloomington: Indiana UP, 1994).

[36] Christa Kamenetsky, "Folklore as a Political Tool in Nazi Germany," in *Journal of American Folklore* 85 (1972): 223.

[37] Kamenetsky, "Folklore as a Political Tool," 223.

[38] Kamenetsky, "Folklore as a Political Tool," 226.

[39] Kamenetsky, "Folklore as a Political Tool," 231.

[40] Cf. Zipes, *Weimar Days*, 25, and Ulrike Bastian, *Die "Kinder- und Hausmärchen" der Brüder Grimm in der literaturpädagogischen Diskussion des 19. und 20. Jahrhunderts* (Frankfurt/Main: Haag & Herchen, 1981), 186.

[41] Cf. Peter Aley, *Jugendliteratur im Dritten Reich: Dokumente und Kommentare* (Hamburg: Verlag für Buchmarktforschung, 1967), 103–5: "Es wäre einfach ergötzlich, zum laut Auflachen, wenn es nicht so todtraurig wäre. Denn es ist abermals unsere, der Deutschen Geschichte. Die deutschen Riesen: Prachtkerle, mit ihren unheimlichen Kräften. Die Welt könnten sie aus den Angeln heben, wenn sie zusammenstünden. Aber alles ist umsonst; ein elender Wicht, der seinen Schabernack mit ihnen treibt, wird ihrer Herr" (104). (It would be hilarious if it were not so sad because

it is once again our, the Germans' history. The German giants: great guys with incredible strength. They could change the world if they stood together. But it is all in vain; they are bossed around by a confounded midget who plays his tricks on them.)

[42] Reinhold Franke, "Das Märchen vom Däumling in deutscher und französischer Sprache," in *Jugendschriftenwarte* 43.11 (1938): 21–25.

2: Heteroglossia from Grimmelshausen to the Grimm Brothers

WITHOUT ATTEMPTING TO BE all-inclusive in its discussion of hetero-glossia in Grass's novel, which would be a Gargantuan enterprise, this chapter presents those texts that through their carnivalesque features have either been acknowledged as having influenced Grass's novel (Rabelais and Grimmelshausen) or with which, upon closer structural analysis, Grass's novel engages in an intertextual dialogue (fairy tales, trickster myth, *commedia dell'arte*). The carnivalesque features that Bakhtin discusses all belong to a popular culture rooted in the trickster myths. In Europe this myth resurfaces in the carnival tradition, the medieval Feast of Fools and the Feast of Asses,[1] and extends to the oral tradition of some folk-tales as well as to literature. The trickster myth has had a substantial impact on such written culture as the picaresque novel, the literary fairy tale, and some twentieth-century novels. In much of this literature it has been used for satire.

Grass's novel engages in a structure-forming dialogue with a multitude of texts from the oral and written tradition and the dwarf-fairy tale tradition, and with Rabelais and Grimmelshausen, both of whom are central sources. Like Rabelais's *Gargantua* and *Pantagruel* (published from 1532 on) and Grimmelshausen's *Simplicius Simplicissimus* (1668), *Die Blechtrommel* is rooted in the Menippean satire, "one of the main carriers and channels for the carnival sense of the world in literature" to this day (*DP*, 113). Texts always feed off and into other texts, deliberately or not. *Die Blechtrommel* is a prime example of such networking with other texts, and it in turn becomes the palimpsest for later texts such as Salmon Rushdie's *Midnight's Children* (1981) or John Irving's *A Prayer for Owen Meany* (1989).[2] The novel explicitly mentions such texts as the Grimm Tom Thumb tales and Wilhelm Hauff's *Der Zwerg Nase* (Dwarf Longnose, 1826/7), yet in its conflation of folklore motifs and totalitarian atrocities it also opens itself up to other texts, such Michel Tournier's *Le Roi des Aulnes* (The Ogre, 1970), Mikhail Bulga-kov's *The Master and Margarita* (1966), Pär Lagerkvist's *The Dwarf* (1945), Friedrich Dürrenmatt's *Der Verdacht* (The Suspicion, 1951), Simon Mawer's *Mendel's Dwarf* (1998), and the story of the female dwarf Trudi in Ursula Hegi's American novel *Stones from the River* (1994).

This chapter discusses some of the sources of Grass's novel. The term intertextuality is a charged term, a can of worms so to speak, because it becomes an impractical concept once we take into account the fact that we are always dealing with a universe of texts. We therefore need to exercise restraint and confine ourselves to a subset of relevant works. Bakhtin's heteroglossia is a more suitable concept for the purposes of this study because it implies those texts and genres that have an actual voice in a given text and not those to which this text may stand in some superficial relation. This chapter therefore focuses only on those texts and genres that have fed into *Die Blechtrommel*, not on later texts that have been influenced by Grass's novel, such as the novels by Rushdie and Irving, nor on those texts that resemble it in their use of the grotesque in relation to the theme of Nazi eugenics, like the novels by Dürrenmatt, Tournier, and Mawer.

Bakhtin's concept of heteroglossia with its principal features of heterogeneity corresponds to his notion of "carnivalized literature." Literature as carnival exists primarily where it parodies other more serious forms of literature, such as tragedy or the Bildungsroman. In his introductory reader on Bakhtin, Simon Dentith mentions the classic representatives of the so-called comic, heteroglot novel: in England, Henry Fielding (1707–54), Tobias Smollett (1721–71), Laurence Sterne (1713–68), Charles Dickens (1812–70), and William Makepeace Thackeray (1811–63), and in Germany, Gottlieb von Hippel (1741–96) and Jean Paul (1763–1825). He also mentions Miguel de Cervantes (1547–1616), Inigo Lopez de Mendoza (1398–1458), Johann von Grimmelshausen (1622–76), François Rabelais (c. 1494–1553), and Alain René Lesage (1668–1747).[3] Grass's novel shows heteroglossia because it fulfills the two main requirements that Dentith envisions for such novels. It consists in its rich use of various genres, that is, it contains diverse literary voices and thus reflects a multiplicity of language systems, and second, it contains a high degree of parody in its rejection of the seriousness of learned culture, above all the Goethean Bildungsroman.

Despite the heteroglossia in Grass's novel, all these different texts and genres are linked via Oskar, who is in varying degrees a reincarnation of the mythological trickster and his descendants, the Tom Thumb of the folk tale, the dwarf of the literary fairy tale, the picaro of the picaresque novel, the harlequin of the *commedia dell'arte*, the Erlking of Germanic mythology, the fool at the medieval court and in medieval church ceremonies, the jesters of the street carnival, and the modern-day circus clown. As such a multi-faceted creature steeped in various traditions of popular culture, Oskar becomes Grass's prime vehicle in positing a counter-culture to the official cultures of the Third Reich and the Adenauer period. Despite this heterogeneity of subtextual genres in Grass's novel there is homogeneity of purpose in this assembly: the representation of Nazi crimes and the subversion of official culture through this carnivalization of literature.

An interesting phenomenon regarding Grass's text is that if we see Oskar not only as a victim, but also as a *Mitläufer,* a supporter of Nazi activities (the text suggests this in several areas, for example when Oskar and Bebra perform for the Nazis), then through this allegory of the folk-tale gnome's participation in Nazi politics, Grass also reveals the Nazis' appropriation of popular culture, much in the same way as Bakhtin reveals Stalin's exaltation of the proletariat and ideological co-option of popular culture. The appropriation of popular culture by a totalitarian regime deprives this folk culture of its revolutionary potential, which seems to take the bite out of Bakhtin's study. It is, however, not the grotesque images discussed by Bakhtin that are revolutionary in themselves, but Bakhtin's study per se as an attack on Stalin's social policy. In Grass's case, on the other hand, there is a defense of the grotesque aspects of popular culture, which the Nazis had suppressed as degenerate, a sort of liberation of popular culture from the ideological manacles that the previous generation had imposed upon it. This chapter discusses the principal genres of popular culture that contribute to the heteroglossia of *Die Blechtrommel* as well as their Bakhtinian images of the carnival.

Trickster Myth

The figure at the root of Grass's revival of grotesque popular culture and of the multiplicity of figures that Oskar represents is the trickster (discussed in detail in chapter 5). Defying any categorization and forever transgressing boundaries, the trickster seems an ideal figure to represent the heterogeneity of life opposed to Nazism's attempt at homogenizing society. No other than the trickster with his multifarious nature, his various roles and functions (if we look at a figure like Hermes with whom Oskar likes to compare himself) can be a better embodiment of the principle of heteroglossia. The protean nature of the trickster is reflected in his various mutations throughout the ages. He is recycled in various cultural traditions as the fool, the picaro, the clown, the harlequin, even the ogre in folklore. In folk-tales he is often pitted against another physically inferior but mentally superior trickster, as is the case in Charles Perrault's *Le Petit Poucet*, for example, where the ogre is outsmarted by Tom Thumb.

Trickster myths share with the carnival tradition the fact that in their capacity as the obverse of restrictive order they are socially sanctioned. The gradual disappearance of the trickster in his incarnation as the picaro of the picaresque novel and the German *Hanswurst* on stage, to give two examples, coincided with the suppression of carnival in the Age of Enlightenment.[4] One task of the trickster is carnivalesque renewal. Frequently, his trickster work initiates creative reflection within his society as to how to change its culture. He can be a culture hero in that he brings about this kind of change and thus exposes his society to cultural transition. This is one of the goals of *Die Blechtrommel* as a trickster story, that it challenges German society during the 1950s, primarily that society's postwar rationalism with its taboos, un-confronted past, and suppression of irrationalism. In addition to

Günter Grass, writers like Arno Schmidt and Heinrich Böll deliberately worked against this postwar trend of suppressing anything irrational. The revival of picaresque literature in the 1950s and 1960s and of its trickster figures in novels like Schmidt's *Das steinerne Herz* and Böll's *Ansichten eines Clowns* can consequently be seen as paralleling individual authors' attempts, like those by Grass and Schmidt, to resuscitate the fairy tale genre that the postwar rational climate had likewise tried to suppress.

Examples from different cultures demonstrate that tricksters are carnivalesque characters to which the Bakhtinian categories of the carnival can be applied. Wakdjunkaga (the tricky one) of the North American Winnebago tribes, studied in great detail by the anthropologist Paul Radin, may serve as a suitable example. He is called not only the "tricky one" but also the "foolish one," and like the picaro is an aimless wanderer. Radin stresses the importance of food for this figure, the Rabelaisian imagery of devouring versus being devoured. Wakdjunkaga kills and eats the children of other animals; he has a huge appetite and often corresponds to the ogres in fairy tales. The Winnebago trickster cycles teem with grotesque body images, primarily of the lower body: like most tricksters this one is obsessed with his penis; he probes a hollow tree with it, which has the effect that it is reduced to human size as its end gets gnawed off by a chipmunk, a scene that Radin explains as the trickster's growing awareness of his sexuality, while the myth explains it as the reason why man's penis is so short today.[5] Trickster burns his anus, plays with his own intestines, coils up his penis and puts it in a box that he carries on his back, and cross-dresses. As in the picaresque tradition, farting and defecation are popular themes in this myth. Breaking wind and laughter both come from the same source and have the same purpose of deflating seriousness. Trickster myths are truly Rabelaisian in their defecation motifs. Wakdjunkaga covers the earth in excrement, there are talking laxative bulbs, he falls into piles of his own dung; and his defecation is accompanied by raucous laughter. All this is reminiscent of the carnival's dichotomy of mocking versus being mocked. The myth's conflation of laughter and death serves as a satire of the savage Winnebago war customs.[6]

The purpose of satire is to deflate the seriousness with which a culture may see itself. Both Grass's novel and the trickster myths do this for their own cultures. Satire also aims at destroying or temporarily relieving society's self-imposed taboos. *Die Blechtrommel* breaks the taboo against talking about Germany's past disrespectfully, and the Winnebago trickster, in cohabiting with a woman during the feast before the tribe goes to war and in destroying the war bundle, becomes a destroyer of the most sacred symbols. The image of the penis being gnawed off is linked to a Winnebago creation myth; with the recovered pieces the trickster creates the earth. This makes him a buffoon-like deity. At the same time the Winnebago consider their trickster a satanic creature. We see this ambivalence reflected in Oskar, who too is a buffoon-like Jesus figure as well as a satanic figure, for he is a victim of human abuse but he also takes revenge. Trickster is an asocial outsider, an aimless wanderer on the margins of society; he breaks the most holy taboos and destroys the most sacred objects.

As useful as Radin's observations of the Winnebago trickster are, one has to be careful about his and other critics' theories of developmentalism. Radin and Jung see the trickster as a sort of inchoate primordial being who in the course of the cycle becomes conscious of his own deeds, primarily his own sexuality, and they draw a line from the trickster to the development of humanity. John Greenway has even gone so far as to compare tricksters with "retarded children," no doubt an attractive theory for the purposes of the present study but one that ought to be highly resisted.[7] Development, as Doty and Hynes argue, is not a dominant feature of this mythological creature.[8] The grotesque images, satirical elements, and the absence of development, of *Bildung*, that the trickster myths share with the picaresque tradition in literature, make Oskar an embodiment of both these genres. The mythological trickster resurfaces not only in the picaresque tradition but also in oral popular culture as the medieval fool, the Harlequin of the Renaissance, and as the Tom Thumb of the folk-tale. In written culture he also appears as the dwarf of the literary fairy tale. Grass's novel partakes of all these cultural traditions.

Dwarf Tales

Die Blechtrommel is first and foremost the story of a dwarf. As such it is part of a whole tradition of dwarf tales in the form of legends, folk-tales and literary fairy tales as well as some novels in the twentieth century. That both the Grimm and the Hauff tales have a specific function in Grass's novel can be seen as early as in Oskar's initial exposure to literature. One of his first mentors, Gretchen Scheffler, keeps giving him "Märchen wie Zwerg Nase und Däumeling" (*B*, 72; "fairy tales such as *Dwarf Longnose* and *Tom Thumb*": G, 91) so that he may identify himself with these figures. It is an interesting detail that she would actually prefer that Oskar read *Soll und Haben* (Debit and Credit, 1855) because Gustav Freytag's (1816–95) anti-Semitic novel was among favorite reading material prescribed by the Nazis for Germany's youth. Oskar, who only wants to read about Rasputin, also rejects Goethe, whose intolerance he fears and whom he suspects would have condemned him as an incarnation of anti-nature. Gretchen Scheffler ultimately succeeds in awakening Oskar's enthusiasm for the Grimm Tom Thumb tale. As in Wilhelm Meister's first central formative experience, his visit to the theater, Oskar is being exposed to the theater at an early age. Grass's reduction of the Classical theater episode of the nineteenth-century Bildungsroman into a "mere" Christmas performance of the Tom Thumb tale is only one of many examples for the parody of the Bildungsroman genre. During the whole performance Oskar identifies strongly with this Tom Thumb figure:

Es wurde das Märchen vom Däumeling gegeben, was mich von der ersten Szene an fesselte und verständlicherweise persönlich ansprach. Man machte es geschickt, zeigte den Däumeling gar nicht, ließ nur seine Stimme hören und die erwachsenen Personen hinter dem unsichtbaren aber recht aktiven Titelhelden des Stückes herspringen. Da saß er dem Pferd im Ohr, da ließ er sich vom Vater für schweres Geld an zwei Strolche verkaufen, da erging er sich auf des einen Strolches Hutkrempe, sprach von dort oben herab, kroch später in ein Mauseloch, dann in ein Schneckenhaus, machte mit Dieben gemeinsame Sache, geriet ins Heu und mit dem Heu in den Magen der Kuh. Die Kuh aber wurde geschlachtet, weil sie mit Däumelings Stimme sprach. Der Magen der Kuh aber wanderte mit dem gefangenen Kerlchen auf den Mist und wurde von einem Wolf verschluckt. Den Wolf aber lenkte Däumeling mit klugen Worten in seines Vaters Haus und Vorratskammer und schlug dort Lärm, als der Wolf zu rauben gerade beginnen wollte. Der Schluß war, wie's im Märchen zugeht: der Vater erschlug den bösen Wolf, die Mutter öffnete mit einer Schere Leib und Magen des Freßsacks, heraus kam Däumeling, das heißt, man hörte ihn nur rufen: "Ach, Vater, ich war in einem Mauseloch, in einer Kuh Bauch und in eines Wolfes Wanst: nun bleib ich bei Euch." Mich rührte dieser Schluß und als ich zu Mama hinaufblinzelte, bemerkte ich, daß sie die Nase hinter dem Taschentuch barg, weil sie gleich mir die Handlung auf der Bühne zum eigensten Erlebnis gemacht hatte. Mama ließ sich gerne rühren, drückte mich während der folgenden Wochen, vor allen Dingen, solange das Weihnachtsfest dauerte, immer wieder an sich, küßte mich und nannte Oskar bald scherzhaft, bald wehmütig: Däumling. Oder: Mein kleiner Däumling. Oder: Mein armer, armer Däumling. (*B*, 87)

[The play was *Tom Thumb*, which obviously had a special appeal for me and gripped me from the start. They did it very cleverly. They didn't show Tom Thumb at all, you only heard his voice and saw the grownups chasing around after him. He was invisible but very active. Here he is sitting in the horse's ear. Now his father is selling him to two tramps for good money, now he is taking a walk, very high and mighty, on the brim of one of the tramps' hats. Later he crawls into a mouse hole and then into a snail shell. He joins a band of robbers, lies down with them, and along with a mouthful of hay makes his way into the cow's stomach. But the cow is slaughtered because she speaks with Tom Thumb's voice. The cow's stomach, however, with Tom inside it, is thrown out on the dump heap, and gobbled up by the wolf. Tom cleverly persuades the wolf to pillage his father's storeroom and starts to scream just as the wolf is getting to work. The end was like the fairy tale: The father kills the wicked wolf, the mother cuts open the wolf's stomach with her scissors, and out comes Tom Thumb, that is, you hear his voice crying: "Oh, father, I've been in a mouse hole, a cow's stomach, and a wolf's stomach: now I'm going to stay home with you." The end touched me, and when I looked at Mama, I saw that she was hiding her nose in her handkerchief; like me, she identified herself with the action on stage. Mama's feelings were easily stirred, and for the next few weeks, especially for the remainder of the Christmas holidays, she kept hugging and kissing me and, laughing or wistful, calling me Tom Thumb. Or: My little Tom Thumb. Or: My poor, poor Tom Thumb. (*TD*, 108–9)]

The passage is a conflation of motifs from the two Grimm versions *Daumesdick* (Tom Thumb) and *Daumerlings Wanderschaft* (Tom Thumb's Travels).[9] Like Tom Thumb, Oskar is in constant danger because of his size. Like Tom Thumb, therefore, Oskar repeatedly has to hide in places that symbolize the protectiveness of a mother's womb. He hides under the skirts of his grandmother, inside a rostrum during a Nazi party rally, and inside war bunkers, and stands under the Eiffel Tower, which combines the phallic with the uterus-like, and so on. Like Tom Thumb, he joins a band of criminals, the "Dusters" and the Nazis themselves, in order not to be crushed by them.

Although he is the size of a thumb, Tom Thumb's journey reflects his pursuit of happiness. Grass elaborates on this concept and puts it into context with the historical background of euthanasia. The physical arresting of Oskar's growth stands in direct contrast to his inner life. The association of arrested intellectual growth with arrested physical growth and the consequent condemnation of the disabled by the Nazis as being *dead souls* and therefore "undeserving of life" are thus critically commented on. Oskar's rich inner life — after all he is capable of telling his own tale — exposes the enormity of the Nazi crimes towards the mentally and physically handicapped that were sent to the gas chambers after a perfunctory medical test.[10] What have been literary topoi for centuries — society's contempt for the dwarf, the view that his physical shortcomings signal his mental inadequacy, and his consequent uselessness — are paradigms that we can observe in most stories of dwarves, among them also the Grimm Brothers' *Der junge Riese* (The Young Giant) and Charles Perrault's *Le Petit Poucet*, the motion picture *Simon Birch* (1998), which is based on John Irving's *A Prayer for Owen Meany*, and even Ursula Hegi's best-selling *Stones from the River*. These literary topoi became a gruesome reality under Nazi euthanasia. The four fairy tales, the two Tom Thumb versions of the Grimm Brothers and Wilhelm Hauff's *Der Zwerg Nase* and *Die Geschichte von dem kleinen Muck*, contain the structural parallels detailed below: moments in the narrative that are all in some way linked to the protagonist's dwarfish body. The tales share these structural features with *Die Blechtrommel* where, as the next four chapters will reveal, they serve the purpose of historical representation. They allow Grass to comment metaphorically and satirically on discriminatory body politics, on patriarchal gender and family politics, bourgeois conceptions of sanity, and the politics of social integration. The structural parallels are:

1) The reduction of the dwarf to his grotesque body (discussed under body politics in chapter 3);

2) The dwarf's desire to hide from harassment and persecution. Oskar and the Tom Thumbs have in common, for example, that they escape into uterus-like places (discussed under Oskar's oedipal relationship with his mother in chapter 4);

3) His parents' questionable love (discussed under dysfunctional family in chapter 4);

4) The theme of mockery and public display of the dwarf. The public interprets the dwarf's lack of size as a reflection of his mental inadequacy and his madness. The dwarf is being mocked but he also mocks others. Tom Thumb is mocked by the highwaymen and he mocks his master's wife. Hauff's Jakob (Zwerg Nase) is mocked in the marketplace and by the Duke, and in turn he mocks the old witch who buys cabbages from his mother. Little Muck is mocked by the neighbors' kids and the King and his courtiers, but he ends up mocking the whole court by putting donkey's ears on them. Oskar is mocked by the neighbors' kids and many of his contemporaries and mocks the authorities of church and state (discussed under insanity in chapter 5);

5) Since the dwarf is always underestimated by fully-grown people around him he needs to prove his usefulness in order to avoid being classified as useless by society and hence become the victim of persecution. He is often equipped with a magical weapon to assist his survival in a hostile environment. Tom Thumb exploits his size in assisting others, Jakob in *Der Zwerg Nase* becomes an exceptional cook, Little Muck exploits his magic running shoes and walking cane at the King's court, Oskar exploits his voice to survive among the Nazis and in postwar society is eager to prove his usefulness as a stonemason's apprentice. As a form of self-protection the dwarf even develops a criminal nature and collaborates with criminals or those in power. Tom Thumb joins a band of robbers, Muck and Jakob offer their talents and services to the cruel rulers of their country, and Oskar joins the Dusters gang and sides with the Nazis when performing for them at the front (discussed under trickster in chapter 5); and

6) His aimless wandering in search of happiness (like the picaro discussed in chapter 6).

Like the trickster myths and the descendants of the Menippean satire, Rabelais's novels and Grimmelshausen's picaresque novel, these tales are steeped in the tradition of the carnival. They display an association of Tom Thumb with carnival food (sausage); his boundless appetite characterizes Tom Thumb as a classic trickster figure; and they are full of grotesque body images: Tom Thumb slips into a sausage and animal stomachs, Muck becomes a fool with donkey's ears, and Jakob's deformities are displayed in the marketplace. Like Tom Thumb of the folk-tale, Hauff's dwarf Jakob is associated with banquet images, most of all at the moment when the Duke threatens to chop him into a pie.

Traditionally, the dwarf in literature often has the role of a spy, as August Lütjens informs us.[11] Dwarves usually serve and entertain their masters; they can charm through their voices, but they are at times truculent. In German literature, the dwarf is frequently associated with hidden treasures (for example Alberich in the *Nibelungen*), and he can be an incarnation of the trickster archetype. The dwarf Alban in a poem from the twelfth century, for example, is like all tricksters mischievous, is a keeper of gates, and has a boundless sexual appetite. There is a long tradition extending all the way up to the Romantic Age of associating dwarves with stones and ore, their life inside mountains, a motif to which Grass alludes by making Oskar the apprentice of a stonemason. The dwarf's association with the cap of invisibility (Alberich) is also interesting. It shows man's fear of hidden evil, an evil that Pär Lagerkvist locates not in the dwarf but in man himself when he has his dwarf Piccoline say: "I have noticed that sometimes I frighten people; what they really fear is themselves. They think it is I who scares them, but it is the dwarf within them, the ape-faced manlike being who sticks up its head from the depths of their souls. They are afraid because they do not know that they have another being inside them" (*D*, 29–30).

A sophisticated portrait of the dwarf as a social outcast who is drawn deeper and deeper into the intrigues of court and the turbulence of war, an evil dwarf who craves blood and combat, and wants to see men fall, see death and destruction around him (which he finally will), this story contains all the key moments of the Hauff tales and the two Tom Thumb versions by the Grimm Brothers. Lagerkvist elaborates on his dwarf's grotesque body, his wizened old face, the attention his body gets when it is painted in the nude, which feels like a sort of rape to Piccoline. The dwarf's public display raises the old question of the body as property. The dwarf's right to his own body varies from case to case. If the fairy tale dwarf is displayed against his will for everyone to ridicule, if Mengele uses dwarves for his experiments, if Master Bernardo, who wants to paint a portrait of Piccoline, is so violent to him that it seems like rape to the dwarf, and if the appropriation of Oskar's body for postwar art resembles the Nazis' victimization of disabled bodies in euthanasia institutions, then we see an infringement upon the dwarf's right, like anyone else's right, to complete ownership of his body.[12] Like the dwarves in Hauff's stories, Lagerkvist's Piccoline is both mocked and mocking others: "they throw dead rats and other foulnesses from the muck-heaps at me. When I draw my sword in rage, they roar with laughter" (*D*, 17). Like Muck, who mocks authority by putting donkey's ears on the King, Piccoline mocks authority, the church. During carnival he gives a mock communion service, comparing Jesus with a dwarf. In this he resembles Oskar even more than the fairy tale dwarves, since Oskar more than once blasphemes in church: he declares himself the savior and desecrates church rituals and the Virgin Mary. In his novella *The Eternal Smile* (1920) Lagerkvist had already used the image of the hunchbacked dwarf cast out by society. As Robert Donald Spector has argued, the dwarf's deformity, which allegorically represents evil, is a common image in Lagerkvist's work.[13] As Oskar's hump symbolizes Germany's burden of the Nazi past as well as his personal guilt in having been the cause of several family members' deaths, so Piccoline's nefarious activities at court cause the deaths of several characters. Lack of parental love becomes the prime source for the dwarf's evil. Oskar's oedipal fixation may lead him to hand over his presumptive father Jan Bronski to the Home Guards, who shoot him, and to press the swastika badge into Matzerath's hand. This leads to Matzerath's death, and, as Bebra points out to little Oskar, these are not the only murders committed by Oskar: "War es nicht so, dass er seine arme Mama ins Grab trommelte?" (*B*, 461; "Is it not true that he drummed his poor mama into her grave?": *TD*, 553). While the fairy tales often end in reconciliation between the dwarf and his parents, this no longer seems to function in twentieth-century literature. Piccoline's hatred of mankind is entirely due to the fact that his mother sold him as a baby, "turning away from me in disgust when she saw what she had borne" (*D*, 15).

The structural similarities between Lagerkvist's novel, a text like Simon Mawer's highly readable novel *Mendel's Dwarf* (1998), and the fairy tales may support the argument that *Die Blechtrommel* transcends its roots in the folkloric tradition by displaying certain features of the structural topography outlined above that belong to a daily reality faced by all dwarves, such as society's mockery and underestimation of the dwarf, or the parents' sense of shame. This reality is ultimately responsible for stock situations in the literature about dwarves from the folk-tale to the twentieth-century novel. It cannot be denied that Grass's book is part of this wider contextual pool of dwarfism that is both a literary and a social phenomenon. After all, it is the reality of the dwarf's marginalization in society that precedes his centralization in various manifestations of popular culture.

When Benedict Lambert, the dwarf in Simon Mawer's novel, asks his school careers officer what kind of job he should take after school, that man tells him that he should join the circus.[14] The old prejudice about the dwarf's mental acumen surfaces here too, and is not limited to the fairy tales. Ben

Lambert, who becomes a genius geneticist, thinks to himself that "people seem amazed when they discover not only that I am not mentally retarded, but that I am actually more intelligent than they are."[15] His dialogue with the careers officer reflects clearly the fact that because of society's prejudice and tendency to ridicule its outsiders, dwarves have been stigmatized as prime candidates for public amusement, for popular culture — to this day in fact, if we look at the circus and at phenomena such as dwarf tossing. And yet there is hope, as nowadays we live in societies in which there are other ways for dwarves to render themselves useful, as Mawer's novel on the genius dwarf demonstrates. In this respect we depart from the dark ages' view, still evident in much folklore and legends, in which the dwarf was often equipped with supernatural powers so that he could hold his own vis à vis his aggressors. This is one detail that speaks for the close proximity between *Die Blechtrommel* and the folkloric tradition. Like the Tom Thumb figures and Hauff's dwarves, Oskar lives in a crude society, which is why Grass equips him with a magical weapon so that he may escape his persecutors. That Oskar develops a criminal nature, that he collaborates with those in power, and that he tries to escape into uterus-like places are likewise all motifs that are not part of the wider context of dwarfism, but stem directly from the fairy tale world.

Menippean Satire: Social Criticism through Carnivalesque Literature

Apart from these carnivalesque fairy tales about dwarves, Grass's book is part of a tightly woven fabric of texts that are steeped in the tradition of the Menippean satire. The revival of this genre in the twentieth century, whether in Russia or Germany, has the function of social criticism. It is subversive literature that forms a carnivalesque culture opposed to official ideology. As for Russia, Bakhtin wrote his book on Rabelais with this intention, and he did for literary theory what Mikhail Bulgakov's *The Master and Margarita* did in fiction. The publication of both books was delayed for many years due to the censorship under Stalinism. Bakhtin's dissertation, on which his book is based, was not completed until 1940, he did not receive his degree until 1951, and the book was not published until 1965. Bulgakov's novel experienced a similar publication history: it was started in 1928 but was not published until 1966, twenty-six years after his death, as a censored version in a Moscow journal. These texts attack the sociopolitical milieu of the late 1920s and the ensuing Stalinist period.

Rabelais's *Gargantua* and *Pantagruel* and Grimmelshausen's *Simplicius Simplicissimus,* works that are, like the fairy tales, central subtexts in Grass's novel, drew on Menippean satire for the same reason, namely to criticize the power structures of their times. The narrative romance *The Metamorphoses* (also known as *The Golden Ass*) by the Roman poet Lucius Apuleius (born c.

123 A.D., died c. 170) is one of this genre's principal representatives and influenced the work of Rabelais, Cervantes, Fielding, and Smollett. It displays the typical features of the Menippean satire: its coarse laughter, which is somewhat sharper and more cynical than folkloric laughter, its protean hero who undergoes metamorphoses (the transformation into an animal, mostly an ass), its utopian aspect and the unrestrained use of the fantastic: its heroes ascend into heaven, descend into the nether world, and wander through unknown and fantastic lands (*DP,* 114). For our discussion, one of the most interesting features that Bakhtin discusses for the Menippea is this genre's "representation of the unusual, abnormal moral and psychic states of man — insanity of all sorts, the theme of the maniac, split personality . . . passions bordering on madness" (*DP,* 116), which we see in Grimmelshausen, but most of all in the twentieth-century versions by Bulgakov and Grass. The Menippea discovered new forms of the scandalous and the eccentric, which are deliberately disruptive of the high tone of the epic and tragic genres. This phenomenon was likely to blame when Grass's novel, whose carnivalesque atmosphere drowns the tragic voice associated with Germany's ominous past, was ill received by many critics. Bakhtin emphasizes the carnivalesque nature of the Menippea that brings together absolutely heterogeneous and incompatible elements. Thus his notion of heteroglossia is itself determined through carnival and a carnival sense of the world, with its blurring of all boundaries between genres, self-enclosed systems of thought, and various styles (*DP,* 134). Bakhtin recognizes that Rabelais and Grimmelshausen were infiltrated by the Menippea, and as Morson and Emerson argue, his description of the genre suggests that "Bulgakov's *The Master and Margarita* and Grass's *Die Blechtrommel . . .* might also be considered almost perfect examples of Menippean satire."[16] Interestingly, Bakhtin also mentions the indebtedness of the Romantic philosophical fairy tale to this tradition, of E.T.A. Hoffmann's (1776–1822) *Klein Zaches* (1819), for example (*DP,* 137). Wilhelm Hauff's literary tales about dwarves *Der Zwerg Nase* and *Die Geschichte von dem kleinen Muck* also belong here with their characters' metamorphoses (Muck grows donkey's ears), their changing luck, and their abundance of carnivalesque images.

Rabelais

Rabelais's novels *Gargantua* and *Pantagruel* display polyphony similar to Grass's text. According to Bakhtin they are carnivalesque because of their heteroglossia and yet Bakhtin may overestimate Rabelais's revolutionary spirit. Rabelais was, like Grimmelshausen, a rather conservative author, who was attached to certain values of the church and the state. His novels are utopian, idealizing rather than destructive, and in their overall perspective of contemporary life and French society of the sixteenth century much less pessimistic than Grass is about Germany in the twentieth century. Grass's novel owes much to the novels of Rabelais, whose books were also condemned for their obscenities.[17] The perspective of giants in Rabelais is the perspective of the dwarf in Grass. Rabelais's novels demonstrate to what extent the carnival and folklore are related, mostly through the images surrounding giants and their counter-parts, the dwarves. Gargantua is a figure Rabelais borrowed from the *Chroniques gargantuines,* a series of folkloric writings that appeared about three months before Rabelais's *Pantagruel.* Moreover, Grass and Rabelais are both writers of human functions. Bakhtin's paradigms of carnivalesque literature, the grotesque body, the principle of mockery, and banquet images, devouring and being devoured, are motifs that *Die Blechtrommel* shares not only with the fairy tales but also with Rabelais's two books. In the carnival world, of which the fairy tales are a substantial part, these three dimensions, the body, mockery, and banquet images are often related. The body and banquet images overlap, for example, in that the giant's versus the dwarf's body is linked to the topic of eating versus being eaten. The body and mockery are related in that bodily images are often used for the purpose of subverting the authority of state and church, and mockery and banquet images converge, for example, in Tom Thumb's complaint that the food is not right. He mocks his master's wife when she neglects her maternal role as nurturer by threatening her that he will write on her door: "Kartoffel zu viel, Fleisch zu wenig, Adies, Herr Kartoffelkönig" (231; "Too much potatoes, too little meat! Bye, bye, potato king!": 164).[18] Rabelais's novels teem with images of the grotesque body that are linked to the principle of mockery and to the banquet. His giants are at the center of Bakhtin's theory of the grotesque body, and where there are giants there are dwarves. Gargantua eats six pilgrims in a salad and the narrator travels into Pantagruel's interior. The grotesque body is thematic during the birth of Gargantua, who comes into the world through Gargamelle's left ear and of Pantagruel, who is so large that he immediately suffocates his mother. With Oskar he shares a guilty conscience with regard to the death of his mother. Bodily protrusions and the body's metamorphosis are themes in both texts, for example Friar John's gigantic nose and Oskar's hump. Oskar shares with Gargantua his obsession with the phallus: as Gargantua exercises his codpiece, Oskar touches the 'watering can' of Baby Jesus, and is very proud of his own. In both texts the art of drumming signals the act of making love: "It's how I can manage to roger all those whores there this afternoon; so that there remain not one that I in common form don't drum" (*GP,* 253); Oskar's "halb schmerzhaft beginnende Versteifung meines Gießkännchens unter dem Badeanzug, ließen mich Trommel und beide Trommelstöcke um des einen, mir neu gewachsenen Stockes willen vergessen" (*B,* 220; "the half-painful stiffening of my watering can under my bathing suit made me forget drum and drumsticks for the sake of the new stick I had developed": *TD,* 269). In both novels, there is a conflation of soaring architecture and bodily processes: as Gargantua urinates from the Towers of Notre Dame, Oskar screams from the Stockturm, a tower in the center of Danzig. In Rabelais there are countless images of eating versus being eaten, such as the famous *tripes* (intestines), which are devoured in large quantities by these giants but are also devouring organs, a motif that resurfaces in Grass's eels. As will be discussed in more detail in chapter 4 of this study, these eels are both eaten by the Matzeraths but they also do their share of devouring. Not only are they shown as feeding on drowned sailors and biting the insides of a woman who tries to please herself with an eel, but ultimately they also consume Oskar's mother Agnes, albeit metaphorically.

As is typical of Menippean satire, these carnivalesque images are used for social satire and allow Rabelais and Grass to mock a) the church, b) the ruler, c) the education system, and d) another fictional genre, in Grass's case the Bildungsroman. Because he supported many of Luther's ideas, Rabelais's criticism is directed mostly against the Catholic Church. Gargantua steals the church bells of Notre Dame and ties them around a mule. The utopian image of the Abbaye de Thélème, a sort of anti-monastery, with its emphasis on the appetites (*thelema*), on desire and freedom, allows Rabelais to parody the norms of the Catholic Church. This satirical criticism of "a Christianity stressing sin and the mortification of the flesh"[19] and the Catholic Church's own transgressions through a utopian counter-model resembles Grimmelshausen's ironic description of the alleged virtues of the clergy in that utopian segment in which Simplicius travels to the empire of the Sylphs at the center of the Earth. Such utopian episodes are typical of the Menippean satire. In Rabelais, there is a constant mixing of processes of the lower body and imagery relating to the church and state. Friar John, for example, refers to the virile member in relation to a man's nose "ad formam nasi cognoscitur ad te levavi" and thus to psalm 122: "by the shape of his nose he is known; I have lifted up [mine eyes] to thee" (*GP*, 127), and Panurge loses control of his bowels at the sight of a large cat that he takes for the Devil: "suddenly he did a bigger pile than you would have expected of nine buffaloes and fourteen arch-priests from Ostia" (*GP*, 595), or: "One day, as King Edward IV was doing his business, he showed Villon a painting of the French coat-of-arms, and said: 'You see what respect I have for your French kings. I keep their armorial bearings in this place only, beside my close-stool'" (*GP*, 595). Chapter 5 of this study will demonstrate how Grass uses popular culture to attack the Catholic Church, its silent support of the Nazi crimes and the Adenauer period's politics of sanity and rationalism. Grass's offensive conflation of grotesque body images with those of the church, his profanities in the sacred realm, hark back to the work of Rabelais and its related mythological background, the trickster who takes great pleasure in disturbing the most sacred, as well as such carnival traditions as the Feast of Fools and Feast of Asses (*festum asinorum*).

While the Second World War and the tyrant Adolf Hitler form a central historical background in *Die Blechtrommel,* the backdrop in Rabelais's books is the Picrochole war and the figure of Picrochole, that "immortal image of the militarist, aggressive politician"(*RW,* 447). Through this figure Rabelais no doubt alludes to the tyranny and imperialist ambitions of Charles V, who considered himself the heir of the Roman Empire, and dreamed of leading all of Christendom.[20] Grass mocks and uncrowns such patriarchal rulers as Hitler and Adenauer. Since Oskar has the duplicitous nature of being both a victim and a participant in fascist activities, his drumming can be read as an allusion not only to his resistance to party politics but also to Hitler himself, who was called *der Trommler* (the drummer). *Die Blechtrommel* uncrowns cultural heroes like Goethe and Beethoven, and, at the level of the family, Oskar's alleged father Matzerath as a patriarchal figure. In his stead a matriarchy is established, the grandmother as *magna mater* and her daughter Agnes, who, although she dies, is the one who takes action by cheating on her husband instead of the other way round. Old Matzerath is an almost entirely passive character (except for his party affiliation and his cooking skills) and his carnivalesque uncrowning, the inversion of the traditional patriarchal gender pattern, can be read as a critique of the gender politics of the Third Reich and its legacy.

Rabelais criticizes the medieval school system (book 1, chapters 14, 15, 21–24) and parodies the scholarship of his time (book 2, chapters 18, 19). His novels reflect his embrace of the new humanistic ideals and his eagerness to leave the Middle Ages behind. His books combine Dionysian popular culture with the Apollonian aims of high culture, the new humanistic ideals of *Bildung.* Although deeply rooted in popular culture, the gigantism in these novels can be interpreted as a representation of this new image of man, who exits from the dark ages into an age of light. In Grass the opposite happens: here the misshapen dwarf is a representation of German guilt and inferiority. Oskar's deliberate rejection of *Bildung* shows that humanistic values had lost their validity after Auschwitz. German *Bildung* had become meaningless after 1945, and the idea and practice of it sank away completely under national shame and the American re-education program. Grass mocks the tradition of a school education in the famous scene in which Oskar attends Miss Spollenhauer's class for one day, and he parodies Goethe and the national German pride in its high culture.

Both books parody a genre: As Rabelais's novels parody the high seriousness of epic and tragedy as well as the medieval *roman de chevalier,* the courtly novel, with its structure of the hero's genealogy, youth, education, heroic adventure, courtship and marriage, Grass parodies the Bildungsroman. The idea of the genealogy of the *roman de chevalier* still appears in rudimentary form in *Die Blechtrommel,* when Grass elaborates on Oskar's grandfather and grandmother. Another relic of this genre in Grass's novel is the comparison of Oskar with Parcifal in various chapters (for example, "Der Igel" [The Hedgehog]). The *roman de chevalier* and the novels that treat the quest for the Holy Grail intended to hold up an idealized mirror to courtly society, a phenomenon that is similar to the optimism of the Bildungsroman that reflects the ideals of nineteenth-century bourgeois society. Both Rabelais and Grass parody these genres through their use of the grotesque. Rabelais parodies the quest motif, for example, through his character Panurge, the central buffoon of his novels. In the same way Oskar, who refuses to develop, who refuses to succumb to *Bildung* in the Classical sense, is a parody of the typical hero of the Bildungsroman. Although both authors evidently parody the serious, official culture by resorting to the folk humor in popular culture, Richard Berrong's intriguing study has shown that both learned and popular culture form integral parts in Rabelais's texts.[21] While Grass's book is a full blown grotesque, in Rabelais there is a subtle shift from an abundance of grotesque popular culture in *Pantagruel* (the third, fourth, and fifth book) towards its suppression in *Gargantua* (the first and second book). Rabelais wrote the three books of *Pantagruel* first, although they generally appear after *Gargantua*. Rabelais's series of books reflects his mental step from the Renaissance world of the senses and its tolerance of the grotesque body to the Enlightenment's abandonment of this world for the sovereignty of reason. As in Grimmelshausen's *Simplicius Simplicissimus*, certain bourgeois values surface in *Gargantua*, for example the suppression of laziness by the dominant class. The defense of the lower classes is therefore not as pronounced as Bakhtin would have it.

Grimmelshausen

One of Oskar's many roles is that of a picaro, an aimless and asocial wanderer like his early, pre-Enlightenment European relatives Don Quixote, Tom Jones, and Simplicius Simplicissimus. Friedrich Gaede has shown to what extent Grass is indebted to Grimmelshausen's picaresque novel *Simplicius Simplicissimus*.[22] The picaro's life story is often told as a retrospective narrative, he is typically a character of low birth, his parents often display a lack of moral integrity, he experiences a problematic childhood, and the genre focuses heavily on its character's wanderings and his changing masters (Oskar after the war becomes an apprentice, a jazz musician, an entrepreneur, and so on). Like Rabelais's books, Grimmelshausen's novel is rooted in the tradition of the Menippean satire, as Stefan Trappen has shown.[23] *Simplicius Simplicissimus* shares two structural features with the Menippea of antiquity, such as Apuleius's *Metamorphoses*: his physical and mental metamorphosis, and the hero's withdrawal from society. As Lucius changes into an ass, a popular motif that also occurs in Carlo Collodi's (1826–90) *Le Avventure di Pinocchio* (The Adventures of Pinocchio, 1883) and Hauff's

Muck, the picaro is a fool who is often depicted as an animal. Simplicius becomes a calf and also has a costume displaying donkey ears. As we have seen, Oskar too is debased to the level of an animal, at the moment when Maria, the chief representative of postwar bourgeoisie, calls him a pig. This degradation of the hero, who is a thief and a transient, is a mode of representation that in Grass's novel is closely linked to the persecution of the physically and mentally disabled whom the Nazis saw either as animals in the shape of humans or even as monsters at a lower level than animals. That *Simplicius* is a picaresque novel (pre-Enlightenment) and not a Bildungsroman, a genre that arose in the age of Enlightenment, has been established since the 1970s, while in earlier research it was still considered a Bildungsroman and compared to Wolfram von Eschenbach's (c. 1170–c. 1225) *Parzival* (c. 1205) and Goethe's *Wilhelm Meister* novels.[24]

The picaresque novel is about a character that typically does not become integrated into society but stays outside of it. Lucius in Apuleius's Menippean satire and Simplicius both escape the ups and downs of life by becoming hermits and turning to religion. That the Nazis managed to ignore Simplicius's aimless wandering, his thievishness, and his withdrawal from society, as well as the grotesque dimension of this novel, shows us how blinded they must have been in their attempt to fit Grimmelshausen into their ideology (discussed in detail in chapter 6). Considering the Nazis' own telos of constructing a nation-state in which everyone had to function, the nineteenth-century Bildungsroman, in which the protagonist in the course of his acculturation is integrated into bourgeois society, was understandably a more popular genre to Nazi ideologues than the picaresque novel, this low genre and *roman comique* of dubious Spanish origin. Particularly because of the fact that none other than Goethe had written one of the great German Bildungsromane, the Wilhelm Meister novels, the Nazis deeply identified with this form of German high culture. Examples for the popularity of the Bildungsroman during the Third Reich are such nineteenth-century novels as Gustav Freytag's *Soll und Haben* and Wilhelm Raabe's (1831–1910) *Der Hungerpastor* (The Hunger Pastor, 1864), both of which juxtapose a cosmopolitan Jewish antagonist with a more rooted, home-loving non-Jewish protagonist. The Jew in these novels succumbs, while the non-Jew finds happiness at the end. The teleology of the Bildungsroman's happy ending is then deconstructed by many postwar authors, including Grass, Arno Schmidt, and Edgar Hilsenrath in their resuscitation of the picaresque tradition. It seems that the blissful times of the Bildungsroman no longer function in our post-Auschwitz, postmodern age, which is characterized by increasing fragmentation and a deeply rooted skepticism towards all happy endings. The picaresque novel is indeed more suited to the representation of our fragmented world.

By returning to the picaresque tradition, Grass's novel is directed against Goethe, his obsession with form and formation, the perfectibility of man.

Grass shows through fiction what Michael Baigent and Richard Leigh have argued, that one can see how Goethe's "insistence on spiritual and cultural leadership, if allied to social and political ambition, could themselves become pernicious, providing a foundation for a theology of racial supremacy."[25] Oskar surmises that had he lived and drummed in Goethe's time, this "man of the Enlightenment," as Ralph Manheim freely translates the term "Alles-wisser, hätte . . . in dir nur Unnatur erkannt, dich als die leibhaftige Unnatur verurteilt und . . . dich armen Tropf wenn nicht mit dem Faust dann mit einem dicken Band seiner Farbenlehre erschlagen" (*B*, 72; "would have thought you unnatural, would have condemned you as an incarnation of anti-nature and . . . poor devil . . . hit you over the head with *Faust* or a big heavy volume of his *Theory of Colors*": *TD*, 91). In opposition to Goethe's dictum that classicism is healthy while Romanticism is sick, Grass's novel shows that Romanticism contains strong humanitarian aspects, as it was tolerant of grotesque forms that had been suppressed in the Age of Reason and its ensuing bourgeois periods, such as the Biedermeier period (1815–48) and bourgeois realism (1848–80).[26] Between Classicism and the Bieder-meier, Romanticism was a counter movement that made room for minorities and social outsiders. No other period between the Enlightenment and 1945 witnesses such sympathy with outsiders as Romanticism. Examples range from fairy tales such as Ludwig Tieck's (1773–1853) *Der gestiefelte Kater* (Puss in Boots, 1797), with its provocative marginalization of the clown Jackpudding, to novellas such as Joseph von Eichendorff's (1788–1857) *Aus dem Leben eines Taugenichts* (From the Life of a Good-For-Nothing, 1826) and Adalbert von Chamisso's (1781–1838) *Peter Schlemihls wundersame Geschichte* (The Wondrous History of Peter Schlemihl, 1814) with their aimlessly wandering characters. It is no coincidence that the Bildungsroman with its socialization process for the hero accompanies Germany's rise of a nationalist awareness. On the other hand, the picaresque novel with its social outsider precedes the beginnings of nationalism and then in the writings of Grass and others resurfaces in reaction to the Nazis' extreme version of nationalism, which implied a rejection of all social outsiders, the insane, but also the aimless wanderers, who because they were without roots were like-wise considered insane. Unlike the hero of the Bildungsroman, who travels for the purpose of Bildung and in order to come to his senses, aimless wan-dering in the bourgeois age implied a permanent physical *Entrücktheit*, a displacement from one's home and hence a form of *Verrücktheit*, insanity. In the Classical Bildungsroman the individual ideally gives up his "poetry of the heart," as Hegel once called it,[27] which particularly in the period of bourgeois realism after 1848 makes this genre support the formation of the nation-state. It is the more liberal picaresque tradition from an age in which there were no nation-states, a genre that showed more tolerance towards social outsiders, to which Grass harks back in his attempt to reconstruct

German culture as a part of European culture and through which he can voice his skepticism about the idea of nationalism.

Goethean thought, Goethe's vision of the "klassisch Gesunde" (the classically healthy) as a seedbed for the racial eugenics of the Nazis — this is undoubtedly a provocative thought. Yet in postwar German culture Grass's novel is not alone in its recourse to the picaresque and its parody of German high culture and the Enlightenment concept of *Bildung*. In this regard, *Die Blechtrommel* can also be compared with such works as Thomas Mann's *Bekenntnisse des Hochstaplers Felix Krull,* Arno Schmidt's *Das steinerne Herz,* and Edgar Hilsenrath's *Der Nazi & der Friseur*. In their return to the world of fairy tales and myth for the representation of the Holocaust and post-Holocaust German society, these artists were all supporters of Richard Alewyn's warning to all Germans in 1949 that between us and Weimar there is Buchenwald.[28] Much has been written on Grass's use of the picaresque and his parody of Goethean *Bildung,*[29] yet these categories have not been discussed in the context of the Nazis' oppression of the grotesque and of low culture. More will be said on this connection in chapter 6 of this study. By recovering what was considered an inferior genre throughout the nineteenth century, namely the picaresque tradition, that is, by salvaging the degenerate and grotesque not only in the human body (Oskar) but also in the literary form, Grass's *Die Blechtrommel* becomes one of the great humanitarian novels of our time.

Notes

[1] These medieval celebrations date back to the Saturnalia, a festival during which a brief social revolution empowered the lower church clergy, usually the sub-deacons. At its core, the Feast of Asses contains the scene in which the prophet Balaam's ass protests to the angels against the cruelty of his rider. This ritual from the eleventh century was eventually incorporated into the Feast of Fools, which was initially celebrated by the lower clergy, then by a guild of fools, and was finally forbidden under severe penalties by the Council of Basle in 1435.

[2] For the intertextuality between these authors see: Henrik D. K. Engel, *Die Prosa von Günter Grass in Beziehung zur englischsprachigen Literatur: Rezeption, Wirkungen und Rückwirkungen bei Salmon Rushdie, John Irving, Bernard Malamud u.a.* (New York: Peter Lang, 1997); Rudolf Bader, "Indian Tin Drum," in *The International Fiction Review* 11.2 (1984): 75–83; Mario Couto, "'Midnight's Children' and Parents," in *Encounter* 58.2 (1982); "Raj Gopal, Saleem Snotnose und Oskar der Blechtrommler: Zum Vergleich von Günter Grass und Salmon Rushdie," in *German Studies in India* (Trivandrum: U of Kerala, 1983); E. W. Herd, "Tin Drum and Snake-Charmer's Flute: Salmon Rushdie's Debt to Günter Grass," in *New Comparison* 6 (1989): 205–18; Patricia Merivale, "Saleem Fathered by Oskar: Intertextual Strategies in 'Midnight's Children' and 'The Tin Drum,'" in *Ariel: A Review of International English Literature* 21.3 (1990): 5–21.

[3] Simon Dentith, *Bakhtinian Thought* (New York: Routledge, 1995), 196 and 204.

[4] Cf. John Walter Van Cleve, *Harlequin Besieged: The Reception of Comedy in Germany during the Early Enlightenment* (Bern: Peter Lang, 1980).

[5] Paul Radin, *The Trickster: A Study in American Indian Mythology* (New York: Schocken Books, 1972), 39.

[6] Radin, *The Trickster*, 29: "he cut off the head of one of the children, put a stick through its neck and placed it at the door as though the child were peeping out and laughing."

[7] John Greenway, *The Primitive Reader: An Anthology of Myths, Tales, Songs, Riddles, and Proverbs of Aboriginal Peoples around the World* (Hatboro: Folklore Associates, 1965), 57.

[8] William J. Hynes and William G. Doty, ed., *Mythical Trickster Figures: Contours, Contexts, and Criticisms* (Tuscaloosa: U of Alabama P, 1993), 15.

[9] The fairy tale subtexts of the novel have been analyzed in only two articles, Janice Mouton's "Gnomes, Fairy Tale Heroes, and Oskar Matzerath," in *The Germanic Review* 56.1 (1981): 28–33, and David Roberts, "Tom Thumb and the Imitation of Christ: Towards a Psycho-Mythological Interpretation of the 'Hero' Oskar and his Symbolic Function," in *Proceedings and Papers of the Congress of the Australasian Universities Language and Literature Association* (Canberra: U of Canberra, 1972), 160–74.

[10] Leni Yahil, *The Holocaust: The Fate of European Jewry* (Oxford: Oxford UP, 1990), 309.

[11] August Lütjens, *Der Zwerg in der deutschen Heldendichtung des Mittelalters* (Breslau: M. & M. Marcus, 1911), 7.

[12] This issue of the dwarf's complete ownership to his body has recently been discussed with regard to the custom of dwarf tossing. Should dwarves be allowed to be tossed for money (up to $500 a day) in bars or should there be a law preventing this custom, which some think ridicules and demeans little people and may tear down the structure and esteem that they are trying to gain? Cf. Robert W. McGee, "If dwarf tossing is outlawed, only outlaws will toss dwarves: is dwarf tossing a victimless crime?" in *The American Journal of Jurisprudence* 38 (1993): 335–58.

[13] Robert Donald Spector, *Pär Lagerkvist* (New York: Twayne Publishers, 1973), 52.

[14] Simon Mawer, *Mendel's Dwarf* (New York: Harmony Books, 1998), 44.

[15] Mawer, *Mendel's Dwarf*, 44.

[16] Gary Saul Morson & Caryl Emerson, *Mikhail Bakhtin: Creation of a Prosaics* (Stanford: Stanford UP, 1990), 462.

[17] Frank-Rutger Hausmann, *François Rabelais* (Stuttgart: Metzler, 1979), 29: on 23 October 1533 the Sorbonne condemned *Pantagruel* for its obscenity (see in novel II, 15, in which Panurge wants to build the walls of Paris out of the private parts of men and women).

[18] The editions used here are: Brüder Grimm, *Kinder- und Hausmärchen* 1 and 2, ed. Heinz Rölleke (Stuttgart: Reclam, 1980) and Jack Zipes, ed., *The Complete Fairy Tales of the Brothers Grimm* (New York: Bantham, 1987).

[19] Jerome Schwartz, *Irony and Ideology in Rabelais: Structures of Subversion* (Cambridge: Cambridge UP, 1990), 83.

[20] Cf. Schwartz, *Irony and Ideology*, 78.

[21] Richard Berrong, *Rabelais and Bakhtin: Popular Culture in "Gargantua and Pantagruel"* (Lincoln: U of Nebraska P, 1986), 38.

[22] Friedrich Gaede, "Grimmelshausen, Brecht, Grass: Zur Tradition des literarischen Realismus in Deutschland," in *Simpliciana: Schriften der Grimmelshausen-Gesellschaft 1* (1979): 367–82.

[23] Stefan Trappen, *Grimmelshausen und die menippeische Satire: Eine Studie zu den historischen Voraussetzungen der Prosasatire im Barock* (Tübingen: Max Niemeyer, 1994), primarily 233–35. Grimmelshausen's novel displays the typical features of the Menippea: Simplicius's metamorphoses, his changing luck, the utopian elements of the text, his trip to the center of the Earth, the scandalous and the slum naturalism of the novel, are all indicators that the text is steeped in this tradition.

[24] Trappen, *Grimmelshausen*, 239.

[25] Michael Baigent and Richard Leigh, *Secret Germany: Stauffenberg and the Mystical Crusade against Hitler* (London: Penguin, 1994), 204.

[26] Grass's "Romantic" fascination with chaos and the grotesque reappears in his travel writing about India, which contrasts with Goethe's own writing about that country. Goethe, who was a worshipper of the classical form in the Greek statues, was appalled by the formlessness of the Indian deities displaying grotesque admixtures of animal and human parts. Cf. Veena Kade-Luthra, ed., *Sehnsucht nach Indien: Ein Lesebuch von Goethe bis Grass* (München: C. H. Beck, 1993), 18–19, 83–84.

[27] Georg Wilhelm Friedrich Hegel, "Die Poesie," part 3 of *Vorlesungen über die Ästhetik* (Frankfurt am Main: Suhrkamp, 1970), 393: "Eine der gewöhnlichsten und für den Roman passendsten Kollisionen ist deshalb der Konflikt zwischen der Poesie des Herzens und der entgegenstehenden Prosa der Verhältnisse . . . ein Zwiespalt, der sich entweder tragisch und komisch löst oder seine Erledigung darin findet, dass . . . die der gewöhnlichen Weltordnung zunächst widerstrebenden Charaktere das Echte und Substantielle in ihr anerkennen lernen, mit ihren Verhältnissen sich aussöhnen und wirksam in dieselben eintreten." (One of the most common and typical collisions in the novel is the conflict between the poetry of the heart and the prose of external conditions, of reality, a conflict that is resolved either tragically or comically, or in such a way that the characters who are initially opposed to the world order learn to recognize its genuine and substantial aspects, learn to become reconciled to its conditions, and to be integrated effectively into this order.)

[28] Georg Bollenbeck, "German 'Kultur,' the 'Bildungsbürgertum,' and its Susceptibility to National Socialism," in *The German Quarterly* 73.1 (Winter 2000): 67–83.

[29] See eg., Rainer Diederichs, *Strukturen des Schelmischen im modernen deutschen Roman: Eine Untersuchung an den Romanen von Thomas Mann "Bekenntnisse des Hochstaplers Felix Krull" und Günter Grass "Die Blechtrommel"* (Jena: Eugen Diederichs, 1971); Volker Neuhaus, *Günter Grass* (Stuttgart: Metzler, 1992); and Volker Neuhaus, *Günter Grass: "Die Blechtrommel"* (München: Oldenbourg Verlag, 1982).

3: The Dwarf and Nazi Body Politics

> *"It is a fact that a hunchback is born into
> the world every minute. It seems, therefore,
> that there exists in the race a definite need
> to be in part hunchbacked"*
> — Pär Lagerkvist, *The Eternal Smile*

Nazi Body Politics

GRASS'S TEXT COMMENTS on National Socialism's obsession with the body, the Nazis' worship of the desirable body and their persecution of the undesirable body. The years from 1933 to 1945 were a time in which the bodies of millions of people were sacrificed for the high ideals of a few. The Nazis, who were convinced that a healthy spirit can only be found in those who have a healthy, well-shaped body, perceived "Körperschönheit als Lebenswert," physical beauty as an indicator of life's value and thus worthiness of life as opposed to the ugly body as life unworthy of life. This view was adopted from Nietzsche and the Stefan George circle, which glorified spiritual and physical nobility and openly despised the *Durchschnittsmenschen* (the average human being) (*NT,* 165). Modernity's cultural despair due to the increasing ugliness of the world is reflected in this aesthetic concern that makes the human body its primary target. Around 1900, journals like *Die Schönheit* (Beauty) and *Kraft und Schönheit* (Strength and Beauty) desire to heal the body from diseases of civilization through nudity and a return to nature, for example in the *Wandervögel* movement, a youth movement that was established in 1901 and was devoted to outdoor activities. This is the time that the cult of beauty becomes increasingly allied with racism. It is now that society becomes divided into *Übermenschen* and *Untermenschen* based on purely aesthetic values. The working class, which was bent over from physical labor, became the main enemy of this cult of the body, and it was associated most of all with *Untermenschen,* because they were farthest from the ideal of the perfect body (*NT,* 173). Yet society's outsiders, primarily the Jews, also became excluded from this vision of beauty. The proletarian and the Jew were regarded as the two manifestations of primordial evil. The question of beauty was increasingly related to the racial question. Beauty was associated with clarity, purity, cleanliness, and order, ugliness with chaos, and after the chaotic times of the Weimar Republic nothing was more frightening to the bourgeois class than a lack of *Ordnung*: order and orderliness. What was condemned in the human body was likewise condemned in the arts, which had to reflect beauty and harmony. Modern art was the epitome of ugliness and became associated with disease and crippled bodies.[1] The extermination of the physically disabled thus went hand in hand with the extermination of undesirable art.

The association between degenerate art and the degenerate body in the Third Reich becomes evident if one listens to the words of Hitler's speech at the opening ceremony of the "Haus der Deutschen Kunst" and the "Große Deutsche Kunstausstellung," in which he mentions "misshapen cripples" who inspire nothing but disgust, men who are closer to animals than humans, children who, if they stayed alive, would be cursed by God.[2] Hitler's speech also appeared in the catalog for the exhibition "Entartete Kunst" (Degenerate Art).[3] In *Die Blechtrommel*, this perception of the disabled is reflected mostly in Maria's verbal abuse of Oskar, by which she strips him of his humanity. Her words reflect to what extent the party's racist ideology colonized the quotidian consciousness of the population, as Ulrike Schulz put it.[4] While Maria is eager to get rid of Oskar during the Nazi years, she still considers him a burden during the Adenauer years. Maria, who used to pray with Oskar, is part of a wide range of means through which Grass attacks the church for its silence in the face of Nazi crimes. Another is the chapter "Madonna 49," which alludes to Hitler's association of disabled people with the degeneracy of modern art. When Oskar poses as a model for the Düsseldorf art students, one of the two art professors refers to him as a "Krüppel" (cripple) (*B*, 383), the other calls him a "Mißgeburt" (freak of nature) (*B*, 385). The church is indicted here in the figure of Professor Kuchen, who wants his students to "slaughter" and "crucify" this cripple, to nail him to their paper with charcoal. Art, the killing of disabled people, and the involvement of the church in the Nazi crimes against the human body and works of art are all woven together in this passage.

The Munich exhibition of degenerate art was divided into two opposite parts, one that propagated the ideal of beauty, the other on *entartete Kunst* that showed cripples, disfigured bodies, and bodies in pieces. The Nazis aspired to the former, the creation of beautiful bodies, but in order to get there they went through the latter, the bodies in pieces. The parallel exhibitions reflect the Nazis' ideal of the desired body versus the body that is to be destroyed. In his speech Hitler pointed out that National Socialism had made it its task to free the Reich from all those influences that might be destructive to its people, and even if this cleansing did not happen in one day, everybody who participated in this destruction ought to know that the hour of his or her elimination would come sooner or later.[5] Just as the greengrocer Greff hides his homosexuality behind his well-trained body, Oskar escapes persecution for a while because initially he hides his dwarfism in the body of a child, and later he proves his usefulness by being an entertainer at the front. Yet his ultimate uselessness to society surfaces more and more as the war progresses.

Oskar's dwarfism is not congenital but the result of his willpower. This element of pure fantasy clashes with the historical reality of the persecution of "diseased" bodies. Oskar is safe from the Nazis for a while because he is not Jewish, although he is racially impure because of his Kashubian background and the fact that he is possibly the son of a Pole. At the time when the letter requesting Oskar's institutionalization reaches Matzerath from the Ministry of Health, euthanasia activities had reached their zenith of ideological frenzy. Oskar's dwarfism would be reason enough to make him the victim of persecution, as Klee informs us.[6] The infamous physician of Auschwitz, Dr. Josef Mengele (1911–79) had a particular fascination with dwarves, and he used Auschwitz to study exceptionally rare individuals. Particularly his studies on twins were used to "confirm a discourse of racial hygiene which lent scientific legitimacy to the institution of the concentration camp and to the genocide to which that institution had been dedicated."[7] Mengele's assistant, Miklos Nyiszli, described the Nazi doctors' particular fascination with dwarves, who were treated with some degree of respect before they were exposed to all sorts of humiliating medical examinations.[8] Spotting physical deformities was a welcome opportunity for the camp doctors to support their theory of the Jewish race's degeneracy, as in the case when Mengele espied a hunchbacked father and his lame son among those lined up for selection.[9]

It was not only the aesthetic appeal of the healthy body that mattered to the Nazis. The main reason for their insistence on a healthy body was more primitive and had immensely practical implications. Since only the healthy body can function well it was considered useful for the building of the Thousand-Year Reich. What was pure aestheticism at the beginning of the century became allied under National Socialism to the practical purpose of an efficient performance in the workplace. This went so far that even people with minor defects were killed.[10] To maintain the health of the individual and the overall health of the collective body, the so-called *Volkskörper*, National Socialism relied largely on the beneficial impact of physical education. Sports had the function of keeping the body in shape so that it could contribute its energy to the *Volkskörper*. The understanding was that if the individual body was not intact the whole body of the people would suffer. Therefore, by cutting away the diseased parts of the collective social body, it could recover its overall health. In a way, the Nazis applied to the *Volk* what the first letter to the Corinthians expresses in its simile of the body and its limbs that are to reflect the diverse make-up of Christianity: chapter 12, verse 26: if one limb suffers, all limbs suffer along with it. National Socialism tried to represent this people's body in its texts and public scenarios, such as the Olympic Games of 1936 (*BK*, 11). Although the national body cult and physical education (*Leibeserziehung*) movements were mostly a means to activate the energies of the people for war and work, (*NT*, 47) at the same time, sports played a part in the Nazis' struggle for racial hygiene. Physical education was regarded as a way to counteract the social and cultural decay, the diseases of the time. Those who were considered responsible for this sociocultural decline, society's *bacilli* in Nazi jargon, the Jews and other groups of the so-called *Asozialen*, were excluded not only from physical education but from the education system in general.

In view of the overall health of the collective body, it was each individual's duty to keep his or her body in good shape. The term that the Nazis created was *Gesundheitspflicht* (the duty to stay healthy).[11] The Nazis attributed the bad body primarily to the Jews, "das weibische zersetzende Judentum" (the effeminate and corrosive Jewry)(*BK*, 84), while the good masculine body was the Aryan body, although it was not limited to it. That the Nazis extended their body cult beyond the national boundaries becomes obvious, for example, in Leni Riefenstahl's (1902–2003) film *Olympia* (1936), which represents the Japanese and the Finns as prime athletes in the marathon. They function as role models to the Germans whose athletes were not victorious in this discipline (*BK*, 89–90). Likewise, it was difficult for the Nazis to deny that Blacks also had 'good' and masculine bodies. Although Hitler was adverse to the international spirit of the 1936 Olympics, there is in Riefenstahl's movie a candid admiration for the black body of Jesse Owens, who won the 100 meters. Black bodies were considered natural miracles, bodies untainted by civilization (*BK*, 72 n. 35). In view of such politics of functionality, Oskar's stunted growth is *artfremd*, alien to the German kind, *entartet*, degenerate, and ultimately damaging to the health of the *Volkskörper*.

The body concept of antiquity that the archaeologist and art historian Johann Winckelmann (1717–68) praised in the Greek statue's reflection of a democratic spirit did at first not appeal to the Nazis. More than the classical beauty of antiquity that was initially considered void of soul, the *völkische* ideology prized the Gothic style because it seemed to reflect the Faustian quest of the German soul. Before 1936, partisans of the idea of the *Volk* had rejected antiquity as corrupting Germanic society and culture, because they saw Greek antiquity as Apollonian, that is, complete in form, empty beauty without soul, that could not aptly represent the Faustian quest of the Germanic soul, which they saw reflected primarily in the figure of Parsifal (*NT*, 92). In Grass's novel, this dichotomy between *völkisch* admiration for the Gothic style on the one hand and the degenerate on the other forms a backdrop in that the redbrick Gothic architecture of the Hanseatic town of Danzig contrasts sharply with the deformed body of Oskar. In the chapter "Fernwirkender Gesang vom Stockturm aus gesungen" (The Stockturm:

Long-Distance Song Effects) we see Oskar climb to the top of a Gothic tower with the intention of liberating himself temporarily from the maze below, but also of screaming holes into an architecture that stands for a concept of beauty he cannot be a part of. Unlike Goethe, who was once humbled by the grandeur of the Strasburg cathedral, Oskar rebels against the authority of high culture and an ideal of beauty, a rebellion against the times he grows up in as well as his personal family situation. The Nazis' preference for Gothic beauty gave way, however, between 1934 and 1937 to their acceptance of the classical beauty of antiquity as expressed in the Greek statue, which the Nazis then related to the ideological construction of the optimal Aryan body (*BK*, 25). Hitler had a vision of German high culture that went well beyond his provincial Germanic cult and included the worship of beauty practiced in Greek Antiquity (*NT*, 83). He clearly saw a connection between the Nordic race and the Greek, thus wedding, as did Goethe in *Faust II*, the Hellenic to the Germanic (*NT*, 87).

> The human of Nordic race is not only the most gifted but also the most beautiful. There stands the slim body of man, erect with victorious expression of bone and muscle build, with magnificent span of broad and powerful shoulders, the broad chest and small waist. There thrives the growth of woman with narrower, rounded shoulders and broader hips, but always slim in most exquisite manner. Man has a sharply cut face, woman has softer features, both have clear fresh skin, blonde hair, bright victorious eyes, both show the consummate motion of a perfect body, a royal breed among mankind.[12]

It is easy to see how this general image of beauty could also be discerned in the Greek statue, which then became the ideal of the body at a time that was characterized by the stigma of decay and the ugliness of everyday life. Art had the function of reflecting the impending regeneration of the *Volk* and anything that did not serve this purpose was considered degenerate. Arno Breker's statues in particular reflect the ideal human body in art. Breker did for sculpture what Leni Riefenstahl achieved for film. With the Olympic Games of 1936, antiquity's ideal of beauty became adopted in theory and practice. As Wildmann points out, Riefenstahl's film on the Olympic Games formulates the official iconography of the body and disseminates it visually (*BK*, 26). Through her images of the marathon runners and the decathlete Erwin Huber, Riefenstahl establishes a link between antiquity and the Germany of her time. Breker and Riefenstahl were obsessed with the myth of the "body beautiful" and after 1945 both denied that their art contained any political message.

The Nazis' adoption of the Greek ideal of the perfect body paved the way for their rejection of the degenerate body. In its rigidity the Greek statue is the classical body in completion, which best shows its perfection as the naked body. The naked body was also associated with a primordial state of health that predates the ailments of modernity brought about by increasing industrialization disguised as civilization. The body was considered to be increasingly in danger of becoming diseased through exposure to city-life and the Jews. The German concept of *Freikörperkultur* (FKK, free body culture) originated in the various youth movements around the turn of the century and implied the idea that the naked body could heal more easily and become a healthy body, because through nudity one was in touch with nature. In the Third Reich, FKK was soon allied to the ideology of racial hygiene. In Grass's novel, we see this celebration of nudity in the greengrocer Greff who undresses to go swimming in the Baltic Sea. His body cult is a way of hiding his homosexuality and effeminate nature, which, if it were discovered by the Nazis, would place him in one camp with the "effeminate Jews" and also make him a victim of persecution.[13] In the chapter "Madonna 49" Grass then distorts the purity of nudity by making Oskar a naked model. His nudity is thus used to contrast his grotesque body with the classical beauty of the fascist worship of Greek statues, and the size of his penis is made to stand in grotesque contrast to his small body. What at the level of history is the Nazis' worship of classical form, the bedrock of the persecution of the disabled body, therefore finds its fictional representation primarily in Grass's chapter "Madonna 49" and in the juxtaposition of Oskar's grotesque body and Greff's classical body.

It is obvious that the historical context of Nazi body politics in *Die Blechtrommel* is conflated with the Bakhtinian image of the grotesque body, a central image of carnival that pervades much of Rabelais and other carnivalesque literature, primarily the dwarf fairy tales. Due to the increasing disappearance of the carnival, what were once scenes belonging to the medieval street carnival have, since the Renaissance, become the material of literature: the grotesque body with its associations of the marketplace, abuse, copulation, and excrement. Rabelais has an intense obsession with the grotesque body's lower stratum, as Bakhtin calls it, the intestines, the uterus, the stomach, the mouth, the nose, as well as the body's excretions: sweating, defecating, urinating, and vomiting. Grass shares this obsession in scenes like the eel episode or the one in which the neighbors' kids force Oskar to eat a soup consisting of urine and dying toads. Another memorable scene in this context is the one in which Oskar visits Dr. Hollatz, whose collection of snakes, toads, and embryos he destroys. Hollatz may remind the reader of Rabelais's physician, who is interested in the body that "is pregnant, delivers, defecates, which is sick, dying, and dismembered" (*RW*, 17).

The Grotesque Body of the Fairy-Tale Dwarf

In all dwarf fairy tales Bakhtin's concept of the grotesque body appears through the same motifs: its mockery, its public display, its underestimation, and the dwarf's urge to prove useful to society. Due to his physical inadequacy, the dwarf's ability to work becomes questionable, which provokes the aggressiveness of mocking laughter and always implies the danger of his persecution in societies that want to eject their useless members. In the Third Reich the mentally and physically disabled were killed also under the pretext of sparing them public ridicule: grotesque logic indeed, in that those mocked are killed so that they may no longer be mocked.[14] Among the philosophers of Enlightenment it was primarily Voltaire who turned against Rabelais's freewheeling laughter and described his books as full of mockery and deserving of being mocked. It is through this kind of pollution by contempt that in the Age of Reason laughter loses the regenerative quality that it still had in the Renaissance and becomes more and more destructive, according to Bakhtin. This development coincides with Foucault's age of the "great confinement," as early as the seventeenth century, which saw the creation of enormous houses of confinement, in which were interned precisely those groups that the Nazis persecuted, the physically and mentally disabled, the unemployed, the idle, and vagabonds (*MC*, 38). The theme of mockery is linked to the public display of the grotesque body. As long as physical abnormality and insanity were quotidian phenomena populating the streets of Europe, the public did not show these people the kind of contempt associated with their marginalization, contempt leveled at those already segregated, society's invisibles, as well as those who had now become rare in public life. As Foucault argues, by confining madness and physical abnormality they became a showpiece and the object of ridicule: "madmen remained monsters — that is, etymologically, beings or things to be shown. . . . In the Renaissance, madness was present everywhere and mingled with every experience by its images or its dangers. During the Classical period, madness was shown, but on the other side of bars" (*MC*, 70).

With the age of the great confinement dwarves too had become victims of persecution, since they were generally considered incapable of contributing meaningfully to society, but above all because everyone thought that they were insane. A common combination in the Middle Ages and the Renaissance was the dwarf-fool, because it was common belief that dwarves had to be insane. The dwarf's sole usefulness in the eyes of society lay in his marketability, his/her objectification in the marketplace. We can look at any tale about a dwarf and it becomes clear how the themes of ridicule, underestimation, and usefulness are related. As the highwaymen want to display the Grimm Brothers' Tom Thumb for money, in Hauff's tale *Der Zwerg Nase* the barber wants to display Jakob as an oddity in his shop. Piccoline in

Lagerkvist's novel is outraged when Maestro Bernardo objectifies his body for a painting that is to become part of a series of "monsters (that which is to be shown) such as never have been seen and do not exist. They were something between men and beasts" (*D*, 48). The public display of the dwarf, of anyone who does not agree to it, implies stripping the individual of the right to his/her body. Piccoline protests against this usurpation of his body: "Thus everything belongs to others! Don't we even own our faces? Do they belong to anybody who chooses to look at them? And one's body? Can others own one's body? I find the notion repellent" (*D*, 51).

The public ridicule of the dwarf results from the widespread conception of his size as a reflection of his mental inadequacy, which in turn forces him to prove himself. This prejudice that associates the dwarf's body with a lack of mental acumen is rooted in the medieval tradition of employing dwarf-fools at court. One can observe the sequence of related motifs of public display and ridicule, underestimation and the dwarf's desire to prove his usefulness in the fairy tales as well as in Grass's novel. The Grimms' Tom Thumbs, Hauff's Jakob and Muck, and Oskar are constantly trying to prove their usefulness in order to avoid being classified as useless by society and becoming the victims of persecution.[15]

Traditionally, the dwarf of the fairy tale has to prove his usefulness in the world of adults more than anyone else because his usefulness for society is questioned more than other people's. In the Tom Thumb tales the dwarf can render himself useful to criminals, but thanks to his size he also manages to survive, invisible to others. Moreover, their voices as they scream from the dark recesses of an animal's belly save both Tom Thumbs. The dwarf's endangerment increases or decreases in accordance with his usefulness. In Hauff's literary fairy tales it is primarily the dwarf's miracle weapons, Muck's high-speed slippers and the cane that finds hidden treasures as well as Jakob's cooking skills that save their lives and render them useful to the higher authorities, the earls, dukes and kings. The dwarf of the literary fairy tale in particular is exposed to society's mockery. Because of his deformity the dwarf in Hauff's *Die Geschichte von dem kleinen Muck* is being harassed by a group of kids, including the narrator's son. Before the King hires Little Muck as a court runner he has to demonstrate his skill. Arrogantly, the courtiers comment on his physical appearance and call him a fool: "Wie, mit deinen Füßlein, die kaum so lang als eine Spanne sind, willst du königlicher Schnelläufer werden? Hebe dich weg, ich bin nicht dazu da, mit jedem Narren Kurzweil zu machen" (*SM*, 87; "What! you, with your little limbs, which are scarcely a span in length, wish to become a royal messenger! Get away; I have no time for joking with every fool": *T*, 66). The passage shows to what extent physical disability is associated with mental disability. The impression of Muck as a fool is of course augmented by his outlandish clothes, his wide robe and the wide slippers. At the sight of him when he appears for the race the audience bursts out with raucous laughter, which enhances the impression of his otherness and status outside the pale of mankind. In implying the didactic message that the disabled should be taken seriously and perceived as complete human beings who are searching for happiness just like anyone else, this tale reflects Romanticism's tolerance for physical difference. A victim of everyone's derision, Muck is enabled by the magic figs he finds one day to give the whole court grotesque bodies. Once mocked, the dwarf now becomes the one who mocks and despises humanity, a theme that Lagerkvist's novel develops even more strongly. At the end of the tale the narrator of the story whips his naughty son for having ridiculed the dwarf, and he closes with the words that life has made Little Muck both wealthy and full of hatred for men, that experience has taught him wisdom, and that notwithstanding his strange exterior, he is worthy of admiration rather than mockery. That Muck has become a wise man touches on the principle of *Bildung*, which in the folk-tales corresponds to an initiation rite. Rather than being a fool, the dwarf of the literary tale is shown to be capable of development, of a stronger pursuit of happiness because of his handicap than many others among his fellowmen.

The themes of ridiculing physical deformity, underestimation of the dwarf, and his consequent urge to prove himself also determine the structure of *Der Zwerg Nase*. Little Jakob, who is a beautiful child, makes a terrible mistake by scolding an old woman in the marketplace and by commenting on her ugly physical appearance. According to Bakhtin, curses in the marketplace are aimed at the grotesque body, and this is what happens at this point in the story (*RW*, 166). The old woman curses Jakob: she tells him that he will have a nose that will reach down to his chin and that his neck will disappear so that his head will sit directly upon his shoulders. In the marketplace herbs and drugs are sold; it is an ambivalent place of praise and abuse, of life-giving humor and death-bringing mockery: "The cries of Paris and the cries of quacks and druggists operating at the fairs belong to the eulogizing genres of folk humor. They too, of course, are ambivalent; they too are filled with both laughter and irony. They may at any moment show their other side; that is, they may be turned into abuses and oaths. . . . They are essentially connected with the lower stratum" (*RW*, 187). In Jakob's abuse of the old woman in the market scene one can see how laughter has turned into mockery, how it has become a negative attribute rather than still being the freewheeling laughter of the Renaissance. The oaths "are ambivalent but it is the negative pole of the lower stratum which here prevails: death, sickness, disintegration, dismemberment of the body, its rending apart and swallowing up" (*RW*, 187). Jakob's abuse of the old woman is the cause of his body's grotesque transformation after she feeds him a magic soup, a transformation in which a certain herb plays a key role. Jakob's haughtiness causes his downfall. Again, as in "*Muck*," this tale contains the didactic message that derision aimed at others' physical shortcomings will be punished. Through his own fault Jakob is taken out into the world and has to learn the lesson of resisting the temptation to ridicule people because of their bodies before he can return to his parents as a beautiful son.

Jakob in turn becomes the victim of ridicule as he enters the marketplace after his grotesque transformation and when he offers his services to the Duke. He must repeatedly dispel everyone's doubts in him. When the chief cook looks at him from head to toe he bursts out into laughter and exclaims that due to his size Jakob would never be able to look into the cooking pots and that whoever has sent him must have made a fool of him. Like the courtiers who called Muck a fool when he proposed that he would run for the king, the chief cook places the dwarf and the fool in the same category. Again the dwarf's size is equated with mental inadequacy, undoubtedly a relic from the days of the dwarf-fool at medieval courts. Like Muck, who has to prove the power of his slippers and the treasure cane, Jakob must again and again dispel everyone's doubts in him and prove that he can hold his own in the world of grown-ups. When the Duke is visited by an earl, Jakob, *Nase* (Nose) as the Duke calls him, must once again prove his skill by baking a complicated pie. If he fails he will die. Bakhtin stresses the connection between mockery, oaths and the dismembered body, "the carnival role of butchers and cooks, of the carving knife and of the minced meat for dressings and sausages" (*RW*, 193). The Duke swears that he will chop up Jakob's body and have him baked into a pie if he fails to prepare the *souzeraine,* the queen of all pies. It becomes clear how the carnivalesque image of chopping meat (in Rabelais's *Gargantua* it surfaces in the figure of Friar John, who is nicknamed *Entommeure,* because he pounds bodies into minced meat) and making pies is linked to cruelty towards the dwarf, the oven motif in some fairy tales. The motif also occurs in the German Tom Thumb tales where the hero becomes the filling of a sausage. That the war breaking out at the end of Hauff's tale is called "war of herbs" is rooted in the tradition of the fifteenth and sixteenth centuries when culinary images would accompany battle scenes, a tradition Grass returns to in mixing the events of the Second World War with Matzerath's cooking experiments.

Oskar's Body and the Fairy-Tale Structure

How does this fairy-tale structure that ties together the motifs of mockery, of the dwarf's usefulness, his display in the marketplace, and society's underestimation of his mental acumen resurface in *Die Blechtrommel?* As Bakhtin notes, "the grotesque concept of the body in some of its essential elements represented the humanist and, above all, the Italian philosophy of that period. It had conceived, as we have seen, the idea of the microcosm (stemming from the Paduan school of Pompanazzi) as adopted by Rabelais. The human body was the center of a philosophy that contributed to the destruction of the medieval hierarchic picture of the world and to the creation of a new concept" (*RW*, 362). We can see to what extent this concept returns to its medieval antecedent during the Nazi period when state authority once again became paramount and subjected the body to destruction. That Oskar is part of a microcosm that is indifferent to higher powers shows itself in the scene when he and his father are discovered by the Russians. Just before Matzerath is shot, Oskar observes a group of ants, which appear to him completely indifferent to what goes on in the world. He identifies with these ants, again a comment on his size, identifies with this microcosm that is so detached from historical events. Like the ants and Tom Thumb, who in spite of all his activity remains invisible to the world around him, Oskar is, as an enemy, invisible to the Russians, those "great lovers of children" (*TD*, 392). Oskar's activity at this moment — for like Tom Thumb he is a very active hero — consists in having just pressed the Nazi party badge into Matzerath's hand, which indirectly causes his father's death.

A central event that *Die Blechtrommel* shares with *Der Zwerg Nase* is Oskar's transformation from a child into an ugly deformed dwarf. Oskar's transformation is clearly modeled on that of Little Jakob,[16] who, however, is transformed twice, into an ugly dwarf and back into a beautiful youth:

> Seine Augen waren klein geworden, wie die der Schweine, seine Nase war ungeheuer und hing über Mund und Kinn herunter, der Hals schien gänzlich weggenommen worden zu sein; denn sein Kopf stak tief in den Schultern, und nur mit den größten Schmerzen konnte er ihn rechts und links bewegen; sein Körper war noch so groß als vor sieben Jahren, da er zwölf Jahre alt war, aber wenn andere vom zwölften bis ins zwanzigste in die Höhe wachsen, so wuchs er in die Breite, der Rücken und die Brust waren weit ausgebogen und waren anzusehen wie ein kleiner aber sehr dick gefüllter Sack; dieser dicke Oberleib saß auf kleinen, schwachen Beinchen, die dieser Last nicht gewachsen schienen, aber um so größer waren die Arme, die ihm am Leib herabhingen, sie hatten die Größe wie die eines wohlgewachsenen Mannes, seine Hände waren grob und braungelb, seine Finger lang und spinnenartig, und wenn er sie recht ausstreckte, konnte er damit auf den Boden reichen, ohne daß er sich bückte. So sah er aus, der kleine Jakob, zum mißgestalteten Zwerg war er geworden. (*SM*, 151)

> [His eyes had become as small as pig's eyes, his nose was enormous and hung down over his mouth and chin; his neck seemed to have disappeared altogether, for his head was deeply stuck on his shoulders, and it was with the utmost pain he could turn it to right or left; his body was the same size as seven years ago when he was twelve years of age, but while others grew in height from twelve to twenty, he had grown in breadth, his back and chest were broad and expanded, and looked

> like a little but well-stuffed sack; this enormous upper part of his body
> was supported by his little thin legs, which did not seem to be suitable
> for such a burden, but his arms were all the longer, hanging down at
> his sides, for they were the size of those of a full-grown man; his hands
> were coarse and of a brownish yellow, his fingers long and spider-like,
> and whenever he stretched them out at full length, he could touch the
> ground without bending. This was how Little Jakob looked. He had
> changed into a deformed dwarf. (*T,* 121–22)]

Jakob has indeed been transformed into a person of monster-like appearance.
When he changes back into a beautiful youth, his grotesque body is mentioned once again: all his limbs begin to twitch and crack, he feels his head
rising from his shoulders and his back and chest straightening, he watches his
nose grow smaller and smaller and his legs become longer. Oskar's metamorphosis, which happens in the railway carriage that takes him west, is clearly a
mixture of motifs from Hauff. His sudden growth is promoted by the shaking
of the train so that he begins to grow lengthwise, his joints relax, his ears,
nose, and sex organ grow perceptibly, and when the train stops he feels acute
pain. Particularly Grass's focus on the joints, the nose, and the pain seems to
derive from *Der Zwerg Nase.* As a consequence of his transformation, Oskar
measures four feet and one inch, and like Jakob, when he was ugly, he carries
his head right between his shoulders on an almost nonexistent neck, while his
chest and a humped back protrude from his body.

The grotesque body in popular culture is the body in the act of becoming
unlike the classical body, which Bakhtin calls the modern body because it
represents the official culture of the bourgeois order. This modern body is
limited, self-sufficient, and closed. Unlike the grotesque body, whose principle
features are the gaping mouth and protrusions such as the huge nose, and its
transformability forever promising the renewal of life, the classical body is
associated with death and never promises renewal (*RW,* 321). Jakob's and
Oskar's bodies resist any sort of closure that the classical body contains. Some
Tom Thumb folk-tales, such as "Der junge Riese," in which Tom Thumb
becomes a giant, reflect this ability of the grotesque body to burst its confines.
Popular culture seems to have a fascination with the telescopic body, that is,
the body that can transform from small to large and back. A famous example
for this motif would be Lewis Carroll's (1832–98) *Alice in Wonderland*
(1865), in which Alice changes from tiny to elongated to gigantic. In the
Grimms' tales *Daumesdick* and *Daumerlings Wanderschaft,* however, the
hero's body merely traverses grotesque locations such as a sausage or a stomach, a motif that we also find in Rabelais when Gargantua eats six pilgrims in
a salad. Tom Thumb's body itself does not change shape.

It is the grotesque protrusions that Grass picks up from Hauff's literary
tales when he transforms Oskar into a hunchbacked dwarf after the war. Bakhtin argues that the grotesque body is closely related to the idea of renewal

and rebirth. Oskar's rebirth in a physical sense occurs after his father dies. The old witch in *Der Zwerg Nase* leaves Jakob grotesquely deformed after he has eaten the soup that she has cooked for him. Yet by teaching him how to cook she also equips him with the kind of miraculous talent that corresponds to the magical objects of others: Little Muck's speed slippers and the walking cane, with which he can find hidden treasures, and Oskar's ability to shatter glass. We can see that a repetitive motif in the stories is the moment of foolishness or guilt of the hero that brings about the grotesque protrusions of his body. Muck's foolishness, his naiveté in dealing with the courtiers and the King, cause his ears and nose to grow out of proportion and Jakob becomes deformed just after insulting the old woman. The relationship between Oskar's grotesque body and his guilt is ambivalent. His humpback is an expression both of his guilt for having caused the deaths of Jan Bronski and Matzerath and the collective guilt of all Germans. That his metamorphosis takes place in the railway carriage is no doubt a reference to his partaking of the collective guilt shared by those who were in one way or another responsible for the Nazi crimes. Despite the initial resistance he puts up with his drum under the rostrum, Oskar eventually performs for the Nazis and thus indirectly supports their mission. The railway car, which in a physical sense turns him into a monster, may be one of those that transported the victims of Nazi crimes east to the concentration camps. At the same time, his physical ugliness represents the ugliness of Germany to the world, a monstrousness that does not fully reveal itself until the end of the war.

Because of its protrusions — the limbs, the humpback, the nose, the ears, the gaping mouth (open orifices are grotesque, closed ones part of the classical body) the bulging eyes, arms and fingers — the grotesque body's confines are drawn differently from the classical body. The nose in particular receives much attention in carnivalesque literature and the carnival itself. It usually symbolizes the phallus and occurs throughout world literature. In *Gargantua* Friar John's "handsome" nose is associated with his phallus by way of a garbled psalm *ad formam nasi cognoscitur* (by the shape of his nose he is known), which corresponds to the popular saying "an der Nase eines Mannes erkennt man seinen Johannes" (by the nose of a man one can tell his penis).[17] Oskar is clearly a part of the Rabelaisian world of hunchbacks with humps of huge proportions, characters with monstrous noses, abnormally long legs, and gigantic ears, of men with disproportionate phalli that are wound six times around their waists and others with unusually large testicles. During carnival week at the art academy where Oskar poses as a model, he emphasizes the size of his phallus, his "ansehnliche Genitalien" (imposing genitals) (*B*, 387), and the ability of his hump to bring good luck to women, "ein Buckel bringt den Frauen Glück" (*B*, 389), a hypothesis that echoes Bakhtin who argues that "various deformities, such as protruding

bellies, enormous noses, or humps, are symptoms of pregnancy or of procreative power" (*RW*, 91).

Die Blechtrommel abounds in passages in which Oskar is being ridiculed
and underestimated because of his size and deformities. As in Rabelais's
novels, in which grotesque debasement is linked to excrement and urine —
the act of giving birth is, for example, linked to the act of defecating — and
in similarity to Little Muck, who is being harassed by a group of kids, Oskar
becomes the victim of ridicule when the neighbors' children force him to eat
the soup one of the children, Susi Kater, has urinated into. These images of
excrement in Rabelais and Grass reveal how deeply rooted their novels are
in the trickster myths, which teem with excremental images. The humanitarian message of both literary tales, that one refrain from derision of people
with physical shortcomings, is irreconcilable with the racist ideology of the
Nazis. It is not surprising that these literary tales were not particularly popular in the Third Reich. One merit of Grass's novel is that it harks back to this
humanitarian spirit of the literary fairy tale. As in Hauff's tales, physical
disability is associated with a lack of mental capacity in *Die Blechtrommel*.
One scene that reflects this is when Oskar goes to school, a place that is built
for *Riesenkinder* (giant children) (*B*, 66), not for him. The water fountain,
the steps, the desk, everything is too high for him, and when his mother
takes him out of school after his scream has pulverized his teacher's glasses,
he becomes excluded from both physical and mental education. His counterpart, the greengrocer Greff, embodies the ideal sportsman, and the boys
with whom he surrounds himself fulfill Hitler's dream of godlike German
youth, strong and beautiful, athletic and heroic, violent and fearless. Ironically, it is Greff who casts a sort of spell on Oskar that aims at excluding him
from both physical and mental education. Having to tread lightly among the
Nazis because of his homosexuality, he is the victim in hiding trampling on
the exposed victim. Not only does Greff not admit Oskar to his sporting
games, but he also discourages him from reading and calls him too dumb
and too little to understand the book that Oskar finds in his shop. In the
novel, the book in question is Greff's pornographic literature, full of naked
boys, and in asking Oskar to put it away Greff shows his fear of discovery.
Volker Schlöndorff's movie version of 1979 gives this moment an ironic
twist in that Greff discourages Oskar from reading the great German classics.
Just as Muck and Jakob are considered fools by their employers, Oskar is
considered retarded by his own family and neighbors during the Nazi years
because he does not grow.

As in the fairy tales, society's mockery and underestimation of the dwarf
results in Oskar's desire to prove his usefulness. Oskar makes himself useful to
a number of people. He is useful to women as a token of luck, and as a child
he is useful to the physician Dr. Hollatz in his research, a reference to the
usefulness of the dwarf's body for the research in concentration camps. Like

Tom Thumb, who thanks to his size can steal coins from a treasury, Oskar is useful to criminals in destroying the glass of windows. His voice is useful to those other criminals, the Nazis, as a source of entertainment. Like the folk-tale dwarf, Oskar survives mainly because he makes himself invisible (under the rostrum, for example) and because he can scream. He is like Hermes, who with his lyre charms Apollo, the principle of order. With his drum Oskar destroys the order of the party rally and brings a Dionysian element into it. With his voice he charms the beast, the Nazis, at the front so that they don't kill him. As long as he makes use of his talents he can escape euthanasia. In this he resembles those concentration camp inmates who managed to live longer thanks to a talent such as being able to play an instrument.

After his transformation into a deformed dwarf Oskar needs to convince West German society of his value. Like Tom Thumb, who becomes an apprentice, Oskar wants to demonstrate his usefulness to postwar capitalist society by becoming an apprentice. His master, the stonemason Korneff, is skeptical about Oskar's strength, whereupon Oskar implores Korneff not to underestimate him. He bares his left arm, flexes his biceps and asks Korneff to feel his "zwar kleinen aber rindfleischzähen Muskel" (*B*, 366; "my muscle, which was small but tough": *TD*, 442). Manheim's translation is imprecise here because in the original version Oskar's biceps are more than just "tough," they are "rindfleischzäh" (tough as beef), an allusion to such Nazi terminology as "zäh wie Leder" (tough as leather), "hart wie Kruppstahl" (hard as Krupp steel), "schnell wie die Windhunde" (fast as a greyhound), the three expectations of youth in the Third Reich.[18] Oskar's display of his biceps can be interpreted as an attempt to assimilate within a society rooted in Nazi ideology, in which there is no place for effeminate men. That he cannot completely hide his feminine side reveals itself in his high-pitched voice as well as some homoerotic tendencies. Ironically, Oskar compares his own demolition of glass and ice with the greengrocer Greff vigorously hacking away at the icy Baltic: "Während Oskar Glas nah- und fernwirkend zersang, gelegentlich Eisblumen vor den Scheiben auftaute, Eiszapfen schmelzen und klirren ließ, *war* der Gemüsehändler *ein Mann* (my italics), der mit handlichem Werkzeug dem Eis zu Leibe rückte (the kind of tool that Oskar cannot hold for more than an hour)"(*B*, 240; "While Oskar sang glass, far and near, to pieces, occasionally thawing the frost flowers on the windowpanes, melting icicles and sending them to the ground with a crash, the greengrocer *was a man* who attacked ice at close quarters, with hand tools": *TD*, 293). Oskar's homoerotic tendencies surface when he thinks about why he is not Greff's type but primarily in the episode where he touches Jesus' uncircumcised "watering can" in the Church of the Sacred Heart and gets an erection. This Jesus statue itself is an expression of hyper-masculinity, thus reflecting the union of the church with National Socialism. The sculptured Jesus hanging over the altar is represented as a decathlon winner, clearly a reference to the Nazis' obsession with that sport (*NT*, 55). Grass's divine athlete recalls those heroic Jesus figures of the 1920s and 1930s, of which Fritz Viktor Meier speaks in the journal *Die Schönheit*, a Christ-figure that became more and more Germanic and in relinquishing his suffering was full of "Nordic pride and heroism."[19] This muscular little Jesus figure serves Grass as an ironic *mélange* of religious images with images from Leni Riefenstahl's film on the 1936 Olympic Games, which in all seriousness uses a similar conflation of images. Wildmann has shown that as the marathon runners in Riefenstahl's film collapse just after crossing the finishing line they remind one of Jesus in his suffering for humanity. For Riefenstahl, Wildmann argues, the athlete's body has to be "gleichzeitig Opferkörper und Leistungskörper," the body that both sacrifices itself and performs for the good of society (*BK*, 111). That Grass intends a reference to this collusion of religious imagery with Nazi ideals in Riefenstahl's movie can be seen specifically in the following passage from the chapter "Kein Wunder" (No Wonder) in the first book. Oskar looks at Jesus and thinks to himself:

> Was hatte der Mann für Muskeln! Dieser Athlet mit der Figur eines Zehnkämpfers ließ mich den Herz-Jesu-Bronski sofort vergessen, sammelte mich, sooft Mama Hochwürden Wiehnke beichtete, andächtig und den Turner beobachtend vor dem Hochaltar. Glauben Sie mir, daß ich bete! Mein süßer Vorturner, nannte ich ihn, Sportler aller Sportler, Sieger im Hängen am Kreuz unter Zuhilfenahme zölliger Nägel. Und niemals zuckte er! Das ewige Licht zuckte, er aber erfüllte die Disziplin mit der höchstmöglichen Punktezahl. . . . Ich kniete, wenn es nur irgend mein Knie erlaubte, nieder, schlug das Kreuz auf meiner Trommel und versuchte Worte wie gebenedeit oder schmerzensreich in Verbindung mit Jesse Owens und Rudolf Harbig, mit der vorjährigen Berliner Olympiade zu verbinden. (*B*, 112)

> [What muscles the man had! At the sight of this decathlon-winner I forgot all about Sacred-Heart Bronski. There I stood as often as Mama confessed to Father Wiehnke, gazing devoutly at the athlete over the high altar. You can believe me that I prayed. Athlete most amiable, I called him, athlete of athletes, world's champion hanger on the Cross by regulation nails. And never a twitch or a quiver, but he displayed perfect discipline and took the highest possible number of points. . . . I knelt down as best I could, made the sign of the Cross on my drum, and tried to associate words like 'blessed' or 'afflicted' with Jesse Owens and Rudolf Harbig and last year's Olympic Games in Berlin. (*TD*, 139)]

Again the translation is faulty in parts; what Grass means by "Disziplin" is a certain sport, while the translation turns it into the discipline of the athletic and erect body thus supporting Michel Foucault's concept of the docile body as the disciplined body. Sport, education, religion, and the physician functioned as the great discipliners during the Third Reich, as Haug informs us, and Oskar resists all of them.[20] Oskar's blasphemous thoughts show us to what extent he resists the authority of the church. He also resists the authority of school and that of Dr. Hollatz. That Grass's satiric conflation of Christian images and sport is a comment on the alliance between the church and Hitler Germany becomes clear immediately after this passage, when Oskar lists all the versions of crosses that he can think of, including, of course, the swastika. This, however, so he says, is a forbidden cross, all other crosses are permitted and especially the position of the church under Adenauer is, once again, fortified.

Jesus' athletic body in contrast to little Oskar, who later develops a hunchback — this odd pair also implies the concept of the erect body held high in Nazi body politics. As Wildmann informs us, the bent-over body was associated with the Jewish body, "der als gekrümmt und degeneriert gezeichnete Jude wird zum auszugrenzenden Feindbild" (the bent-over, degenerate Jew is the image of the enemy), and was a target also for euthanasia if Aryans were afflicted by it (BK, 79). Walter Benjamin spoke of the "bucklicht Männlein," man bent over by the burden of patriarchal history.[21] The bent-over back expresses man's alienation from nature and according to Siegfried Kaltenecker, while Benjamin attempted through his critical thinking to straighten man, the Nazis tried to straighten man through violence.[22] The Nazis' ambition to straighten out man to its original natural shape from the time preceding the malaise of civilization was therefore one reaction of modernity to the ubiquitous symptoms of its own degeneracy. It was an attempt to recover what Rousseau had called "retour à la nature," while insisting on German high culture, the cultural heritage of Goethe and Schiller. This is definitely where one of the inconsistencies of Third Reich ideology lay, for how can man be liberated from the burden of civilization while retaining its cultural climax? At times, Grass's novel displays irony with regard to such inconsistencies of Nazi politics, for example in the figure of Gauleiter Löbsack, whose hump represents the very opposite of Nazi body politics. Paradoxically, the party regards Löbsack's hump as a sign of keen intelligence and therefore makes him district chief of training. He derives "all seinen Witz aus seinem Buckel" (all his wit from his hump), and his hump is always right and so is the party, "woraus man schließen kann, daß ein Buckel die ideale Grundlage einer Idee bildet" (B, 94; "whence it can be inferred that a hump is an ideal basis for an idea": TD, 117). The idea behind the hump in reality was the ideology to straighten it, that is, to do away with figures like Löbsack, who through poetic license here becomes a leading Nazi figure. At the same time, however, the Nazis' reverence for Löbsack's hump demonstrates Kaltenecker's theory that fascism needs its others to sustain itself. That they make Löbsack one of their own instead of victimizing him forms a parallel to their temporary tolerance of Oskar, the dwarf.

As Bernd Jürgen Warneken has shown, the disciplining of the body into an erect one was a sign of bourgeois emancipation, a sign of the citizen's autonomy of will over his own body in the Age of Enlightenment.[23] What held true for the beginnings of the bourgeois age had even more validity for National Socialism, where an erect body was considered to reflect a strong character and a strong will. Among the sports that had a primary function in straightening the body was *Turnen,* gymnastics, which gained increasing significance during the nineteenth century, which overall saw a general disciplining of the body that pervaded not only the military but all other institutions of discipline: school, where the erect posture was introduced for the pupil's desk, and even the work place.[24] What started as a trend to liberate the individual was perverted by the Nazis into a general subjection of the body. The Swing-movement in postfascist Germany then became a reaction to the Nazis' perversion of the erect body posture, a disruption of the erect body back into relaxation. In Grass's novel, too, we can see this juxtaposition of erect bodies next to their relaxation, in the rostrum chapter where Oskar sits beneath the bandstand and drums the rhythm of a Charleston, Jimmy the Tiger, by which he disrupts the official party rhythm, the marching music. The stiff bodies produced by the march finally break down and everyone dances in a relaxed style.

Classical and Degenerate Art

Art in the Third Reich had the function of representing the ideal body, because it was only an ideal that nobody could really fulfill, least of all the Nazis themselves. Nowhere else is the concept of beauty related more to the question of race than in the theories of biologist Konrad Lorenz (1903–89). He declared beauty to be the sole standard of worthiness of life and advocated that whoever did not correspond to the ideal of beauty should be cut away from the *Volkskörper* like a cancerous growth. Yet since nobody really corresponds to this ideal of beauty other than a statue like Breker's Dionysos, all humans would have to be eliminated. The history of the Second World War suggests that it was an attempt in this direction. By sacrificing millions of people, the Nazis indirectly declared the whole nation as *lebensunwert,* unworthy of life, and it could therefore easily be fed to the all-devouring war machine. Since they were considered as worthless, bodies could be easily sacrificed. Only in the work of art could this kind of ideal of beauty be achieved.

This obsession with beauty in real life and in the arts is parodied by Grass in the chapter entitled "Madonna 49" in which Oskar becomes an *objet d'art* in the Academy of Art in Düsseldorf. In putting Oskar on a pedestal at the art school Grass borrows the motif of the dwarf's body on display from medieval market conventions. As we have seen, the motif occurs in

Daumesdick, whose central character the men want to exhibit for money, and in *Der Zwerg Nase*, where the barber wants to display Jakob in his shop. The dwarf's grotesque body under scrutiny by the clinical gaze (Dr. Hollatz) or the artist's gaze is also a theme in Pär Lagerkvist's *The Dwarf*. When Maestro Bernardo, who in Rabelaisian fashion reads the future in intestines, paints Piccoline's naked body, it feels like rape to the dwarf:

> Then, placid as ever, he began to take off my clothes and exposed my body most shamelessly. I resisted desperately, fought with him as for my life, but all in vain, for he was stronger than I. When he had completed his vile task he lifted me onto a scaffold in the middle of the room. I stood there defenseless, naked, incapable of action, though I was foaming with rage. And he stood some distance away from me, quite unmoved, and examined me as though, scrutinizing my shame with a cold and merciless gaze. I was utterly exposed to that outrageous gaze which explored and assimilated me as though I were his property. (*D*, 45)

The dissecting gaze is shared by art and medicine. Lagerkvist's novel smacks of the crimes committed on the physically disabled. Like Mengele, Bernardo "had always been greatly interested in dwarfs" (*D*, 48), a detail that is exploited also in Friedrich Dürrenmatt's *The Suspicion*, where the concentration camp doctor Emmenberger keeps a dwarf, and in milder fashion in Thomas Mann's *Magic Mountain*, where we find another clinic that employs a dwarf.[25] The history of medicine abounds in this obsession with the grotesque body, an interest that in the Third Reich became destructive. When as a child Oskar destroys the preserved misshapen embryos in Dr. Hollatz's practice, this could be perceived as the heralding of a coming age that witnesses the destruction of misshapen bodies.

In the chapter "Madonna 49" Grass unmasks the hypocrisy of the postwar period, the new age's capitalist exploitation of its own past. Oskar, who is obliged to make a living, partakes of this spirit, since he quickly learns to exploit his grotesque hunchbacked body at a time when a new art was established in reaction to the rigid understanding of art under the Nazis. He becomes a model for charcoal drawings, sculpture and painting, both dressed and in the nude. By way of ironic contrast, this chapter conjures up the Classical statues that were considered high art during the Third Reich. It develops a contrast between the grotesque and classical body, between the Dionysian and Apollonian principles that pervade the structure of the book. Two understandings of art are juxtaposed in this chapter, an avant-garde art full of accusation for the fascist art of the previous generation and that fascist art that worships classical forms and harmony. On the one hand, there is Professor Kuchen's admiration of Oskar's grotesque crippled physique as an expression of the damage caused by the Nazi years and the subsequent suffering during the postwar years. Kuchen represents the darkness of the postwar years. Everything about him is black, a charcoal beard, charcoal eyes, a black hat, and charcoal under his finger nails, no doubt also a reference to Germany's legacy of the concentration camp ashes. As so often, Oskar is once again stylized into a Jesus figure. By being associated with the crucified Christ in the scene in which Kuchen asks his students to nail him to their paper with charcoal, Oskar takes German guilt upon his back. After all, as we have seen, his hump is also an expression of the burden of German guilt that he takes upon himself. Oskar becomes the carrier of the German cross. As in the scene where Oskar admires the divine athlete in the Sacred Heart Church, Grass once again makes fun of Riefenstahl's conflation of Christian and Olympic icons of sacrifice. By combining Oskar the cripple with the idea of sacrifice, he conjures up the very counter-image of Riefenstahl's sportsmen. On the other hand, this scene, in which the crippled body becomes a central image for the madness of the century, and by which Grass undoubtedly refers to the crimes of German fascism, also reflects the American re-education program imposed on Germany, which ultimately led to a climate of self-imposed philo-Semitism and society's tolerance toward its outsiders. Oskar notices as the students draw his portrait that they all focus on his cadaverous features, thundering condemnation, and that instead of drawing his blue eyes they represent them as narrow holes of charcoal. What Grass describes here as a phenomenon just after the war was the beginning of a trend that was to last to the present: Professor Kuchen and his disciples create a type of art that deliberately abstains from Aryan images such as blue eyes, and embraces the colors and shapes of victimization: Oskar's black gypsy look and his deformity. Through identification with the victims it has, ever since the war, been possible for many Germans to distance themselves from the crimes of their fathers and grandfathers. Only a few German artists, first and foremost Anselm Kiefer, radically broke with this trend. It is Oskar himself, victim and perpetrator, deformed but blue-eyed, who points out that there can be no coming to terms with the past if one merely swings along with the pendulum to whatever is politically correct at a given time. By ignoring the blue radiance of his eyes, that bright sparkle in him, and merely focusing on his dark side, the art students ignore the dual nature of his personality, his Rasputinian side which exists next to his Goethean side, his irrationalism next to his rationalism.

This corresponds to postfascist Germany's eager acceptance of rationalism in response to the Nazis' irrationalism and the chaos of the war years. It was not until the 1970s that those who rebelled against the crimes of their fathers finally understood that rationalism may smack just as much of fascism as irrationalism. After all, National Socialism was a movement that had the same duality of ideologies that Oskar applies to himself: it was made up of dark, inchoate forces as well as strong rationalist principles: "Den Rasputin in dir haben die jungen Musensöhne und kunstverstrickten Mädchen zwar erkannt;

ob sie wohl jemals jenen in dir schlummernden Goethe entdecken" (*B*, 384; "These sons and daughters of the Muses, I said to myself, have recognized the Rasputin in you; but will they ever discover the Goethe who lies dormant in your soul": *TD*, 463). This is an important thought, since post-Nazi society was as little able to integrate these two sides, the Apollonian and the Dionysian, within it as these art students were able to perceive them in Oskar.

Kuchen and his disciples have a counterpart in Professor Maruhn, "ein Liebhaber klassischer Formen, blickte [er] mich meiner Proportionen wegen feindselig an. Seinen Freund verhöhnte er: er, Kuchen, habe wohl nicht genug an seinen Zigeunermodellen, die er bislang angeschwärzt habe. . . . Ob er sich nun auch an Mißgeburten versuchen wolle, ob er sich mit der Absicht trage, nach jener erfolgreichen und gut verkäuflichen Zigeunerperiode nun eine Zwergenperiode noch verkäuflicher, noch erfolgreicher anzuschwärzen?" (*B*, 385; "a lover of classical form. He thoroughly disapproved of my build and began to poke fun at Kuchen: couldn't he be satisfied with the gypsy models. . . . Must he try his hand at freaks? The gypsy period had sold well, there was that to be said for it; did the charcoal-crusher entertain hopes that a midget period would sell still better?": TD, 464–65). While Kuchen profits from the widespread postwar hypocrisy and sympathy for those groups that the Nazis had persecuted and killed in concentration camps, Maruhn remains true to the past's ideals. He is a key figure, demonstrating that Grass saw a continuity of the Nazis' discriminatory body politics in the Federal Republic. Although repulsed by Oskar's physique, Maruhn is lured by the "Goethean clarity" of his eyes, Oskar's one physical feature that contains classical beauty, whereupon Maruhn selects him as a fit model for sculpture. As Wolbert has shown, sculpture was the most important form of art for the Nazis' idealization of the perfect human body. It is therefore all the more ironic that Maruhn chooses Oskar for his representation of classical beauty. Grass's irony reveals to what extent the Nazis' quest for the perfect body was a ludicrous undertaking, an ideal that could exist only in dead sculptures but never in reality. His irony turns into the macabre when he shows Maruhn, Promethean-like putting clay, that is, flesh, on his skeletons for projected sculptures of wire, iron, and bare lead tubing, only to realize that the truly perfect body is the skeleton bare of any clay/flesh. Under Maruhn the representation of Oskar's body becomes a devastated body reflecting that harvest of body parts, that *assemblage monstrueux* also found in Rabelais's novels: "da fiel mir der Kopf zwischen die Füße, da klatschte der Ton von den Bleirohren, da rutschte mir der Buckel in die Kniekehlen, da lernte ich den Meister Maruhn schätzen, der ein so vortrefflicher Gerüstbauer war, daß er das Kaschieren des Gerüstes mit dem billigen Stoff gar nicht nötig hatte" (*B*, 387; "My head fell between my feet, the clay parted from the tubing, my hump drooped nearly to my knees, and I came to appreciate Maruhn, the master, whose skeletons were so perfect that there was no need to hide them beneath vile flesh": TD, 467). It is especially Manheim's translation of *Gerüst* (framework) as *skeleton* that is highly macabre in view of the fact that to the Nazis too, who could never realize true perfection in the human body, perfect bodies could only be skeletons, the dead bodies left in the wake of mass sacrifice to the idea of the Thousand-Year Reich — whether as victims of racial hygiene or as victims of the war.

Greff

Grass achieves the contrast between the grotesque body and the Nazi ideal of the classical Aryan body mainly by juxtaposing Oskar and his physical counterpart, the greengrocer Greff. Like Oskar, Greff is in danger of being persecuted by the Nazis, whose understanding of asocial individuals included prostitutes, homosexuals, pimps, and other types of *Sittlichkeitsverbrecher*, that is, people who committed moral crimes, and were consequently classified as *gemeinschaftsunfähig*, socially not adaptable.[26] Even Oskar, whom Maria calls a pimp, fits into this category, not only because of his provocative sexual behavior in church but primarily because he is quite possibly the offspring of an incestuous love affair between his mother and her cousin Jan Bronski. A vegetarian like Hitler, Greff is a homosexual who is attracted to teenage boys, with whom he engages in boy-scout games. In the end, his sexual orientation leads him to commit suicide, partly because of the death of his favorite boy scout Horst Donath, but also because he gets a letter from the police, "eine Vorladung vors Gericht, der man den Stempel der Sittenpolizei mehrmals aufgedrückt hatte" (*B*, 260; "a summons to appear in court on a morals charge": *TD*, 317).

One of Grass's most memorable characters, Greff celebrates his own body and those of young boys: "Greff liebte das Straffe, das Muskulöse, das Abgehärtete. Wenn er Natur sagte, meinte er gleichzeitig Askese. Wenn er Askese sagte, meinte er eine besondere Art von Körperpflege. Greff verstand sich auf seinen Körper" (*B*, 240; "Greff liked everything that was hard, taut, muscular. When he said 'nature,' he meant asceticism. When he said asceticism he meant a particular kind of physical culture. Greff was an expert on the subject of his body": *TD*, 293). Through his exaggerated body culture Greff chastises himself for his desire for teenage boys and thus follows a strange logic that Hitler once outlined in *Mein Kampf*: "The youth who achieves the hardness of iron by sports and gymnastics succumbs to the need of sexual satisfaction less than the stay-at-home fed exclusively on intellectual fare."[27] What Michel Tournier says of his pro-fascist protagonist Abel in *The Ogre* is also true of Greff, namely that he prefers "the rigor of cold" because it "symbolizes that of morality."[28] Greff is an incarnation of National Socialist body politics: their dislike of the grotesque body, and their idea of hardening the male body into a likeness of the statuesque Classical body:

Er . . . begann sich . . . nackt auszuziehen; denn wenn Greff sich aus-
zog, zog er sich nackt aus. . . . Greff nahm . . . zweimal in der Woche
ein Bad in der Ostsee. Mittwochs badete er alleine am frühesten Mor-
gen. Um sechs fuhr er los, war um halb sieben da, hackte bis viertel
nach sieben das Loch, riß sich mit raschen, übertriebenen Bewegungen
die Kleider vom Leib, sprang in das Loch, nachdem er sich zuvor mit
Schnee abgerieben hatte, schrie in dem Loch, singen hörte ich ihn
manchmal: "Wildgänse rauschen durch die Nacht," oder: "Wir lieben
die Stürme . . ." sang er, badete, schrie zwei, höchstens drei Minuten
lang, war mit einem Sprung schrecklich deutlich auf der Eisdecke: ein
dampfendes krebsrotes Fleisch, das um das Loch herum hetzte, immer
noch schrie. (B, 241)

[He began to undress. He took off his clothes and he was soon stark naked, for Greff's nakedness was always stark . . . twice a week during winter months, Greff the greengrocer bathed in the Baltic. On Wednesday
he bathed alone at the crack of dawn. He started off at six, arrived at half-
past, and dug [a hole into the ice] until a quarter past seven. Then he
tore off his clothes with quick, excessive movements, rubbed himself with
snow, jumped into the hole, and, once in it, began to shout. Or sometimes I heard him sing: "Wild geese are flying through the night" or
"Oh, how we love the storm . . . ." He sang, shouted, and bathed for
two minutes, or three at most. Then with a single leap he was standing,
terrifyingly distinct, on the ice: a steaming mass of lobstery flesh, racing
round the hole, glowing, and still shouting. (TD, 294)]

One of the principal characteristics of Greff is that he exaggerates everything
he is and does. Greff's exaggerated subscription to the Nazis' body ideal and
body culture reveals his own fear of discovery and persecution at a time that
sees manliness in crisis and aspires to reassert its own heterosexuality not
only by eliminating all homosexuals but also by rooting out any effeminacy
in the male body, whether in real life or in its artistic representations.[29] Kaltenecker shows persuasively to what extent representations of the fascist
imagination of the body reflect the way in which it is expected to "pull itself
together" (sich zusammennehmen) as opposed to a society in which the
body is allowed to "let itself go" (sich gehenlassen).[30] Physical tautness is
possibly best represented in the Hitler salute, which, ironically, was often
relaxed from a straight line to a crooked wave by Hitler himself and other
leading figures of National Socialism, such as the Reich Marshal Hermann
Goering. If we look at Greff's pursuit of a taut body from a psycho-analytic
perspective we can assume that he tries to hide his effeminacy behind an
exaggeratedly male body. Unlike the Nazis, who assert their own identity by
persecuting those groups to whom they do not wish to belong, Greff hides
his true identity through self-denial, by coating his effeminate inner self with
a male body. Yet like the Nazis Greff accentuates his masculinity through his

body culture, thus reflecting the Nazi party's own struggle in imaging their patriarchal, heterosexual politics. Greff is the typical bodybuilder who is unsure of his masculinity and therefore eager to emphasize through his body that part of his identity that he fears is missing. As Alan M. Klein has pointed out, "bodybuilders tend to be hypermasculine and there is a link between their hypermasculinity and gender-based insecurity."[31] Quoting Theodor Adorno's *The Authoritarian Personality* (1950), Klein says that "hypermasculinity is an exaggeration of male traits, be they psychological or physical" and that "there is embedded in it a view of radical opposition to all things feminine. Male self-identity is the issue here. The more insecure the man, the greater his tendency to exaggerate, to proclaim his maleness."[32] We can observe this tendency in Greff because "alles an Greff war übertrieben" (*B*, 239; "everything about Greff was overdone": *TD*, 292).

Greff's body culture is, however, more than a psychological problem. It represents a sort of camouflage and is a way to hide from the homophobic Nazis, who, in order to uphold the image of a healthily heterosexual society, killed those who did not fit into this image: the effeminate Jew[33] and the homosexuals. As Klein informs us, it is the athlete's identity that society rarely questions. As the highest embodiment of masculinity in our society, male athletes are allowed to behave in a way that other men are not. They are, for example, allowed to hug in public, precisely because their masculinity is beyond doubt. Klein is talking about American society, but the same holds true for other conservative societies, and National Socialism was no exception.[34] Greff's athleticism also stems from a preoccupation with youth and health. After all, the Nazi persecution of minorities was the result of the politics of racial hygiene, and Greff's concern with a healthy lifestyle, signaled both by his asceticism and his profession, can also be explained by a desire to comply with a society that thinks along these lines of public health: "Es konnte gar keine Krankheit geben, die den Gemüsehändler ans Bett hätte fesseln können"(*B*, 255; "There existed no ailment that could have fastened the greengrocer to his bed": *TD*, 311). Although he hardens his body through exercise, his body corresponds to what Foucault in *Discipline and Punish* has described as the "docile body." His eagerness to please the boys with whom he surrounds himself is accompanied by an eagerness to please a society that would condemn him if it knew the truth about him. Discipline, according to Foucault, produces subjected docile bodies,[35] and Greff makes his feminine body docile, that is, obedient to a patriarchal society that through hypermasculinity tries to eradicate any femininity that it may contain. He does so not only through his bathing routine in the icy Baltic but also through his sleeping routine, since he despises soft mattresses, instead preferring to sleep on camp beds and wooden planks. In the Third Reich the obedient, docile body was the one that the state could use for work and war. More than in any other period "a policy of coercions" was made to "act upon the body"³⁶ and the less docile the body was, the less useful it was to society and consequently the more this society felt threatened by it and was eager to get rid of it. The disabled body eludes this process of being made docile, and no amount of discipline can increase the potential of such a body in economic terms.

Notes

¹ Klaus Wolbert, *Die Nackten und die Toten des Dritten Reiches* (Giessen: Anabas, 1982), 223: "Als Inbegriff alles Häßlichen wurde die Kunst der Moderne diffamiert, deren Menschenbild Schultze-Naumburg in seinen Kampfbund-Vorträgen wie in seinen Schriften stets mit klinischen Krankheitsfällen und körperlichen Missbildungen verglich. Womit er eine Praxis ideologisch vorbereitete, die nicht allein die Eliminierung der häßlichen Kunst forderte, sondern auch die Liquidation des als häßlich ausgesonderten kranken oder behinderten Menschen mitkonzipierte." (Modern art was considered the epitome of all ugliness. Schultze-Naumburg used to compare this art's images of humans with clinical cases and physical deformations, thus ideologically preparing a practice that demanded not only the elimination of grotesque art but also the liquidation of diseased and disabled humans who were singled out as ugly.)

² Klaus Peter Schuster, ed., *Die "Kunststadt" München 1937: Nationalsozialismus und "Entartete Kunst"* (Munich: Prestel-Verlag, 1988), 250.

³ Cf. also Ernst Klee *"Euthanasie" im NS-Staat: Die "Vernichtung unwerten Lebens"* (Frankfurt am Main: Fischer, 1989), 84. Klee describes the discussion between the manager of the chemistry department of the *Reichskriminalpolizeiamt* (the Reich Police Department), Dr. Albert Widmann, and his boss in 1939, who asks him if the *Kriminaltechnische Institut* (KTI) (Criminological Institute) could order larger quantities of poison. Widmann asks why, for the killing of people? No. For the killing of animals? No. What then? The killing of animals in the shape of humans, "Tiere in Menschengestalt," the killing of the mentally disabled.

⁴ Ulrike Schulz, *Gene mene muh raus mußt du: Eugenik von der Rassenhygiene zu den Gen- und Reproduktionstechnologien* (Munich: AG SPAK, 1992), 59.

⁵ Schuster, *München*, 252: "Der Nationalsozialismus hat sich nun einmal zur Aufgabe gestellt, das Deutsche Reich und damit unser Volk und sein Leben von all jenen Einflüssen zu befreien, die für unser Dasein verderblich sind. Und wenn auch diese Säuberung nicht an einem Tage erfolgen kann, so soll sich doch keine Erscheinung, die an dieser Verderbung teilnimmt, darüber täuschen, dass auch für sie früher oder später die Stunde der Beseitigung schlägt."

⁶ Ernst Klee, *"Euthanasie,"* 38: "Zu sterilisieren ist . . . bei Epilepsie, erblicher Blind- und Taubheit sowie bei schweren erblichen Mißbildungen. . . . Zu den körperlichen Mißbildungen werden unter anderem Kleinwuchs und spastische Lähmungen gerechnet." (To be sterilized are those with epilepsy, congenital blindness and deafness, as well as severe deformations such as dwarfism and spastic paralysis.)

⁷ Mario Bagioli, "Science, Modernity, and the 'Final Solution,'" in *Probing the Limits of Representation: Nazism and the "Final Solution,"* ed. Saul Friedlander (Cambridge, MA: Harvard UP, 1992), 202.

[8] Dr. Miklos Nyiszli, *Auschwitz: A Doctor's Eyewitness Account* (New York: Frederick Fell, 1960), 57–58. See also Robert Jay Lifton, *The Nazi Doctors: Medical Killing and the Psychology of Genocide* (New York: Basic Books, 1986), 360–64.

[9] Cf. Nyiszli, *Auschwitz*, 175.

[10] Klee, *"Euthanasie,"* 347, gives the examples of Johann Fr., who was killed because (ironically like Goebbels) he had a clubfoot and limped although he was otherwise perfectly healthy, and Karl M. whose only fault was that he could not see much without glasses.

[11] Daniel Wildmann, *Begehrte Körper: Konstruktion und Inszenierung des "arischen" Männerkörpers im "Dritten Reich"* (Würzburg: Königshausen & Neumann, 1998, 70: "Der einzelne Körper ist immer auch Teil des Volkskörpers, und so wird die Gesundheit des einzelnen die Voraussetzung für die Gesundheit des Volkskörpers, und so wandeln sich Gesundheit und die Gesundheit fördernde Maßnahmen wie Sport zur Pflicht gegenüber der 'Volksgemeinschaft.' Der 'Arier' und die 'Arierin' mögen und sollen ihn hegen und pflegen, aber ihr Körper gehört letztlich dem Staat." (The individual body is always a part of the body of the people, the *Volk*, so that each person's health contributes to the health of the body of the *Volk*. Hence health and activities that promote health, like sports, become a duty towards the entire national community. All Aryans, male and female, are to look after their bodies, which in final analysis belong to the state.)

[12] Wolbert, *Die Nackten und die Toten*, 226, quoting Hans F. K. Guenther, *Ritter, Tod und Teufel: Der heldische Gedanke* 4th edition (Munich: n.p., 1935), 180.

[13] On this topic cf. for example Günter Grau, ed., *Homosexualität in der NS-Zeit: Dokumente einer Diskriminierung und Verfolgung* (Frankfurt am Main: Fischer, 1993); Robert N. Proctor, *Racial Hygiene: Medicine under the Nazis* (Cambridge, MA: Harvard UP, 1988), 212–17. Nazi persecution of homosexuality, which was thought to be a genetically determined disorder, started on June 30, 1934, as what came to be known as the Röhm putsch or "the night of long knives." By the mid-1930s thousands of homosexuals were sent to the concentration camps so that they would not "infect" the general population.

[14] Cf. Klee, *"Euthanasie,"* 22.

[15] The association of smallness with stupidity is not limited to the four tales discussed here. Possibly the best example is the Grimm tale of "Simple Hans" (Hans Dumm) that makes this link its central theme. Hans's physical shortcomings — he is a dwarf and a hunchback — are wrongly associated with a lack of intelligence. The princess blames Hans for their marriage and her father, the King, ends up dropping them in a barrel into the sea. He had vowed to give his daughter to whoever in church would receive a lemon out of the hands of her illegitimate child. Although only handsome men were invited, in typical trickster fashion Hans manages to sneak into church unobserved and receives the lemon and thus the hand of the princess. Luckily, Hans has magic powers by which he can adapt to the princess's high expectations of happiness. He wishes for a ship, and a castle, and that he might become a handsome young prince. After his wishes come true, their happiness seems to be perfect and this could be the end of the tale were it not for the fact that the King has yet to learn his lesson. When he visits the Prince and the Princess she conceals her own identity from her

father. Before he leaves she slips a golden chalice into his coat and sends her knights after him to search him. He swears to her that he did not steal the chalice and that he does not know how it had got into his pocket. "You see," the princess said, "one should never pronounce anyone guilty before there is proof of his guilt," and with these words she reveals herself as his daughter. Their happiness is now complete, all three are reconciled, and after the death of her father Simple Hans becomes King. This story of the hunchback who in the end is happily married to a princess shares a number of motifs, such as parental neglect and the question of guilt, with *Die Blechtrommel,* with Lagerkvist's novel, and the other two Tom Thumb tales. The closest link, however, is the underestimation of the dwarf by the grown-ups, which all stories share. The tale of "Simple Hans" illustrates what Foucault discusses in the first chapter of *Madness and Civilization.* Whereas the fools still roamed free on city streets in medieval times, in the Renaissance period they were segregated by way of the "Stultifera Navis," the Ship of Fools, which marked the beginning of their increasing separation from society. Although thus marginalized from society, the insane were still allowed to roam. And yet their segregation in boats implies a bitter irony because "confined on the ship, from which there is no escape, the madman is delivered to the river with its thousand arms, the sea with its thousand roads, to that great uncertainty external to everything. He is a prisoner in the midst of what is the freest, the openest of routes" (Foucault, *Madness and Civilization,* 11). Whereas the fairy tale still ends happily for the dwarf who had been put out to sea, Oskar Matzerath may escape being killed by the Nazis but he never escapes his ultimate imprisonment in a mental ward in the Federal Republic.

[16] According to Manfred Pfister, this parallel between the two texts would be an example of what he calls high intertextuality. Cf. Manfred Pfister, "Konzepte der Intertextualität," in *Intertextualität: Formen, Funktionen, anglistische Fallstudien,* ed. Ulrich Broich and Manfred Pfister (Tübingen: Niemeyer, 1985), 28.

[17] The carnival tradition of the *Nasentanz* (Dance of the Noses), introduced by poet and playwright Hans Sachs (1494–1576), also belongs to this phallic symbolism.

[18] Cf. Klee, *"Euthanasie,"* 52: In a speech in 1935 Hitler demanded these qualities from the Hitler Youth.

[19] Fritz Viktor Meier, "Der nordische Mensch das Kunstideal aller Zeiten," in *Die Schönheit: Familiensinn und Rassenpflege* 20.12 (1924): 546.

[20] Cf. Wolfgang Fritz Haug, *Die Faschisierung des bürgerlichen Subjekts, die Ideologie der gesunden Normalität und die Ausrottungspolitiken im deutschen Faschismus: Materialienanalysen* (Hamburg: Argument-Verlag, 1987), 23.

[21] Cf. Walter Benjamin, *Illuminations. Essays and Reflections,* ed. with an Introduction by Hannah Arendt (New York: Schocken, 1969), 6.

[22] Siegfried Kaltenecker, "Weil aber die vergessenste Fremde unser Körper ist: Über Männer-Körper Repräsentationen und Faschismus," in Marie-Luise Angerer, ed., *The Body of Gender, Körper, Geschlechter, Identitäten* (Vienna: Passagen, 1995), 91: "Der gekrümmte Körper wird gewissermaßen in ein stählernes Korsett gezwungen, das das Sich-Zusammennehmen zum Konstituens einer neuen männlichen Identität erhebt." (The bent-over body is forced into a steel corset, so to speak, which makes the act of pulling oneself together the constituent of a new male identity.)

[23] Bernd Jürgen Warneken, "Bürgerliche Emanzipation und aufrechter Gang: Zur Geschichte eines Handlungsideals," in *Das Argument: Zeitschrift für Philosophie und Sozialwissenschaften* 179 (1990): 45.

[24] Warneken, "Bürgerliche Emanzipation," 48.

[25] Thomas Mann, *Der Zauberberg* (Frankfurt am Main: Fischer, 1952), 95. Mann's text may have served as a source for Dürrenmatt's *Der Verdacht.*

[26] Klee, *"Euthanasie,"* 357.

[27] Adolf Hitler, *Mein Kampf,* trans. Ralph Manheim (Boston: Houghton Mifflin, 1943), 253.

[28] Michel Tournier, *The Ogre* (Baltimore: Johns Hopkins UP, 1997), 312.

[29] See Kaltenecker, "Über Männer-Körper Repräsentationen," 99: "[Die] Abgrenzung des faschistischen Mannes vom weiblichen, homosexuellen, jüdischen oder proletarischen Anderen macht die aggressive Expansion zum modus vivendi einer zwanghaften Identität, die alles Nicht-Identische konsequent zum Verschwinden bringen muß." (Distancing himself from the female, homosexual, Jewish or proletarian Other makes aggressive expansion the *modus vivendi* of the fascist man's compulsive identity, which therefore demands the disappearance of everything that is not identical with it.)

[30] Kaltenecker, "Über Männer-Körper Repräsentationen," 99.

[31] Alan M. Klein, *Little Big Men: Bodybuilding Subculture and Gender Construction* (Albany: State U of New York P, 1993), 222.

[32] Klein, *Little Big Men,* 221.

[33] Cf. Monica Rüthers, "Der Jude wird weibisch — und wo bleibt die Jüdin? Jewish Studies — Gender Studies — Body History, in *Traverse: Zeitschrift für Geschichte* 3.1 (1996): 136–45.

[34] Klein, *Little Big Men,* 219.

[35] Michel Foucault, *Discipline and Punish: The Birth of the Prison* (New York: Random House, 1995), 138.

[36] Foucault, *Discipline and Punish,* 138.

4: Oskar's Dysfunctional Family and Gender Politics

I N THE THIRD REICH the persecution of the physically disabled and other groups of so-called asocial life was linked to the perception of them as *nutzlose Esser* (useless mouths to feed). The parents' abandonment of their children, the question of food (especially in the war years) and the grotesque body connect the historical level of Grass's novel with the fairy-tale world. Grass's portrayal of his dysfunctional family, the Matzeraths, parodies the patriarchal gender patterns of the fairy tales discussed in this study. *Die Blechtrommel* shares with the Tom Thumb tales and Hauff's dwarf tales such motifs as the complicated relationship the dwarf has with his parents, particularly with his mother, the motif of parental neglect, the sense of shame felt by his parents, and the dwarf's desire to hide from persecution. In the majority of those tales that Aarne and Thompson have identified as the type "The Children and the Ogre," to which the Grimm Tom Thumb tales and *Hänsel und Gretel* belong, the abandoned children are reunited with the father at the end, while the mother or stepmother epitomizes a menacing cruelty that needs to be obliterated.[1] This patriarchal order in the tales no longer functions in *Die Blechtrommel*, where Oskar is clearly responsible for the death of his two putative fathers, and where his relationship with his mother is intensely oedipal. Yet, as we shall see, Oskar's behavior towards his mother also contains much duplicity, marked both by cruelty as well as desire to return to her womb. To some extent Agnes is a realization of Bettelheim's theory that the mother in *Hänsel und Gretel* becomes "a target of the child's hostility and of a projected form of oral aggression" because she withholds her love and nourishment.[2]

Within the context of euthanasia the theme of parental neglect is of particular interest. To what extent did parents resist Nazi ideology? After all, the Nazis' euthanasia program only functioned because parents would give away their children. There was on the whole little resistance by the parents because the true nature of the killing institutions was well camouflaged, starting with the victims' initial institutionalization all the way to their death. Through the sequence of letters that Matzerath receives from the Ministry of Public Health, *Die Blechtrommel* shows quite clearly the kind of persistent pressure that party officials exerted on the parents so that they would give up their disabled children. Although most parents were assured that their children would be treated well in these institutions,[3] there were some cases in which the parents actually desired their children's and relatives' "salvation,"[4] but these cases were rare. The fact remains, however, that in Grass's novel there are moments when Oskar has the impression that his parents want to get rid of him. The theme of parental participation in the institutionalization process of the euthanasia victim is exposed at several moments: when Oskar thinks that to his mother he was never anything but a gnome, "abgetan hätte sie den Gnom, wenn sie nur gekonnt hätte" (B, 138; "She would have got rid of the gnome if she had been able to": TD, 171), when Matzerath finally signs the ominous letter, and above all when his stepmother Maria shows her readiness to part with Oskar. Her insistence that it's the modern way, "das macht man heut so" (B, 298), recalls Klee's argument that some parents desired the death of their children because it was in tune with the spirit of the times, "im Sinne des Zeitgeistes."[5]

While one salient feature in the fairy tales is the relationship between the dwarf and the mother figures, the nurturing principle, the dwarf's usefulness in the workplace is often reflected in his relationship with his father. Grass inverts this traditional gender pattern in that Agnes neglects her motherly function towards Oskar through her premature death and Matzerath, who reigns in the kitchen, adopts the role of nurturer. Bakhtin has argued that in Rabelais the food images are closely interwoven with those of the grotesque body (RW, 279), and that eating and drinking are among the most significant manifestations of the grotesque body because of its open unfinished nature and interaction with the world (RW, 281). Euthanasia is a denial of this growth, since useless members of society are not supposed to eat (euthanasia patients were often starved to death), a denial of this interaction between the handicapped person and the world. This ideology conjures up such peasant sayings as "wer nicht arbeitet, soll auch nicht essen" (if you don't work, you don't eat), as well as Bakhtin's words that "food was related to work," that "work triumphed in food," and that "collective food as the conclusion of labor's collective process was not a biological, animal act but a social event" (RW, 281). Oskar's categorization in the Third Reich as a useless mouth to feed is a concept that Grass addresses through the foil of fairy tales that belong to the type "The Children and the Ogre," in which the children are a burden to their families if they cannot be useful to them.[6] In these tales the theme of abandonment is directly related to the issue of the child's usefulness or the parents' incapacity to feed their children, a motif that resurfaces in Oskar's stepmother Maria's comment after the war that he is a drain on their budget and that he should look for a job: "du liegst uns auf der Tasche, Oskar. Fang etwas an" (B, 366). Tom Thumb's and Oskar's greatest fear is that their inability to work will exclude them from a society that shares the food after labor. Their desire to make themselves useful reflects how eager they are to become part of society, since not participating in the banquet means death. We see this clearly in Oskar's mother Agnes, who refuses to eat the eel Matzerath has prepared, an act that results in her loneliness, her hypercorrection of this refusal through bulimia, and ultimately her death.

Oskar's problematic relationship with his parents is a theme that is thus closely connected with the grotesque body in the fairy tales, where the dwarf is an embodiment of the lack of food in the lower social sphere. The Grimm tale *Der junge Riese* may serve as a suitable example to illustrate how body size is closely related to the question of food, its presence or absence. Here, Tom Thumb turns into a giant, who walks the world, punishes the greedy and deals with all sorts of adventures such as the nocturnal terror of a haunted mill. This tale shares with the other Tom Thumb tales the question of his usefulness, the moment in which he has to prove himself a useful apprentice, and the dubiousness of his parents' love. When, still the size of a Tom Thumb, he asks his peasant father to take him along to the field, his father responds that he had better stay home, as he is of no use to him and could get lost.[7] He does indeed get lost because a giant comes along, picks him up and carries him away. The giant nurtures him for a number of years until Tom Thumb becomes a giant himself, and one of incredible strength to boot. He returns home but his parents do not recognize him and are afraid of him, a scene that is reminiscent of Hauff's *Der Zwerg Nase,* of Jakob's return to his parents after his transformation.[8] The young giant's parents want to have nothing to do with him. His father is sure that the returned child is not his son, and when he takes him home his mother also exclaims that he cannot be their son, that they never had one that large, and that their son was only a tiny thing. In all Tom Thumb tales the size of the son seems to be related to the parents' incapacity to love and feed him. That the old giant nurtures little Tom Thumb is a motif that undoubtedly stems from the lower classes' fear that there may not be enough food for the children. The old giant is an image for the positive desire to find nourishment for the child while it also implies the negative fantasy of getting rid of one's children, a desire that surfaces in the form of different motifs in the fairy tale, whether as the father who sells his son to strangers (*Daumesdick*), the mother who tells her son to look into the cooking pot, whereupon he is carried away by the steam (*Daumerlings Wanderschaft*), or the even more brutal variant of deliberately losing the children in a forest (*Hänsel und Gretel,* Perrault's *Le Petit Poucet*).

The presence or absence of food determines the main action in many of these fairy tales. When the young giant realizes that his poor parents cannot feed him, he wanders off into the world but not before asking his father to equip him with an appropriate iron stave, which the father, however, cannot provide. No matter which stave he brings home his son can break it. The parents in this fairy tale are completely inadequate providers. It seems to be the father's function to equip his son with a weapon because this motif also occurs in *Daumerlings Wanderschaft* (the father gives his son a long knitting needle as a dagger) and after his father's death Hauff's Little Muck takes with him a long Damascus dagger. Yet in all these tales there is also a conflict between the father and son(s). That Little Muck takes his father's dagger and clothes is an initiation rite echoed in Charles Perrault's tale, where little Tom Thumb finally takes the boots of the ogre, who is a representation of a negative father figure.[9] Like the German Tom Thumbs and Simon Mawer's dwarf in the novel *Mendel's Dwarf,* who says that most people are surprised when they find out that he is actually more intelligent than they are, Perrault's Tom Thumb is considered stupid,[10] but is in fact "the shrewdest" among the children, because he ends up liberating his six brothers from the ogre's den. He is a trickster figure like the German Tom Thumb figures, the brave little tailor, Little Muck and many others. Tricking as an initiation rite in fairy tales of this type often removes the competing father or terrible mother figure. The nourishing mother and the terrible, devouring mother are the two principal figures associated with the question of food in the fairy tale world. The child-devouring witch in *Hänsel und Gretel* is a double of the stepmother who neglects her role as nurturer. In contrast to this German tale, in Charles Perrault's *Le Petit Poucet* it is the mother who wants to keep the children, while the father wants to get rid of them. The mother's protectiveness is reflected in that of the ogre's wife, who tries to hide the children from her husband. Here the fatherly principle is the devouring one. The little boys' bodies that are to be devoured by the ogre are associated with banquet images. The verb "to dress" when the ogre tells his wife to go upstairs and dress the little rascals that she took in the night before reveals the connection between the body and food as it is used ambiguously, as putting on clothes (nurturing) and putting dressing on a salad (being devoured). Mourey's argument that Perrault's tale oscillates between eating and being eaten[11] evokes the carnivalesque world of Rabelais, his central image of *tripes* as edible as well as digesting organs.

The descent into the stomach in the folk-tale and in Rabelais reflects both archetypes: the terrible mother who does not feed the child but wants to devour him, and the child's subconscious wish for rebirth and consequent possibility of mending the family situation. Being swallowed and devoured is part of the initiation rite of the fairy tale hero and is linked to rebirth. The devouring oven in *Hänsel und Gretel,* the man-eating ogre in *Le Petit Poucet,* the German Tom Thumb's journeys through stomachs and sausages, and Oskar's fall into the open grave all bring about this sort of rebirth. The witch's death in the oven causes a healing of the defective family situation in *Hänsel und Gretel* as does Tom Thumb's emergence from an animal's stomach. In *Hänsel und Gretel,* the witch, a double of the evil stepmother and thus a representation of the terrible-mother archetype, burns in her own oven, the womb that devours instead of giving birth. Like the cow's stomach of the Tom Thumb tale, the oven has an ambiguous function. It can kill but also cause rebirth. Bakhtin refers to this ambivalence in the womb/grave image when he points to the "earthly element of terror" in the womb, which is the bodily grave but also "flowers with delight and a new life."[12]

As in *Hänsel und Gretel*, where the threat of the cannibalistic terrible-mother archetype subsides to allow for the children's rebirth into a new family situation, in which the terrible mother has disappeared, in *Daumerlings Wanderschaft* the mother, who neglects her nourishing function, is expelled at the end. Initially, the little boy asks his mother what there is to eat and the mother answers that he should see for himself. The mother's reply in the original German "sieh du selbst zu," renders more clearly the ambiguity of her remark, namely that he should not only look into the pot himself but also that he should not rely on her for food but look after himself. That the steam takes him into the world just after this remark is a fulfillment of the latter meaning of her words. The family is poor, since the father is a tailor, and their son's size reflects this poverty. In the course of Tom Thumb's journey it is characteristically the female figures that make his life difficult. His first master's wife is a substitute mother, who also does not feed him properly. When he complains about the food she chases him with a rag, a motif that Grass uses too at the moment when Maria, Oskar's substitute mother, gags him with a towel to stop him from screaming. Later on Tom Thumb becomes the apprentice of an innkeeper, whose maids are stealing money and trying to kill him. One of them mows him down along with the grass and feeds him to the cow, and the innkeeper's wife goes for him with a knife as she cuts up the sausage that holds him inside. The overall message he gets is that mother figures want to get rid of him. In this context it is also interesting that he dislikes sitting in the cow's stomach. This is not surprising, one might argue, yet if one interprets the cow's stomach as symbolic of a uterus, then this becomes an important detail because unlike Oskar, Tom Thumb does not seek to return to the uterus, to his mother, "denn es war da ganz finster und brannte auch kein Licht" (for it was very dark, and there was no light).[13] While Oskar, who is aware of his vulnerability and wants to hide from persecution, escapes *into* places that symbolize the uterus, the Tom Thumb of this version tries to escape *from* such places, away from the mother and back to the father. Upon his return his father is beyond himself with happiness whereas the text no longer mentions the mother, who seems to have mysteriously disappeared. The father happily gives the fox all the chickens he owns in order to get his son back. The tale ends with Tom Thumb's question as to why the fox got all those poor little chickens to eat, and the father answers: "Ei, du Narr, deinem Vater wird ja wohl sein Kind lieber sein als die Hühner auf dem Hof." (Oh, you fool, don't you think that your father would care more for his child than for all the chickens in his barnyard?).[14] As a didactic message this ending evokes the father's regret for the earlier parental neglect through which his son has been endangered. Birds in folk-tales are a symbol of fertility. The chickens therefore also represent the mother and the yard in which they live is yet another uterus symbol. By giving away the chickens to the fox the father is saying that his son is worth more to him than his wife who had neglected their boy. As in *Hänsel und Gretel,* the bad mother who neglects her nourishing function is expelled from the tale. In the end the male principle rules supreme, a fact that is also indicated by the coin that Daumerling brings back, since earning money corresponds to the patriarchal principles of the folk-tales.

Grass parodies the successful resolutions of the conflict between parents and son that take place in the fairy tale. The initiation rite for the fairy tale hero is often a journey away from home, a journey that Oskar likewise completes as he goes to France. During this journey the fairy tale hero (or heroine) usually overcomes obstacles and dangers, his/her initiation rite, and returns home to a mended family situation. In this group of tales, the Tom Thumb tales and *Hänsel und Gretel,* the family situation is either completely mended at the end in that the son is happily reunited with both parents who are overjoyed and swear that they will never give their child away again, or partially mended in that the evil parent is eradicated so that the good parent can bestow his/her love on the lost son who has come home. It becomes clear that despite their carnivalesque residue, the German tales, in which the evil mother figure disappears at the end, embody a patriarchal value system, the Christian, or male, value system that, since the Reformation, has systematically tried to expel pagan, or female, elements from its midst. *Die Blechtrommel* subverts this patriarchal value system; it paganizes it, so to speak, through its female figures, Oskar's grandmother Anna Koljaiczek, the magna mater who shelters his grandfather in the middle of a potato field[15] and Agnes, the "whore," that is, pure nature and therefore sin. Yet Agnes's sinning with her cousin Jan is the fleeting moment of carnival that eventually subsides again in deference to the Christian high value system that it reinforces, a value system that has fatal consequences for sinful women, for the fallen angels of the nineteenth-century Bildungsroman and for Agnes, who dies from the conflict between her moment of *jouissance* and her Catholic conscience. The only parental figure who survives the war years in Grass's novel is Oskar's stepmother Maria, who wants to sacrifice him on the altar of euthanasia, and in the postwar years still laments that he is a burden to them. Agnes and Maria are devouring rather than nurturing mother figures, Agnes in an oedipal sense and Maria in that she nearly causes Oskar's death. In contextualizing this problematic figure of the mother (whom the patriarchal fairy tale eradicates at the end), Grass's novel mocks the ideal image of the mother promoted by the Nazis and in the postwar years, thus adopting a stance vis à vis family and gender politics that was representative for the Social Democrats in the 1950s.[16]

Uncrowning the Father Figure

The Matzeraths contrast starkly with the ideal of the Aryan family the Nazis desired for the building of the Thousand-Year Reich.[17] Oskar's dysfunctional family also demonstrates how disorder at the level of the family resulted in the lower middle class's desire for order at the political level. Matzerath is the typical *Mitläufer* who joins the Nazis almost immediately after they rise to power although he never attains any higher position than unit leader. Oskar describes him as a man who always has to wave when other people are waving, and to shout, laugh, and clap when other people are shouting, laughing, and clapping. The Matzeraths' frustration releases itself in blaming and denouncing each other, a mentality that in the 1930s pervaded most of the German social sphere but revealed itself primarily in the middle class's desire for an order that it felt lacking in its own ranks.

Although Matzerath actually saves Oskar from being taken to a euthanasia institution through his hesitation at signing the ominous letters from the Ministry of Public Health, his wife and her mother constantly blame him for having caused Oskar's disability. They blame him for having forgotten to close the basement door, an omission which causes Oskar's fall down the steps, after which he stops growing. This alleged guilt of neglect causes a major rupture between Matzerath and his wife. Oskar's grandmother too never forgives him for this; Matzerath becomes the scapegoat of his family. His wife cheats on him with her cousin, and he is unsure of his own fatherhood regarding Oskar, who eventually kills him in oedipal fashion. Yet everyone becomes guilty in this family, most of all Oskar himself. Oskar's grandmother is also quick to blame her grandson for his mother's death, saying that he drummed her to death (the English version does not do justice to Anna's words in dialect: "Maine Agnes, die starb, wail se das Jetrommel nich mä hätt vertragen megen" (*B*, 140), an argument that reduces Oskar's drum to the weapon of a murderer. Among the many functions of Oskar's drum, it is revealed by the text as a bonanza ("Goldgrube," [*B*, 463]) and as a healing instrument that helps the Germans come to terms with their past by making them remember. Oskar's greatest guilt, however, is that he causes the deaths of his two fathers, Jan Bronski and Matzerath. He assumes truly evil dimensions in destroying the family into which he refuses to grow.

The uncrowning of the husband/father figure is one of the carnivalesque inversion principles in Grass's novel that it shares with Rabelais's *Pantagruel*, where Panurge wants to get married but fears that his future wife will cuck- old him: "All his friends' advice, all the novellas about women which they quote, all the studies of the nature of women by the learned physician Rondibilis lead to the same conclusion. The woman's bowels are inexhaustible and never satisfied" (*RW*, 242). That her bowels are inexhaustible and never satisfied is something we also discern in Agnes, whose sexual appetite is insatiable, a fact for which her excessive fish consumption becomes a central metaphor. Bakhtin points out that Panurge's fear of being cuckolded by his wife "is in tune with his fear of the son, the preordained robber and murderer" (*RW*, 243), a constellation that *Die Blechtrommel* also reflects, for here Matzerath is being cuckolded by his wife as well as displaced, "uncrowned" in the terminology of Bakhtin's carnival, by Oskar. Matzerath's role as patriarch is weakened since he only reigns in the kitchen. In carnival all hierarchies disappear. In his discussion of the theme of oedipal constellations in carnival, Bakhtin refers to Goethe's description of the Roman carnival in his *Italienische Reise* (Italian Journey, 1786, 1787), more precisely, its fire festival in which "a young boy blows out his father's candle, crying out, "Death to you, sir father!" (*RW*, 251).This uncrowning of the father in carnival is often indicated through the symbols of fire, birth, and the dagger (*RW*, 249). In Hauff's *Die Geschichte vom kleinen Muck* the son inherits a dagger after his father has died as well as his father's clothes, and Tom Thumb in *Daumerlings Wanderschaft* receives a long knitting needle from his father before he sets off into the world.[18] The dagger is an ambivalent metaphor. It denotes the father's desire to help his son in his initiation rite, while at the same time it is a symbol of displacement and of the uncrowning of the father by his son. This image of the dagger reveals to what extent the fairy tales are inseparable from their nonliterary forerunner, the street carnival. Oskar displaces his father by killing him when he places the Nazi badge into his raised hand as the Russians invade their basement. To hide the badge Matzerath puts it into his mouth and chokes on it, whereupon he gets shot by a Russian soldier.

Oskar's Bulimic Mother

The most problematic figure in Oskar's family is his mother Agnes, whose story resembles that of her husband in that it mocks the Nazis' patriarchal understanding of gender. As has been pointed out, under National Socialism all forms of female sexuality that lay outside of the marital desire of conceiving children were seen as being degenerate.[19] It was woman's duty to bear genetically healthy offspring and the health of the children was considered to be largely a result of the health and the lifestyle of the mother: "The *völkisch* state sees its ideal of mankind in the defiant embodiment of male virility and in women who can once again give birth to real men."[20] Since sexuality and sensuality were considered to be a menace for National Socialist population politics, the sexuality of women was to be channeled into a motherhood whose quality was subject to state control. For this purpose women were seen as desexualized and became the property of the state in its fight against the decreasing population. Woman's monogamy was regarded as a valuable quality thanks to which men could be sure that they were the fathers of their own sons.

The Nazis' vision of the ideal woman and mother becomes the target of parody in a number of works of art after 1945, for example Edgar Hilsenrath's Mother Holle figure in *Der Nazi und der Friseur* (1971) or Parsifal's mother in Anselm Kiefer's painting *Herzeleide* (1979). For the education of their youth the Nazis emphasized the traditional patriarchal gender patterns that they saw reflected in the folk-tales. By parodying the patriarchal fairy tale, artists after 1945 reacted not only against the tales' manipulation by the Nazis but also against their renewed use in the conservative family politics of the Adenauer period, for which the original Grimm tales were ideally suited.[21] Like Hilsenrath's Mother Holle, whom the author turns into a prostitute, Oskar's mother Agnes serves as a parody of the folk-tale's patriarchal gender pattern. She gives in completely to her sexual impulses and sleeps with Jan, not only her cousin, but a Pole to boot. The question of Oskar's fatherhood remains unanswered throughout the novel. Seen from the vantage point of the Nazis' gender ideology, Oskar's disability would have to be taken as the result of his mother's unchaste lifestyle. Although the text avoids this issue, Agnes's lifestyle would make her a victim of Nazi persecution, too. As Schulz points out, the sterilization politics of the 1920s affected women who were "masturbating, nymphomaniac, lesbian, who had illegitimate children without paying fathers, who were *erziehungsunfähig,* that is, incapable of raising their children, seduced or raped girls, transient and 'hysterical' women, child murderesses."[22] In National Socialism the control over such women became increasingly more refined. "Asocial" women in particular, who suffered from *moralischem Schwachsinn* (moral dementia), were the victims of state-organized repression: enforced institutionalization, sterilization, and labor that would lead to their death. The charge of moral dementia is interesting in connection with Grass's novel, which addresses precisely what the Nazis thought of such women, that their promiscuous lifestyle was responsible for their madness and hysteria. We see this process in Agnes, whose insanity and eventual suicide result from her guilt at her incestuous adultery and her failure to be a good mother to her crippled son. She completely fails to fulfill her function as preserver of the blood.[23]

In *Die Blechtrommel* the loss of parental love and the theme of parental neglect are not related to the problem of food shortage, since the presence of food and the theme of cooking are omnipresent in Grass's works. From a conservative point of view, the central moment of neglect occurs when Oskar's mother leaves her son with the toy maker Sigismund Markus during the hours she spends with her cousin. Interestingly, she accuses Matzerath of carelessness in having left the basement door open, which reflects the kind of transference of one's own guilt onto others that became widespread after the war. Agnes cannot live with the guilty conscience caused by her promiscuity with her cousin, and is broken by it. Oskar's own perception of her is ambivalent, since on the one hand he thinks that the shadow of his poor

Mama prevents his institutionalization for euthanasia, while on the other hand he is also convinced that if she had been able to she would have gotten rid of him. The child's abandonment and consequent exposure to evil forces from which he is forced to hide is a key moment in the Tom Thumb folk-tales. Due to his size the dwarf may be able to render himself invisible by hiding, but he is still vulnerable. Tom Thumb, for example, can hide in a sausage, but he dexterously avoids the butcher's knife which cuts through the sausage. The dwarf is forced to hide from the adult world that threatens him, but in order to protect himself he may also side with those who threaten him. Both Tom Thumbs in the Grimm tales side with nefarious characters. For the hero, running with the wolves thus becomes an act of self-preservation. By making himself useful to the enemy he ensures that he can survive. Oskar hides from the adult world in places that protect him like a uterus, and he sides with those who threaten him, the Dusters and the Nazis. This is his dual nature of victim and criminal.

We observe Oskar's repeated escapes back to the mother from a world ruled and terrorized by men.[24] The hiding places of the dwarf have an ambivalent function: they allow the dwarf to escape from his persecutors while observing his surroundings and being able to act from within them. Patricia Pollock Brodsky is correct in pointing out that "Oskar possesses an obsessive love of enclosed spaces."[25] It is his journey through enclosed spaces — for Oskar largely an urge to return to the shelter of the mother's womb — which he shares with the Tom Thumbs of the folk-tales. The Tom Thumbs of the Grimm Brothers hide in mouse holes, snail shells, under a thimble, under a rag, in the crack of a table, in a drawer, and under coins. They become imprisoned in a sausage and are in danger of being chopped to pieces, a motif which also occurs in Hauff's *Der Zwerg Nase*, where Jakob is likewise threatened with being chopped up and put into a meat pie.[26] They travel through the belly of a cow or an animal of prey, and can slip through keyholes, iron bars, and a crack in the door that leads to a treasury. Oskar hides under the skirts of his grandmother, in wardrobes, under tables, and so on; he is imprisoned in the mental institution, and he tries to slip away from his persecutors, the Dusters, through a hole in a fence. The folk-tale figure's symbolic and involuntary return into the womb happens as he gets swallowed by the cow, stuffed into the sausage, or ends up in the stomach of a wolf or fox. Particularly the image of the cow, however, "shows us the principle of nourishment, on which the entire world relies and which penetrates all nature" (*RW*, 253).

Images of birth, death, eating, and being eaten are closely related in popular culture. Bakhtin discusses this "material lower bodily stratum" in relation to grotesque realism and carnivalesque elements in Rabelais' work, where images of being swallowed and images of the bodily underworld are legion. In chapters 32 and 33 of book 2, a whole army of men descends into Pantagruel's mouth and stomach. This visit into the underworld through the gaping jaws into the fertility of the bodily depths clearly parallels the folk-tale Tom Thumb's journey into the depths of the cow's stomach or into the sausage. Bakhtin argues that "birth and death are the gaping jaws of the earth and the mother's open womb," and images of the well, the cow's belly, and the cellar are equivalent to the gaping mouth (*RW,* 329). In the Grimms' tale *Frau Holle* (Mother Holle) the well, in the Tom Thumb tale the cow's belly, and in *Die Blechtrommel* the cellar are all symbols of rebirth. Oskar's fall into the basement, a fall that stops his growth, signifies his wish to return to the womb where he wants to stop his development. Essentially, he wants to stay in the womb, fossilized like his unborn sibling whom his mother takes to the grave.

Rabelais and the folk-tales thus inspire Oskar's journey through hiding places that give him the possibility of corrupting the male world without through action from within. A central image of this corruption from within is the scene in which Oskar drums apart a Nazi Party rally. Like Tom Thumb, who screams from the belly of the cow or the wolf, which then is slaughtered, Oskar manages with his drum "unter Tribünen hockend, mehr oder weniger Erfolg beobachtend, Kundgebungen gesprengt, Redner zum Stottern gebracht, Marschmusik, auch Choräle in Walzer und Foxtrott umgebogen [zu haben] (*B,* 99; "huddling under rostrums, observing successful or not so successful demonstrations, breaking up rallies, driving orators to distraction, transforming marches and hymns into waltzes and fox trots": *TD,* 123). Oskar compares his position under the rostrum with Jonah sitting in the whale and refers to the "Eingeweide einer Tribüne"(*B,* 99; "bowels of a rostrum": *TD,* 123), which again reminds us of the stomach of the cow and the wolf. We can see to what extent Grass uses Tom Thumb's activity from within the uterus-like space within a political context, thus pitting a feminine image against the patriarchal world of politics. The image of Oskar under the rostrum triggers the question of political resistance or its absence during the Third Reich. Oskar stresses the significance of the position that the onlooker adopts vis à vis the rostrum. While the masses in front of the rostrum are in a position in which they can be easily captivated and manipulated, as they are in front of altars, the view from behind or from within allows for a more critical confrontation with ideology and religion and will lead to resistance:

> Haben Sie schon einmal eine Tribüne von hinten gesehen? Alle Menschen sollte man — nur um einen Vorschlag zu machen — mit der Hinteransicht einer Tribüne vertraut machen, bevor man sie vor Tribünen versammelt. Wer jemals eine Tribüne von hinten anschaute, recht anschaute, wird von Stund an gezeichnet und somit gegen jegliche Zauberei, die in dieser oder jener Form auf Tribünen zelebriert wird, gefeit sein. Ähnliches kann man von den Hintenansichten kirchlicher Altäre sagen; doch das steht auf einem anderen Blatt. (*B,* 96)

[Have you ever seen a rostrum from behind? All men and women — if I may make a suggestion — should be familiarized with the rear view of a rostrum before being called upon to gather in front of one. Everyone who has ever taken a good look at a rostrum from behind will be immunized ipso facto against any magic practiced in any form whatsoever on rostrums. Pretty much the same applies to rear views of church altars; but that is another subject. (*TD*, 119)]

This is only one of the links that the narrator makes between the two patriarchal superstructures, the Nazis and the church, although Oskar is far from seeing himself as a resistance fighter.

One of the central hiding places for Oskar is the four skirts of his grandmother. A place of fertility, in which Koljaiczek fathers Agnes,[27] these skirts symbolize a substitute for the mother's womb, to which Oskar wants to return ("dem Wunsch nach Rückkehr in meine embryonale Kopflage" [*B*, 37; "my desire to return to the womb": *TD*, 49]). Oskar takes refuge under these skirts, which he can reach "mit einem einzigen Daumensprung" (*B*, 289) (the English translation "with a snap of my fingers" [*TD*, 349] loses the folk-tale subtext), to look inward to his own memories. His grandfather had managed to hide and escape his persecutors, who searched for him in every *Mauseloch* (mouse hole) (*B*, 16), one of the locations in which Tom Thumb also hides. The political dimension of the dwarf's return to uterus-like spaces also extends to the chapter "Im Zwiebelkeller" (In the Onion Cellar). Onions are like the four skirts of Oskar's grandmother, "sieben Häute sagt man der Zwiebel nach"(*B*, 437; "onions are said to have seven skins": *TD*, 524), but Grass's onion cellar is a restaurant in which Germans learn how to weep and mourn. As such, the onion cellar stands for the Germans' suffering after the war, both for their crimes and the food deficit caused by total destruction, to a point that there was nothing left to eat but onions. If the onion is a mother symbol via its connection with the grandmother's skirts, then it stands for the mother archetype that refuses its nurturing function, the terrible mother. This connection between a sociopolitical situation and the mother archetype can also be found in Rabelais. Bakhtin argues that the good ruler "is the mother nursing her child. . . . The bad ruler is given the grotesque nickname of people-eater" (*RW*, 450). In Rabelais's texts Guillaume du Bellay is the good ruler, who nurtures his people like the good mother archetype, while Picrochole, who represents Charles V, is the bad ruler and people eater. The image of Charles V obviously reminded Bakhtin of Stalin and in Grass's novel the people eater is no other than Hitler, who causes the onion-diet poverty after the Second World War.

Other uterus-like spaces in the novel include the attic to which Oskar escapes after he has been tortured by the neighbors' kids who feed him the ghastly soup consisting of urine and live frogs. The cruelty of children reflects the cruelty of adults in the Third Reich. Oskar also stands under the Eiffel Tower, reminiscent of both the uterus and phallus; he is inside and on top of a bunker on the Norman coast, where he witnesses the preparation of fish; and he hides in a wardrobe. Here he can spy on Sister Dorothea and masturbate to the image of a black leather belt that reminds him of the eels that are the cause of his mother's death. The image of the fish inside the abdomen recurs several times throughout the novel, which plays with the image of man in fish — Jonah in the whale — versus fish in man or woman: "Die gehen ja auch in den Pferdekopp, sagte er. Und in menschliche Leichen gehen sie auch, sagte der Stauer. Besonders nach der Seeschlacht am Skagerrak sollen die Aale mächtig fett gewesen sein. Und mir erzählte noch vor einigen Tagen ein Arzt der Heil- und Pflegeanstalt von einer verheirateten Frau, die sich mit einem lebendigen Aal befriedigen wollte. Aber der Aal biß sich fest, und sie mußte eingeliefert werden und soll deswegen später keine Kinder bekommen haben" (*B*, 122; "They crawl into the horse's head, don't they? And into human corpses, too, said the longshoreman. They say the eels were mighty fat after the Battle of the Skagerrak. And a few days ago one of the doctors here in the hospital told me about a married woman who tried to take her pleasure with a live eel. But the eel bit into her and wouldn't let go; she had to be taken to the hospital and after that they say she couldn't have any more babies": *TD*, 152).

The towers in this novel are a particularly interesting symbol that can evoke the uterus as well as the phallus. According to Bakhtin the belfry (tower) is the usual grotesque symbol of the phallus (*RW*, 310), and in Rabelais the tower is a representation of femininity and fertility: "only the shadow of an abbey-steeple is fruitful."[28] Since Oskar is seen climbing on top of the Stockturm as his mother and Jan are reaching their climax, this tower denotes the phallus more than the Eiffel Tower, which offers him a glimpse of that womb-like protection he is yearning for, "wurde mir jenes zwar Durchblick gewährende, dennoch geschlossene Gewölbe zur alles verdekkenden Haube meiner Großmutter Anna: wenn ich unter dem Eiffelturm saß, saß ich auch unter ihren vier Röcken" (*B*, 272; "the great vault, which seems so solidly closed despite spaces on all sides, became for me the sheltering vault of my grandmother Anna: sitting beneath the Eiffel Tower, I was sitting beneath her four skirts": *TD*, 330). This symbolic treatment of Parisian architecture is reminiscent of Panurge's project of building the walls of Paris out of female sexual organs in Rabelais's story. Oskar's urge to return to the womb during the war forms a stark contrast to all military acts, as much as "Panurge's walls uncrown and renew the fortified walls, as well as military valor, bullets, and even lightning, which is powerless to crush them. Military power and strength are helpless against the material bodily procreative principle" (*RW*, 314). This indestructibility of the motherly procreative principle reveals itself also in the scene on the western front when Oskar and Roswitha dance on the bunker, and when Roswitha gets killed by a bomb, he concludes that dwarves and fools have no business dancing on concrete made for giants, that they had better stay under the rostrums where no one suspects their presence. The images during the war scenes vacillate between male aggressiveness and female protectiveness. The bunker and the rostrum contain both elements. While their inside gives shelter, aggressiveness emerges from them: the troops shoot from the bunker and the party official preaches destruction from the rostrum.

Both Oskar and his mother are obsessed with the lower body, Oskar in the sense that he is phallus-centered and that he desires to return to the womb, his mother in that she wants to fill her own void by filling her abdomen. Yet although she cannot stop making love to her cousin, she is also deeply afraid of her own obsession. Her eel consumption demonstrates this ambivalent feeling towards her sexuality. Oskar's relationship with his mother is intensely oedipal. She shares his desire that he return to the protective uterus because she wants to reverse his destiny, to undo the damage that was done. After all, Oskar is a Tom Thumb or dactyl, that is, a finger, and as such also symbolizes the phallus his mother desires. Tom Thumb's plunge into the abdomen (the cow's stomach and the sausage as a representation of intestines) evokes the moment in the *commedia dell'arte* when Harlequin talks to a man who stutters. Since the stutterer cannot get the word out, Harlequin "rushes head forward and hits the man in the abdomen. The difficult word is 'born' at last" (*RW*, 304). Oskar too rushes towards the abdomen not only in search of uterus-like spaces but also quite literally, when he lunges at Maria's vagina with his fists, after she has slept with Matzerath, and sinks his teeth into her. His biting into her vagina parallels the motif of the eel biting into the inside of the woman seeking pleasure with it. Oskar is associated with the phallic eel also in the episode where he sits in the wardrobe masturbating with a black belt that looks like an eel. Since the eel is the central phallus symbol for the mother, the association of Oskar with it also makes him a phallus symbol. As the eels kill his mother so does he, at least in the eyes of his grandmother, who blames him for having drummed Agnes to death. As we shall see in the next chapter, Oskar is related to Hermes here in his function as the messenger of death. Yet "drumming," as we know from Rabelais, also alludes to the sexual act. Consequently, the sex that kills her is not just the incest with her cousin but is ultimately also her oedipal obsession, a sort of Freudian carnival diametrically opposed to the official party ideology.

Her bulimia is indicative of the mother's mixed feelings of both desire and repulsion towards her son, inasmuch as it reflects the sequence of copulation, wanting to take in, and giving birth, wanting to release what's inside. The eel episode occupies a central position with regard to motifs such as the womb, the aggressiveness of the male phallus, the folk cultural dichotomy of eating versus being eaten that the carnival world shares with the folk-tales, and, related to these motifs, the themes of death, the underworld, and birth.

As a parody of Faust's Easter walk, the famous scene in which the fisherman pulls out several eels from a dead horse's head continues to trigger feelings of disgust in most readers and audiences of Schlöndorff's film version. Matzerath purchases a few of these eels and cooks them for their Good Friday dinner. Agnes, who throws up when she sees the live eels being disentangled from the grinning horse's head, refuses to eat the eel, which leads to a bad fight between her and Matzerath and her ultimate insanity and suicide through excessive fish consumption. The scene is rich in symbolism and folk cultural images. The grinning horse's head, for example, a symbol for the underworld, links carnival laughter and mockery to death, Agnes's death, which it prefigures. The scene is a perfect blend of those images that Bakhtin discusses under his "banquet imagery," which is related to the lower bodily stratum of the grotesque body: eating, drinking, swallowing, wide-open physical orifices, primarily the mouth and the vagina during childbirth, the spaces to which these orifices lead, the womb and its related organs, the stomach and intestines. The female organs of procreation and digestion have their male counterparts, the penis and again the intestines in view of their elongated shape. Intestines in Rabelais are the organs that both digest and are being digested, like Grass's eels that eat the dead men of the Battle of the Skagerrak and are eaten by the Matzeraths. In Rabelais, especially when Gargantua is born, the consuming and consumed organs are fused with the generating womb. The keyword in Rabelais is *tripes*, which are eaten in large quantities, but as Gargamelle gives birth to Gargantua, her own intestines, which fall out of her, are mistaken for the baby. In *Die Blechtrommel* something similar happens. The intestine-like eels merge with Agnes's unborn baby in the sense that she wants to get rid of both, the eel through her vomiting and the embryo through her suicide: "sie hat noch etwas im Leib, das heraus will: nicht nur den drei Monate alten Embryo . . . da gibt es noch Fisch . . . ein Stückchen Aal meine ich" (*B*, 132; "there was something more inside her that wanted to come out: not only that fetus aged three months . . . there's more fish . . . a little chunk of eel": *TD*, 163). That Agnes's pregnancy and the act of giving birth are associated with bulimia makes this scene the most obscene one of the book and completely aberrant from the perspective of all principles of postwar rationalism. It is entirely Rabelaisian. What is consumed by Gargamelle — sixteen quarters, two bushels, and six pecks of tripe after her husband has warned her against overeating on tripe because of the excrement that sticks to them[29] —, wants to leave her body again and it is expelled when she is giving birth. Victor Hugo, for whom the belly "is the center of Rabelais' topography . . . offers the grotesque image of a serpent inside man; these are his bowels" (*RW*, 125), an image that Grass exploits for his motif of the eel inside woman, Agnes as well as the woman who tries to give herself pleasure with a live eel, which then digs its teeth into her abdomen. This image shows to what extent the delineation between eating and being eaten is erased in Grass's text, something it shares with both Rabelais and many folk-tales. Hänsel and Gretel eat from the gingerbread house, in search of a nurturing mother. Instead they encounter the terrible mother, the witch/stepmother, who wants to devour them. In *Die Blechtrommel*, Oskar's mother is forced to consume the eel that ultimately consumes her like those eels of the battle on the Skagerrak that became extremely fat because of the dead bodies they fed on. Likewise Oskar's grandfather Koljaiczek was likely eaten by eels, the text stresses, when he fell under the raft, which might explain why Agnes initially does not want to eat eel. Her fear is one of incestuous cannibalism that would add to the incest she is already committing with her cousin Jan.

The eel is clearly a phallic symbol that inspires both yearning and terror in Agnes. The spilling forth of the eels from the horse's head, through the hollow eyes and the grinning mouth, is like the sexual act but also like the act of giving birth. Agnes's reluctance to give birth again after being with Jan implies her fear that her first child's gnome-like appearance can only be a form of punishment, if indeed he did issue from this relationship. It is in this scene in particular that we see how far removed this mother figure is from the Nazi ideal of the healthy mother giving birth to genetically healthy Aryan offspring. Yet in spite of her fear, she initially refuses to eat the eel, which as Lenten food is also an image of abstinence. We can see to what extent images of food, sexuality, and giving birth are all related. That Agnes initially does not want to eat the eel could be interpreted in the sense that she does not want to abstain from making love to her cousin. She is the carnival queen adverse to Lenten food, with her sexual hunger closely corresponding to that other image of indulgence in popular culture, an appetite for meat. Like this association of images, Tom Thumb's journey into the sausage is expressive of his physical hunger but also relates the lack of food in his life to the womb symbol and his early birth. By going through the sausage and the cow's stomach he symbolically returns to the womb, from which he has emerged too early, which is also an explanation of his size.

Lack of food and health, and the return to the womb in order to fix this deficit are related motifs in the folklore of different cultures. Andrey Toporkov has pointed out, for example, that the Russian version of *Hänsel und Gretel*, the Baba-Yaga tale, is related to an Eastern European rebirth ritual, in which a sick baby is put on a shovel and shoved into a hot oven with the intention of re-baking it, that is, to put it back into the womb so that it can be reborn as a healthy baby (the Russian word for this process is *perepekanye*).[30] Yet in Grass's context of patriarchal gender politics, Agnes's "sinful" womb and its relation to food images take on an entirely new meaning. Her ultimate surrender to the eel as the Lenten food that Matzerath himself has prepared, by which on a metaphorical level he implores her to be abstinent, and the fact that she quite literally consumes fish *ad nau-*

seam, can be seen as a form of penitence, an exaggerated version of her trips to the confessional, that inevitably leads to her death.

Agnes's and Oskar's insanity harks back to an old belief that "the cause of hysteria is in the womb, but the seat of the disease is to be sought, as in the case of hypochondria, in the stomach and intestines."[31] According to this belief, which also states that hysteria is accompanied by fits of vomiting due to the rising womb, "the vomiting that generally accompanies the inflammation of the womb," i.e., pregnancy (*MC,* 153), Oskar and his mother are the victims of their own passions and appetites, of their obsession with their lower bodily stratum, which is the seat of their madness. Oskar's eagerness to return to the womb is a form of hysteria, his scream a manifestation of this hysteria. If we compare Agnes with Greff, it becomes clear how one of them falls victim to this malady, while the other defends himself against it. According to eighteenth-century beliefs, "the more easily penetrable the internal space becomes the more frequent is hysteria and the more various its aspects; but if the body is firm and resistant, if internal space is dense, organized, and solidly heterogeneous in its different regions, the symptoms of hysteria are rare and its effects will remain simple" (*MC,* 149). Unlike Agnes, whose sexuality makes her internal space easily penetrable, Greff, who fears "the torment of all effeminate souls whom inaction has plunged into dangerous sensuality" (*MC,* 157), suppresses his sexuality, and makes his body impenetrable and firm through excessive exercise. He is eager to avoid being classified as feminine and hysterical, his true nature. Through his self-immersion in the icy waters of the Baltic Sea he aims at curing himself of his "madness," his passion for young boys, a practice of immersion that reaches far back into the history of madness. In the Middle Ages, as Foucault points out, this was the traditional treatment of maniacs so that they would forget their fury (*MC,* 167). Since cold baths were considered to consolidate the organism and give tone to the parts, for Greff they consequently have the twofold benefit of curing him of his "hysteria" and working on his ideal, classical body. Physical activity as a panacea against madness and cold water as a cure for it and a means of shaping the perfect body: these views of earlier centuries determine the European consciousness deep into the twentieth century, as they reoccur in German fascism, where, for example, war hysteria in men became highly punishable. Sanity on account of the body's density contrasts with the protrusions of the dwarf and his purported insanity. Hence Oskar's grotesque body is an embodiment of his insanity.

To summarize: The dysfunctionality of the Matzerath family reveals itself primarily in the relationship between Oskar and his parents. Oskar's fear that his mother wants to get rid of him, and his father's ultimate surrender to the higher authority of the euthanasia killing institution are manifestations of an oedipal constellation that at the level of metaphorical language Grass takes to extremes. I would argue that Oskar as a phallic figure is a direct manifestation of his mother's insatiable sexual appetite. Her fear of eels is her fear of her own son and ultimately of her own sexuality, in whose grip she is forever torn between her cousin and the confessional. If her cousin Jan Bronski is Oskar's father, which the novel more than once seems to imply, then Agnes's suicide-by-fish has to be interpreted in the sense that on the one hand she wants to reincorporate her own son (Oskar=phallus=eel) in order to undo her first act of incest, and on the other hand, being pregnant with yet another child by Jan, she also tries to blot out her second act of incest. The original Oedipus complex, the mother's and son's desire to sleep with one another, is transmuted into the Rabelaisian dimension of devouring and being devoured. As Agnes wants to bring Oskar back into her belly, Oskar wants to return to the uterus from fear of the hostile world that surrounds him. The return to the uterus is a central motif that Grass's novel shares with the Tom Thumb folk-tales. This sort of mother-son relationship is a far cry from the Nazis' ideal.

Notes

[1] Maria Tatar, ed., *The Classic Fairy Tales* (New York: Norton & Company, 1999), 182.

[2] Tatar, *Classic Fairy Tales,* 181.

[3] Ernst Klee, ed., *"Euthanasie" im NS-Staat: Die "Vernichtung unwerten Lebens"* (Frankfurt am Main: Fischer, 1989), 304.

[4] Ernst Klee, *"Euthanasie,"* 308, mentions the example of the director of Eglfing-Haar, who reported after the war that he knew of half a dozen parents who in the spirit of the times ("im Sinne des Zeitgeistes") demanded the death of their children. He recalls one father in particular who asked whether it would not be best to eliminate his child from the *Volkskörper,* since that, he thought, was also in the interest of the State.

[5] Klee, *"Euthanasie,"* 308.

[6] The Thumbling tales and *Hänsel und Gretel* are closely related, a fact that becomes especially clear if we look at Perrault's *Le Petit Poucet.* Cf. Antii Aarne and Stith Thompson, "The Types of the Folktale: A Classification and Bibliography," in *The Classic Fairy Tales,* ed. Maria Tatar (New York: Norton & Company, 1999), 374.

[7] Jack Zipes, ed., *The Complete Fairy Tales of the Brothers Grimm* (New York: Bantham, 1987), 328.

[8] This detail demonstrates to what extent certain motifs that have their roots in the oral tradition of folk-tales are adapted in literary tales.

[9] Lilyane Mourey, *Grimm et Perrault: histoire, structure, mise en texte des contes* (Paris: Lettres Modernes, 1978), 64: "prendre les bottes, c'est prendre le pouvoir du père." According to her, taking the boots signifies an acquisition of the ogre's virility as well as the power of the father.

[10] Jack Zipes, ed. and trans., *Beauty and the Beast* (New York: Signet Classics, 1989), 23: "[he] was very delicate and rarely spoke, which they considered a mark of stupidity."

[11] Mourey, *Grimm et Perrault*, 64: "Le conte oscille en outre entre deux pôles qui renvoient au même code: manger, être mangé."

[12] Bakhtin, *Rabelais and His World*, 92. In connection with the oven as a symbol of the motherly womb, see also C. G. Jung, *The Archetypes and the Collective Unconscious* (Princeton: Princeton UP, 1969), 81.

[13] Brüder Grimm, *Kinder- und Hausmärchen* 1, ed. Heinz Rölleke (Stuttgart: Reclam, 1980), 234; Zipes, *The Complete Fairy Tales*, 166.

[14] Grimm, *Kinder- und Hausmärchen* 1, 265; Zipes, *Complete Fairy Tales*, 167.

[15] Richard Sheppard, "Upstairs-Downstairs — Some Reflections on German Literature in the Light of Bakhtin's Theory of the Carnival," in *New Ways in Germanistik*, ed. Richard Sheppard (Oxford: Berg Publishers, 1990), 292: "it is significant that Murner should locate the source of all Folly/sin in the fact that all people derive from the 'acker' (field or ploughland) of a woman's body."

[16] See Maria Höhn, "Frau im Haus und Girl im *Spiegel*: Discourse on Women in the Interregnum Period of 1945–1949 and the Question of German Identity," in *Central European History* 26.1 (1993): 81: "The 1953 creation of the Ministry of Family, against the strongly voiced opposition of the Social Democrats, who favored legislation that would acknowledge the changing role of women in society, is an indicator of how central Christian democratic policies assessed the 'traditional' family. The reemergence of the patriarchal family in the 1950s as *the* ideological bulwark against communism suggests that the decisions in 1949 were closely connected to the question of what kind of a society the new Germany was to be. Despite all of the good intentions for a new beginning that the debates of the early postwar years clearly reflected, Germany failed to make a decisive break with the past." On the topic of the roles of women in West Germany after 1945, see also Robert Moeller, "Reconstructing the Family in Reconstruction Germany: Women and Social Policy in the Federal Republic, 1949–1955,"in *Feminist Studies* 15 (1989), 137–69, and his *Protecting Motherhood: Women and the Family in the Politics of Postwar Germany* (Berkeley: California UP, 1993).

[17] Höhn, "Frau im Haus," 81, n. 100: "The Nazis declared the family to be the most important foundation of society. The family would protect the *Volk* community from all kinds of social ills and communism." On this topic see also Irmgard Weyrather, *Muttertag und Mutterkreuz: Der Kult um die deutsche Mutter im Nationalsozialismus* (Frankfurt am Main: Fischer, 1993).

[18] Zipes, *The Complete Fairy Tales*, 164: "now you've got a sword to take with you on the way."

[19] Ulrike Schulz, *Gene mene muh raus mußt du: Eugenik von der Rassenhygiene zu den Gen- und Reproduktionstechnologien* (Munich: AG SPAK, 1992), 64.

[20] Schulz, *Gene mene muh*, 69.

[21] Cf. Jack Zipes, "The Struggle for the Grimms' Throne: The Legacy of the Grimms' Tales in the FRG and GDR since 1945," in *The Reception of Grimms' Fairy Tales: Responses, Reactions, Revisions*, ed. Donald Haase (Detroit: Wayne State UP, 1993), 169.

[22] Schulz, *Gene mene muh*, 91.

[23] Schulz, *Gene mene muh*, 93: "Hüterin des Blutes."

[24] In this context see also David Roberts, "Tom Thumb and the Imitation of Christ: Towards a Psycho-Mythological Interpretation of the 'Hero' Oskar and his Symbolic Function," in *Proceedings and Papers of the Congress of the Australasian Universities Language and Literature Association* (Canberra: U of Canberra, 1972), 160–74.

[25] Patricia Pollock Brodsky, "The Black Cook as Mater Gloriosa: Grass's *Faust* Parodies in *Die Blechtrommel*," in *Colloquia Germanica* 29.3 (1996): 243. The motif of the dwarf/child wanting to hide from his persecutors is interesting in view of the historical detail that, according to James Glass, some children during the euthanasia actions "tried to escape by hiding in privies, literally holes in the ground behind buildings. But someone — the Jewish police, the Germans — always found them. This effort to avoid selection, by those small enough to fit into these reeking holes, was well known." Cf. James Glass, *Life Unworthy of Life: Racial Phobia and Mass Murder in Hitler's Germany* (New York: Harper Collins, 1997), 21.

[26] See Sheppard, "Upstairs-Downstairs," 311: "we make mincemeat of the natural."

[27] Bakhtin, *Rabelais and his World*, 338, "the bodily depths are fertile."

[28] François Rabelais, *Gargantua and Pantagruel* (Harmondsworth: Penguin, 1955), 137.

[29] Cf. Agnes's mother's warning: "Nu iß nicht soviel von dem Fisch, als wenn man dich zwingen würd" (*B*, 129; "For the Lord's sake stop eating so much fish like someone was making you": *TD*, 160).

[30] Andrey Toporkov, "'Rebaking' of Children in Eastern Slavic Rituals and Fairy tales," in *The Petersburg Journal of Cultural Studies* 1.3 (1993): 15–21.

[31] Foucault, *Madness and Civilization*, 145 and 150: "we have a formulation of the old moral intuition that from the time of Hippocrates and Plato had made the womb a living and perpetually mobile animal, and distributed the spatial ordering of its movements; this intuition perceived in hysteria the incoercible agitation of desires in those who had neither the possibility of satisfying them nor the strength to master them."

5: Oskar as Fool, Harlequin, and Trickster, and the Politics of Sanity

> *The clown may dare to challenge the nomos of the gods as did the hero in Greek tragedy but, like the hero of tragedy, he must not eventually get away with such freedom. While the hero suffers his catastrophe in grand style, the clown is chased around the ring before an applauding audience. What a spectacle, what a twofold pleasure, to experience vicariously the assault on order and to witness simultaneously the reduction to nothingness of the transgressor!*[1]

The Politics of Sanity

IN *DIE BLECHTROMMEL* Grass harks back to the Grimms' international vision of the folk-tale and revives the *Kunstmärchen*, the literary tales by Wilhelm Hauff. He revives the grotesque in the dwarf tale that the Nazis suppressed or misinterpreted and makes use of a key theme in the literary history of the dwarf tale. The dwarf is typically seen as not only physically disabled but, because he looks like a child, as mentally less developed, even insane as well. It is interesting in this context that Oskar Matzerath is not only persecuted by the Nazis, but also locked up in an institution in the postwar years. It is from within this institution that he tells his whole story. In *Madness and Civilization*, Michel Foucault has traced the archaeology of madness in the West, from the Middle Ages and the Renaissance, when insanity was still a part of everyday life, when all sorts of mad people populated the streets of Europe, to the time when such people began to be considered as a threat, asylums were built, and a wall was erected between the insane and the rest of humanity (*MC*). Nazi euthanasia was the climax of this process of segregation. The Age of Reason reached an extreme during the Third Reich, so that all manifestations of unreason and social malfunctioning were to be eliminated. Like Bulgakov's *The Master and Margarita* and Bakhtin's theoretical work on Rabelais, Grass's novel is a polemic against enlightened rationalism that excludes anything irrational.

The shamelessness of *Die Blechtrommel* is reflected to a large extent in the reactions it has inspired both at home and abroad. What these reactions ignore is that Oskar, as an embodiment of the Lord of Misrule, has a specific function in the novel. He is Grass's response to political developments after the war and serves to represent a historical chapter that in the 1950s Germans were loath to talk about. As a fusion of central characters grounded in popular culture and mythology — the clown, fool, trickster, harlequin/Erlking, and their literary relative, the picaro — Oskar Matzerath represents different groups on the margins of modern society: criminals, psychopaths, and transients, groups that the Nazis labeled as asocial and *nutzlose Esser* (unproductive mouths to feed).[2] Hitler intended to get rid of those people who were kept in mental asylums and other institutions and were of no more use to the Reich. He thought that through their elimination doctors, nurses and other personnel, as well as beds, could be made available for the armed forces. The persecution of asocial life was, especially during the war years, largely a matter of economics. Since the Nazis believed there was no value in these lives, they were not willing to spend any money on them.

The insane and schizophrenics in particular were considered to be passive social parasites.[3] Oskar also fits into these categories, at least in the eyes of others. Greff, for example, thinks that he is too dumb and too little. That Oskar is schizophrenic reveals itself primarily in the style of his narration, the switch from first-person narrative to third person, at times even in the same sentence. The so-called "passive" social parasites were regarded as being beyond hope of any social integration because their mental inadequacy resulted in their inability to work independently.[4] Particularly suspicious were the so-called *Hilfsschüler,* students who needed a lot of help to make it through school. To the Nazis an early inclination toward crime, and conflicts with school and police were characteristic features of a youth's mental debility. Oskar, who is without a job, has conflicts with both school and the police. *Bildung* in the sense of *Schulbildung,* that is, getting an education at school, was considered invaluable to the individual's integration into society. Those who could not be educated at school, the *Ungebildeten,* were in danger of being classified as asocial and therefore suspicious to the party. Since Oskar does not get a school education, he falls into this category of lacking in *Bildung.* His private predilection for Goethe and Rasputin would not count as sufficient education to free him from the party's suspicions. Although he reads Goethe, whom the Nazis considered the very cornerstone of German education, Oskar remains uneducated and *asozial* in the official sense of the word. He is suspect in the eyes of a society that prides itself on its high culture, since he refuses to be educated. This choice turns him into a social outcast at a level below the *Hilfsschüler,* a person who at least tries to get an education. Oskar falls into the category of *schwachsinnig* (mentally disabled) because his development remains invisible due to the absence of physical growth and spiritual/mental growth, since he claims he has been fully developed since birth. His neighbors' perception of him as too small and too dumb, as too dumb *because* he does not grow, corresponds to the fascist belief that those who performed menial labor and had no ambition to work their way up were weak-minded. As Ulrike Schulz informs us, even these people were sterilized.[5] That Oskar does not pursue teleological *Bildung* in the sense of a Faustian quest qualifies him in Nazi eyes as weak-minded.

Although the mentally disabled were no longer killed in Germany after 1945, postwar psychiatry in that country undoubtedly bore the stamp of its Nazi precursors. Drs. Thomas Röder, Volker Kubillus, and Anthony Burwell have argued that in postwar Germany "psychiatry has proven incapable of self-criticism, self-condemnation and self-policing, and even today remains nothing more than the modern incarnation of its Third Reich progenitors."[6] They show to what extent the newly founded concept of *Lebenshilfe* (help in living) owed a debt to the earlier *Sterbehilfe* (help in dying), how racial hygiene reappeared in a new disguise, that of human genetics, the new eugenics, as Simon Mawer's dwarf calls it.[7] Röder and his colleagues document the fact that many of the psychiatrists who ran German institutions after 1945 came directly either from the old generation of Nazi psychiatrists or from the ranks of their students.

Fool in Decline

In reaction to bourgeois conceptions of sanity and the tradition of modern psychiatry, Grass not only places Oskar in a German institution, but he creates with him a configuration of a whole range of insane and subversive characters found in popular culture. Bakhtin has discussed these characters for the modern novel as "life's maskers." He mentions three related types, the rogue, the clown, and the fool, whose privilege it is "to be 'other' in this world" and "not to make common cause with any single one of the existing categories that life makes available."[8] While Bakhtin's rogue corresponds closely to the picaro, or *Schelm*, discussed in the next chapter, the circus clown closely resembles the fool. Whether as dwarf-fool, as naturally insane, or as artificially insane, this figure used to entertain royalty from the Romans through the Middle Ages to the Renaissance before he disappeared after the French Revolution, in the bourgeois age. Oskar's words, that he is "Yorick der Narr. Doch wo gibt es einen König, den du narren könntest" (*B*, 388; "Yorick, the fool. But where is the king for you to play the fool to?": *TD*, 468), apply to postwar Germany and imply that there once was a king to whom he played the fool, namely Hitler and his entourage, whom he entertained at the front. In taking on the role of just such a court dwarf-fool to the Nazis, Oskar fulfills the traditional functions of the fool discussed by Enid Welsford in her remarkable study of this historical figure.[9] The tradition of the dwarf-fool reaches back to the Egyptian Danga, a pygmy at the court of Dadkeri-Assi, a Pharaoh of the Fifth Dynasty. The Danga's chief attraction was that he was a sort of mascot guarding against malignant influences

(*FSLH*, 61). The Danga was a hunchback with an enormous phallus often represented also in Greco-Roman terra-cotta figures, a token of luck for women. Touching the hump of a dwarf was considered a sign of good fortune. The association of Oskar's hump with his phallus and women's adoration of his hump — "allen Frauen bedeutet Buckelstreicheln Glück" (*B*, 359; "it's good luck to touch, pat, or stroke a hump": *TD*, 434) — can clearly be read as a relic of these old superstitions. Politically and for the church, this figure served as a token of good luck, diverting the Evil Eye and political calamities, but the dwarf-fool also served as a scapegoat "whose official duty it is to jeer continually at his superiors in order to bear their ill-luck on his shoulders. Who better fitted for such a post than a misshapen dwarf or fool?" (*FSLH*, 74). Oskar's hump as a representation of the German burden of history that he carries on his back and his eventual institutionalization as a madman who identifies himself with Jesus is clearly a remnant of this tradition in many cultures, when "at certain seasons of the year people collect all their diseases and sins and misfortunes, and bind them upon some unfortunate animal or man whom they then proceed to kill or drive off from the community"(*FSLH*, 68).

In the Third Reich too, Oskar holds a paradoxical position between being a sort of mascot to the Nazis in their warfare on the French front and, on the other hand, being a victim of their racist ideology. Yet this ambivalent position reflects precisely the position in which the dwarf-fool found himself in earlier periods. In many cultures, like the Tibetan New Year's festival for example, it is the fool who for a brief spell uncrowns the real ruler, whom he ridicules at sometimes mortal cost to himself (*FSLH*, 69). It is this temporary power of the underdog, the power of abuse and mockery of the highest authority that endangers his life, something we have also observed in the two Hauff tales. The danger to which the dwarf-fool was often exposed due to his physical infirmity manifests itself for example in the tradition of serving him up to the banquet guests in the midst of food. This prank, alluding to the possibility of the dwarf being devoured, was played upon the dwarf Jeffrey Hudson under the Stuarts, who at an entertainment was presented in a cold baked pie to King Charles (*FSLH*, 179). One can find this very motif in Hauff's *Der Zwerg Nase*, where the Duke threatens to hack Jakob to pieces and bake him in a pie. What was a joke in the Middle Ages became a sinister reality during the Third Reich, when the physically disabled were "devoured" by a vicious killing machinery. When Oskar is playing the clown for the Nazis, we see how he tampers with authority in the scene where his voice shatters a beer bottle in the hands of a Nazi corporal. His beer-bespattered face writes finis to Oskar's act, which is followed by long and thunderous applause mingled with the sounds of a major air raid on Paris. As jocular as this fool's moment may appear, it also contains an element of threat to the provocateurs.

While the position of the fool at court was still widely respected in the Renaissance, he became extinct in most countries in the eighteenth century. Natural fools, that is, the insane, and dwarves increasingly became the victims of mockery and abuse, a development that corresponds to Bakhtin's description of the history of laughter and to what Foucault says about the segregation of the insane:

> Until the Renaissance, the sensibility to madness was linked to the presence of imaginary transcendences. In the classical age, for the first time, madness was perceived through a condemnation of idleness and in a social immanence guaranteed by the community of labor. This community acquired an ethical power of segregation, which permitted it to eject, as into another world, all forms of social uselessness. It was in this *other world*, encircled by the sacred powers of labor, that madness would assume the status we now attribute to it. If there is, in classical madness, something which refers elsewhere, and to *other things*, it is no longer because the madman comes from the world of the irrational and bears its stigmata; rather it is because he crosses the frontiers of bourgeois order of his own accord, and alienates himself outside the sacred limits of its ethic. (*MC*, 58)

The disappearance of the fool in the bourgeois age is a product of the waning power of aristocracy after the French Revolution and of the increase of rational thinking since the Enlightenment, which no longer allowed for folly. Enid Welsford laments this decline of the court-fool when she says that "scientific enlightenment is good, yet it would also be good to regain the sense of glory, which does somehow seem to be connected with humility, and the acceptance of limitation" (*FSLH*, 193). For it was the fool's function to remind the powerful of their limitations and thus teach them a lesson in humility. When Oskar laments that there is no king that he can fool, he refers to his own marginalization as a madman in a society that no longer wants its fools to remind the rulers of their own hubris.

Trickster on the Run

As historically tangible lords of disorder, the clown and the fool are rooted in the trickster mythology, which is located entirely in the popular imagination. According to Kerenyi, the trickster's function in anarchic society's tales about him is "to add disorder to order and so make a whole, to render possible, within the fixed bounds of what is permitted, an experience of what is not permitted."[10] This is what the historical fool did too, when he would temporarily uncrown the ruling authority and establish his own disorder, and Oskar follows suit by merging the Apollonian with the Dionysian: "Wenn Apollo die Harmonie, Dionysos Rausch und Chaos anstrebte, war Oskar ein

kleiner, das Chaos harmonisierender, die Vernunft in Rauschzustände ver-
setzender Halbgott" (*B*, 265–66; "If Apollo strove for harmony and Diony-
sus for drunkenness and chaos, Oskar was a little demigod whose business
it was to harmonize chaos and intoxicate reason": *TD*, 323).

Fools and tricksters typically alternate their imitation of the satanic with
that of the divine. Church ceremonies of the fifteenth century, for example,
often referred to the fool as a denier of God.[11] Oskar blasphemously denies
God whenever we see him in church, but he is also associated with Christ.[12]
His trickery implies an imitation of Christ, the ultimate blasphemy that
shows his truly demonic nature. Glenn Guidry has shown that Oskar's drum
and voice are common trickster instruments, especially in African tricksters.[13]
He also interprets Oskar as a culture hero, who in the course of the novel
attempts to purge the trickster infantilism in himself and German society,
thus contributing to Germany's attempt to come to terms with its past, a
rather idealistic view that I do not share entirely. Although I agree with
Guidry that Oskar is clearly a typical trickster, I interpret his trickster work
at best as an initial and rather feeble subversive act vis à vis Nazi Germany
and the rationalism of the postwar years rather than being conducive to what
came to be called *Vergangenheitsbewältigung*.

Oskar clearly corresponds to Jung's perception of the trickster as both
subhuman and superhuman, a bestial and divine being.[14] He is the *Untermensch* par excellence, but like Hermes he walks with the gods, and even
calls himself a semi-god. Although present in the mythologies of all cultures,
in some the trickster is tolerated by society, while in other cultures he is
marginalized. According to Claude Lévi-Strauss, there are two types of
societies, those which absorb their troublemakers and those which eject
them: leave them in the woods or build jails for them (*TMW*, 224). Unlike
the Winnebago, for example, who integrate their tricksters, conservative
societies, insisting on their rational bourgeois values, typically suppress their
irrational members of society. Because of his degeneracy the trickster went
underground in German fascism as well as in the postwar period, a time that
insisted on rationalism in response to the Third Reich and its alleged irrationalism. While in the *commedia dell'arte* the trickster archetype appears as
the figure of the Harlequin, he corresponds to Hermes and Mercury in
antiquity and to various figures in folklore and universally known fairy tales:
Tom Thumb, Stupid Hans, or *Hanswurst*.[15] To what extent the trickster
archetype was misinterpreted and suppressed during the Third Reich can be
illustrated by the *völkische* reception of folk-tales as early as the 1920s. The
valiant little tailor in the Grimm Brothers' tale of that name (*Das tapfere
Schneiderlein*), for example, who kills seven flies on his sandwich and then
intimidates a giant with that trick by saying that he killed seven with one
blow ("sieben auf einen Streich") is such an unwanted trickster. He was
interpreted as a Jew duping the German giants, a reading that deliberately

misses the moral of the story, which encourages the powerless in their desire to survive among the strong.[16] The Jungian interpretation of the trickster implies that since European cultures had ejected their trickster, suppressed him into the unconscious, he resurfaced as the shadow in the shape of Adolf Hitler, in whom he became a truly demonic reincarnation. In contrast, those cultures who admit their tricksters, like the Native American cultures, are less inclined to commit evil deeds, because trickster myths teach of the sacredness of life.[17] In these cultures, animals down to the tiniest insect, and even plants, have souls, something that Christianity ruled out a long time ago. A phenomenon like Nazi euthanasia can arise only in a society that disregards this sacredness of life, disregards the soul in a multiplicity of life forms. In connection with the Native American trickster, we should remind ourselves that the Nazis defined the mentally disabled as soulless beings (*tote Seelen*), at a level lower than animals.

Tricksters are closely associated with the grotesque body. While in the Renaissance the classical body became an aesthetic standard that also structured the "high" discourses of philosophy, statecraft, theology, and law, the grotesque body was a *modus vivendi* with its own set of discursive norms, as Stallybrass and White point out: impurity; heterogeneity; masking; protuberant distension; disproportion; exorbitance; clamor; eccentricity; a focus on gaps, orifices and symbolic filth; physical needs and pleasures of the "lower bodily stratum"; materiality and parody.[18] While the classical was the domain propagated by the ruling classes and their institutions, and was widely embraced by the bourgeoisie after the Age of Reason, the grotesque increasingly came to be regarded as the offensive behavior of the simple folk, the lower classes. As Barry Sanders has argued in his history of laughter, "life at the top is a stylized affair, expressed through a series of carefully articulated, meticulously learned gestures. The lower classes felt most alive, not by channeling their lives through the narrow gauge of rule and law, but by fully unbridling their passions and desires."[19] The Nazis' contempt for the *Unterschicht* (lower classes), which they saw as a breeding ground for *Untermenschen,* is deeply rooted in this social evolution. The fool and the trickster are incarnations of the grotesque body and of that folk humor that the Renaissance, with its rediscovery of the classical ideal, had already started to stifle. Both in body and in actions the dwarf-trickster Oskar is a harbinger of this grotesque, nonclassical sensibility. The discursive norms of the grotesque listed by Stallybrass and White all have their validity for Oskar: his hump is a protuberant distension, his scream and drumming are full of clamor, he is obsessed with sex, he focuses on gaps and orifices (as we have seen in the previous chapter), and he parodies church rituals. In myth we frequently find this clash between the classical and the grotesque: the forces of order and chaos. The latter are associated with the dirt-work of the trickster: dirt, according to Mary Douglas, is "matter out of place, . . . what we exclude when we are creating order" (*TMW*, 179). As "order can become cruel in the name of its own imagined impurity" (*TMW*, 185), eugenics, racial hygiene, was an attempt to create order by getting rid of the impurities, the "human dirt" that, so the Nazis believed, obstructed their quest for order. In Oskar, who engages in dirt-work and whom the classical mind regards as dirt, Grass created an inchoate being, one who temporarily disturbs National Socialism's attempt to create perfect order and who is eventually rejected by an order-loving society. The trickster's reappearance in German culture after 1945 was a reaction to the forces of order and reason in German society. Apart from Grass's revival of this figure, we encounter him in other well-known texts. Thomas Mann's Hermes-figure Felix Krull, Heinrich Böll's clown Hans Schnier, and Max Schulz, the shape-shifting picaro in Edgar Hilsenrath's *Der Nazi und der Friseur,* all belong to this type.

Oskar has much in common not only with the protagonists of these novels but also with tricksters of other cultures, above all with Hermes, with whom he likes to compare himself. Both are fully developed at the moment of birth and their paternity is unclear. Hermes is the son of a concubine, Oskar the result of Agnes's promiscuity. Both are associated with artisans, merchants, and thieves; Oskar is a traveling circus oddity and assists thieves in their work. Yet the "trickster isn't a run-of-the-mill liar and thief. When he lies and steals, it isn't so much to get away with something or get rich as to disturb the established categories of truth and property and, by so doing, open the road to possible new worlds" (*TMW*, 13). After Oskar and the Dusters have desecrated the Church of the Sacred Heart, they are harassed by the Nazis because they have disturbed "the categories of truth" established by the church as well as the "established categories of property." As a cripple and thief, Oskar has become a double target for the Nazis, whose written appeal for Oskar's institutionalization reaches Matzerath right after the church's desecration.

Hermes and Mercury's thievishness cannot be clearly seen apart from their role as the gods of merchants. Lewis Hyde argues that in societies "where the dominant values are kin ties and agrarian wealth, (that is, *Blut* and *Boden,* blood and soil) those whose identity is bound up with trade are typically consigned to a subordinate place in the order of things" (*TMW,* 207). Such societies often think of merchants as thieves. While Oskar says of himself that Mercury, the God of thieves and commerce, would bless him since, born under the sign of Virgo, he possesses his seal, in the Homeric Hymn to Hermes the association of thievishness and trade is established for Hermes at the moment he teaches Apollo to play the lyre. Apollo distrusts Hermes and exclaims: "I'm still afraid you might steal both my curving bow and my lyre, for Zeus has given you the honor of initiating deeds of exchange trade among men all over the fruitful world" (*TMW*, 329). The "fruitful world" is none other than the marketplace for which the hymn does not distinguish between theft and trade. A traditional locus for carnival activity, the marketplace was viewed with suspicion by such reactionary modernists as Werner Sombart in the Weimar Republic, whose views were echoed by the Nazis' attitude towards profit-oriented capitalism, which they associated primarily with the Jews. As advocates of rootless international finance, the Jews were persecuted not only because they were considered a racial threat but also because they were seen as criminals trying to enrich themselves at the expense of the German *Volk*. Their trade, first and foremost the practice of lending, was seen as thievishness. Foucault even goes so far as to relate mercantile liberalism to madness. Continental thinkers of the eighteenth century directed their attention to the phenomenon of frequent suicides in England and considered madness the *maladie anglaise*, which they tried to explain by the great liberties of this nation of merchants. Since the mercantile world is allegedly opposed to truths, this has to be where insanity reigns: "liberty, far from putting man in possession of himself, ceaselessly alienates him from his essence and his world" (*MC*, 214). According to this dubious understanding, the effects of mercantile liberalism are the same as those of sexual liberalism that we have observed in Agnes, who has become alienated from her essence, whereas Greff tries to be a man who is "in possession of himself." And yet in the end both commit suicide. The defenders of reactionary modernism also associated the merchant's traveling and aversion to a sedentary lifestyle with his purported madness, since the nomadic lifestyle takes man outside of his center, marked by his roots in the home soil, and disperses his essence throughout the world. It forces him to a life of wandering.

Hermes and Oskar are simultaneously enchanters (Oskar's voice and drum) and disenchanters and both are connected to the underworld. Hermes's ambivalence — Hermes of the Dark who leads into the underworld, enchants, and Hermes of the Light, who leads out of the underworld, disenchants — is that of Oskar, who tries to unify within himself the Apollonian in the form of Goethe and the Dionysian in the form of Rasputin. He enchants the Nazis and at the same time tries to disenchant them by means of his subversive acts. Hermes and Oskar both play an instrument and are artists in the sense of *ars* as skill, artifice, or craft. Hyde defines tricksters as "joint-disturbers," since the word *art* is also related to the Latin *articulus* and the Greek *arthron*, joint, but he points out, "not that they are much involved with making the firm and well-set joints that lead to classical harmony. What tricksters like is the *flexible* or *movable* joint" (*TMW*, 256). Their own grotesque bodies display these movable joints, for example, during Oskar's transformation in the railway car, where his swollen joints are given an opportunity to relax, and during the metamorphosis of Hauff's Jakob, whose limbs twitch and crack. That the trickster is an artist "unmaking old harmonies and sometimes, especially if he has a lyre of his own, singing new ones to fill the ensuing silence" (*TMW*, 257–58), also holds true for Oskar's drum, which he uses disruptively under the rostrum in order to undo the established harmony of the fascist marching music. He uses it on his first day at school to undermine the authority of the teacher, he uses it in church where he sits on the knee of the Virgin Mary in order to accompany the mass that he blasphemously re-enacts with the Dusters, and he uses it in order to make Germans aware of their guilt, for "die Kunst des Zurück-trommelns" (*B*, 393). Through his art of drumming back the past, he does indeed "fill the ensuing silence" after the Holocaust.

The trickster in myth is often persecuted because of his duplicitous nature. He is an amoral figure. This mythological pattern in Grass's novel serves the representation of the Nazis' persecution of criminals and schizophrenics. Like all schizophrenics, the trickster constantly crosses the boundaries by which groups articulate their social life, boundaries between right and wrong, sacred and profane, clean and dirty, male and female, young and old, living and dead. In every case tricksters cross the line and confuse such distinctions, since they attempt to obliterate any form of categorical thinking, even dialectic thinking (*TMW*, 7). The Homeric hymn calls Hermes wily, polytropic (turning many ways), cunning, versatile, much-traveled (*TMW*, 317), attributing to him a lifestyle that the Nazis regarded as Jewish cosmopolitanism and gypsy nomadism. The association of cunningness and roaming the land is interesting and will occupy us further in the discussion of the picaro and the politics of social integration in the next chapter. Oskar, who alternates his identity between Jesus and Satan, between victim and Nazi accomplice, is highly polytropic. As the shape-shifter and guardian of multiple personalities he stands for the opposite of the Nazis' categorical, rational thinking, through which people were divided into groups and valuable people were separated from worthless life. Frequently under Nazi rule, categorical thinking, which at its worst is reduced to thinking in binary oppositions, determined life and death, like the decision whether somebody should walk right or left at the ramp in Auschwitz, or the difference between a plus sign and a minus sign on the medical questionnaires for the euthanasia institutions. The trickster deliberately blurs such categories and destroys order through chaos. He can be a wise fool, an ancient baby, or a cross-dresser, and he destroys the distinction between the sacred and the profane. As John Money has shown, prematurely aged children are also neglected children, something one can observe in Little Father Time, for example, the boy who returns from Australia in Thomas Hardy's novel *Jude the Obscure* (1894–95).[20] Oskar too, who suffers from constant parental neglect, is an example of a wise but ancient baby of this type. He belongs to that ancient race of which Lagerkvist's dwarf speaks. At birth Oskar is already fully developed. We encounter the old man in the child's body also in Bebra, the circus clown, who, however, does not remain loyal to his mediating position and instead immediately sides with the Nazis to save his own skin. Oskar, of course, is also a speaker of sacred profanities, a fact that manifests itself whenever he enters church. Trickster "is the mythic embodiment of ambiguity and ambivalence, doubleness and duplicity, contradiction and paradox" (*TMW*, 7).

Furthermore, Oskar is a typical trickster in the sense that he is ridden by lust. Typically, the trickster is a psychopath,[21] not only because of his criminal nature but also because he is at the mercy of his sexual appetites. He embraces obscenity and conflates amorous with excretory functions, an idiosyncrasy that explains the decline in his popularity in the prudish times that arose from the Enlightenment. The scene in which Oskar and Maria derive sexual pleasure from Oskar's spitting onto a mound of fizz powder in Maria's hand is a perfect example of such a confusion of amorous and excretory functions.

The motif of the trickster's appetite, whether sexual or purely food-related, is prevalent in Native American trickster tales. In these stories, the central tricksters Raven or Coyote build traps to catch fish, but often end up getting ensnared in their own devices, a detail that moves these stories into the vicinity of the Bakhtinian carnival, with its opposition of devouring versus being devoured, as well as the Tom Thumb folk-tales. When he wants to eat, Coyote must be careful not to be eaten. His intelligence is directly linked to this process. Likewise Tom Thumb, whose appetite is huge, must be vigilant to avoid being eaten. Here too his cleverness springs from this duplicity linked to appetite. Oskar's appetite is mostly of a sexual nature, while his mother's sexual appetite is linked to her appetite for food and the loss thereof. As in the North American trickster myths, the fish in Grass's novel is caught with a trap, in this case a horse's head, a central image of the underworld in which tricksters feel at home. In the North American trickster tales, Coyote and Raven often devour the organs of appetite, the intestines of other animals. As in the carnivalesque literature of Rabelais, eating and death caused by being eaten, are related in these trickster tales. All who eat will also be eaten at some point. This circularity is contained in Rabelais's image of the *tripes*. Eating tripe in Rabelais also conjures up the image of the consumption of excrement contained in the North American Raven stories, and just as the trickster ravens eat excrement, Oskar is forced to eat the soup concocted by the neighbors' children, which is full of urine, dying frogs and spittle. This soup kills Oskar's appetite for food and yet his appetite for sex is boundless, an obsession he shares with the Winnebago trickster who carries his long penis coiled in a box on his back (the sort of hump that Oskar displays, which is supposed to bring luck to women) and his intestines wrapped around his belly, the perfect image of someone obsessed by his own appetites. Oskar's sexual prowess, his big penis, and his hump (the box on his back) mark his sexual appetite, since bodily protrusions in folk humor tend to be phallic symbols. Trickster tales are concerned with the question of desire, lust, craving, and how to end it: "To end our craving we must eat the organs of craving, and craving then returns" (*TMW*, 31). This is precisely what Agnes is trying so desperately to accomplish when she starts eating all that fish, when she fries and drinks the oil from sardine cans. The trickster is an inventor of fish traps, who traps with his own intestines what then becomes food. Oskar is seen near the horse's head that contains the eels, an image for the archetypal intestines, which then in turn become food for his mother. If the eels are both intestinal and phallic symbols as parts of the trickster, then she is devouring her own son, who has trapped her with these organs, another variant of the incest motifs pervading the novel and one that would support the theory, developed in the previous chapter, of their oedipal relationship. In that case the words of Oskar's grandmother that he has 'drummed' his mother to death acquire a strangely ambiguous meaning. Oskar becomes her "gatekeeper who opens the door into the next world" (*TMW*, 159), yet another function of the trickster archetype. Like Hermes, Oskar is a messenger of death. Since the eel is clearly a phallic symbol, by eating it she wants to end her craving; yet it keeps returning, and so she keeps eating more and more fish until she ends her own craving through her death. The effect of erasing her sexual appetite through food is also achieved by the woman in Grass's novel who uses an eel to stimulate herself. The eel bites into her vagina, crippling her desire, an act which could be read as a version of the vagina-dentata motif that occasionally appears in trickster tales (*TMW*, 31).

In analyzing texts like Grass's *Die Blechtrommel* or Thomas Mann's *Felix Krull*, one may ask the question, What distinguishes the trickster from the picaro? Since one is a mythological archetype and the other the anti-hero of a literary genre, they are indeed close relatives. I would argue that the picaro's salient feature is his aimless wandering, his vagrant lifestyle, while one of the main features of the trickster is his trickery, by means of which he shamelessly disturbs order, his function of situation-inverter: "Profaning or inverting social beliefs brings into sharp relief just how much a society values these beliefs. These profanations seem to exhibit a clear pattern of proportionality: the more sacred a belief, the more likely is the trickster to be found profaning it."[22] He shares this desire for profanation with the medieval tradition of Saturnalia, the Feast of Fools, the Abbeys of Misrule, Charivaris, and the Feast of the Ass. Their purpose was to upset the established order and power of the church, albeit only temporarily, because in the end they helped reinforce the church's authority.

Church Blasphemies

"Es gibt Dinge auf dieser Welt, die man — so heilig sie sein mögen — nicht auf sich beruhen lassen darf!" (*B*, 114; "There are things in this world which — sacred as they may be — cannot be left as they are": *TD*, 141).

The difference between aboriginal peoples and pagan societies, which manage to wed the forces of chaos with the forces of order, and Christianity, which started separating these two principles by distinguishing between Jesus and Satan, becomes interesting within the context of Grass's novel. The novel reflects this pagan union of the Apollonian and Dionysian sphere, merging in Oskar the figures of Jesus and Satan, of victim and fascist. Oskar can never be just one: the dividing line of any dialectic juxtaposition is blurred in this book, and like all tricksters he finds himself on the threshold between two domains. The trickster's typical location in European culture is the marketplace. In the Middle Ages and the Renaissance this was the place, which Bakhtin calls *billingsgate*, in which curses, profanities, and oaths reigned.[23] While the sacred was reserved for church, the profane (*pro-fanum* means "before the temple") reigned outside of church, primarily in the marketplace. The marketplace and the church correspond to the opposition of the grotesque and the classical body, the former open at its boundaries, the latter closed. The protrusions of the grotesque body that violate the classical ideal correspond to the marketplace's extension beyond itself as a place where commerce brings the local community into contact with the outside world. In early modern European culture the grotesque became most visible in the marketplace, a place not only of multicultural interaction but also a venue for all sorts of groups that later became increasingly segregated from society: gypsies, transient musicians, exotics of doubtful origin, freed slaves, and midgets and giants.[24] Yet with the formation of the bourgeois class, socially inferior classes in marketplaces and fairs increasingly became the "object of the respectable gaze"[25] by which this class was able to confirm its own superiority. Particularly the slave from the colonies, the dwarf, and the pig were displayed and celebrated at the fair because of their low status. These groups also became increasingly banished from church, which manifests itself in the Grimm Brothers' folk-tale of *Hans Dumm*, the dwarf who has to sneak into church where he is normally not admitted.[26] Oskar's presence in church is in itself a violation of the sacred through the profanity of his grotesque body and all his body stands for, as opposed to one of his counterimages, the classical body of the athlete on the cross, who is flexing his muscles and expanding his chest over the main altar of the Sacred Heart Church. In addition, Oskar repeatedly violates this physical division between the sacred and the profane by taking profane language and actions into church. As a culture of shame and guilt, Germany in the 1950s had its areas of silence — the Holocaust, euthanasia. A central moment of breaking the silence about the Holocaust, in which Oskar accuses the church, that sacred domain opposed to the grotesque, of its passivity in the face of Nazi atrocities, occurs when he gives the Jesus figure his drum and tells him to use it. Of course, nothing happens. This is a double disruption of the sacred, both in the sense that Germans in the 1950s did not want to hear about the Holocaust and the war, and in locality, the desecration of the sacred ground.

The Catholic Church in particular is the target of Grass's satire. As Günter Lewy has shown, the Catholic Church silently supported the Final Solution, while it followed the general public in its outcry against the practice of euthanasia.[27] The main reason for the Catholic Church's protest against euthanasia was that here Germans were killed while the Final Solution targeted the Jews, who had killed Jesus Christ.[28] In 1939, Archbishop Gröber argued that because the Jews had killed God, Christianity was not to be regarded as a product of the Jews but was "in the most intimate union with the Germanic spirit."[29] This appropriation by the German church of Jesus into its own ranks is reflected in Grass's aryanization of the Jesus figure à la Riefenstahl.

The church scenes exhibit some of the most offensive passages in the book, conflating sacred images with those of the material lower bodily stratum, as Catholicism never ceases to inspire Oskar with "Lästerungen" (blasphemies) (B, 111). Oskar mutters commentaries on the Mass while moving his bowels, he equates Jesus with the philandering Jan Bronski, he touches the little Jesus figure's penis, his watering can, as he calls it, thus giving himself a massive erection, and he comes to sit on the Virgin Mary's thigh in the same way as he sits on the nude left thigh of the Art Academy's favorite model Ulla, the Madonna 49. In the marketplace, Bakhtin argues, "the most improper and sinful oaths were those invoking the body of the Lord and its various parts, and these were precisely the oaths most frequently used" (RW, 192–93). Oskar's drumming and especially the drumsticks belong to a series of phallic symbols. A variation of the drumstick motif is the finger Oskar finds towards the end of the novel. Being dactyls like Oskar himself (a Tom Thumb figure), these represent grotesque images of potency that contrast starkly with Jesus' own flaccid penis as a symbol of the church's political impotence. These carnivalesque images subvert the authority of the church, conflating the theme of the Holocaust with folk humor.

Oskar's blasphemies turn into crime when he and his gang, the Dusters, steal nativity figures from numerous churches. In these later church scenes Oskar uncrowns the church Jesus by adopting his name as leader of the gang and by sawing him off along with the other two figures, John the Baptist and the Virgin Mary. He has his "disciples" perform Catholic rituals such as genuflections by the holy-water font or enact an impromptu Mass and invoke the ite missa sunt, a line that was also the object of derision in the medieval Feast of Fools, where it was converted into the threefold braying of an ass performed by the priest.[30] In synchrony with other tricksters who muddy high gods and "are made in and for a world of imperfections," in which they "do not wish away or deny what seems low, dirty, and imperfect" (*TMW*, 90), Oskar's blasphemies in church challenge religious idealism and indict the church's silence towards the Nazis' practice of doing away with what seems low, dirty, and imperfect. This union between the church and the totalitarian state is explicitly addressed in Grass's equation of the classical body of Jesus and the perfect Aryan body, the athletes of the 1936 Olympics and Jesus' blue eyes, and the equation of the holy cross and the swastika. Oskar questions the concept of Jesus as a culture-hero and concludes that "eher ist Oskar ein echter Jesus" (*B*, 115; "Oskar is a realer Jesus": *TD*, 143) than the other, for at least Oskar drums resistance under the rostrum. His actions seem to imply the question: where was God during the Holocaust? Where were Jesus' miracles then? Oskar's desire to scream glass to pieces in church, "während ich doch Scherben wollte"(*B*, 117; "I was praying for nothing but broken glass": *TD*, 145), could then be read as a form of protest against the broken glass during Reich Kristallnacht and the church's silence.

Oskar is a shape-shifter in true trickster fashion. While he initially just wants to destroy the church windows, he later becomes a kind of cultural healer. Typically, the trickster does not observe boundaries between the sacred and the profane, and typically tricksters target their victim's sense of shame, in this case Germany's collective silence. Oskar's activities in church and the Onion Cellar are possibly the best examples of this iconoclasm. The trickster sometimes invents "the 'inner writing' of memory" and "what tricksters quite regularly do is create lively talk where there has been silence, or where speech has been prohibited" (*TMW*, 76). In his Mephistophelean role, Bebra makes it possible for Oskar to participate in the rising prosperity of the Adenauer years as a musician who strikes it rich. Oskar and his drum become healers of the body and soul: "Gedächtnisschwund könne sie [the drum] beseitigen, hieß es, das Wörtchen 'Oskarnismus' tauchte zum erstenmal auf und sollte bald zum Schlagwort werden" (*B*, 464; "And what we cured best of all was loss of memory. The word 'Oskarism' made its first appearance, but not, I am sorry to say, its last": *TD*, 556). By thawing the Germans' cold hearts and stirring them to tears he exploits their guilty conscience. The German past becomes his commodity. Ironically, German society attempts to be healed by one of its own victims, an irony that gives Oskar truly Christian proportions. After Oskar has "uncrowned" the athletic Jesus of the Church of the Sacred Heart by sawing him off his pedestal, he forgives those who wanted to kill him, the ultimate satire of Christian faith. This is not *Vergangenheitsbewältigung*, it is a satire of it.

Subversion of State Authority

Despite the Nazis' ideological appropriation of the carnival, the party was suspicious of the revolutionary carnival spirit that Bakhtin visualizes, with its free-wheeling laughter that had filled the streets before the onset of the bourgeois age. Oskar's reprehensible behavior in church and his disruptive activities in the famous scene in which he hides under a rostrum and with his drum dissolves a Nazi party rally into free-wheeling dance and laughter are therefore heroic acts amidst the lethal seriousness of the official culture. His wild drumming inside the rostrum harks back to a central motif in the German tales of Tom Thumb, who screams from the stomach of a cow, fox, or wolf, which is then slaughtered. In Grass's novel this motif represents the rebellion of the grotesque world in fear of being "swallowed" by the official culture. The chapter "Die Tribüne" abounds in carnivalesque inversions. When Bebra asks Oskar to guess his age and he says 35, the clown turns out to be 53. It is the chapter in which the Matzeraths replace the gloomy Beethoven portrait with the even gloomier Hitler portrait. While Matzerath senior quickly bends to Hitler, the newly installed power figure, Oskar is far from doing the same. This is reminiscent of Bakhtin's comments on *Don Quixote*, that "the hero's madness permits a whole series of carnival crownings and uncrownings, of travesties and mystifications. This theme (madness) permits the world to abandon its official routine and to join the hero's carnivalesque fancies" (*RW*, 104). Oskar's temporary uncrownings, in this case of several party officials, harks back to a trickster theme that we encounter quite literally in Charles Perrault's *Le Petit Poucet*. Here the little boy steals the crowns of the ogre's daughters and puts them on his and his brothers' heads, thereby also uncrowning the ogre himself, who by mistake butchers his seven daughters instead of the seven little boys. The trickster deflates the power of the mighty. Under the rostrum Oskar drums the rhythm of *Jimmy the Tiger*, a Charleston that Bebra, the circus clown, performs during the circus performance where the two dwarves meet for the first time. That they share the same music points to their secret union, which is also sealed by the kiss that Bebra imprints on Oskar's forehead, a strange magical act that seems highly suspicious to his mother. Appalled that he was with the midgets and that a gnome kissed him on the forehead, she hopes that it doesn't mean anything. It means that the persecuted bond with one another in their trickery of the persecutors.

The actual physical position of various characters with regard to the rostrum indicates their political stance. While Matzerath is a passive supporter *in front* of the rostrum, Bebra warns Oskar that as a dwarf he should never be a member of the audience. Unlike Oskar he tricks the Nazis by — metaphorically speaking — joining them *on* the rostrum. He survives the Nazi years by becoming a partisan. One of the leaders of the rally, Gauleiter Löbsack, makes this his own principle in that he can best hide his disability, his hump, by exposing himself as a leading political figure (which is reminiscent of Goebbels and his clubfoot). Oskar chooses to inspect the rostrum at first from behind and then from inside, which has the same sobering effect on him as a look behind church altars. Oskar's position behind and beneath the rostrum, the symbolic structure whence Nazi politics are orchestrated, corresponds precisely to the status of the trickster figure on the margins of society. Victor Turner has shown that the trickster disrupts community from the margins: "Communitas breaks in through the interstices of structure, in liminality; at the edges of structure, in marginality; and *from beneath structure* (my italics), in inferiority."[31] Oskar's size is also a reflection of his marginality in this position of inferiority and it allows him to engage in action from beneath. Dwarves are therefore ideal trickster figures because they are literally physically marginalized. By virtue of his marginal position the trickster gains a unique perspective of his community that allows him to offer new visions of the world, which is what Oskar does as he is drumming his own rhythm.

As Oskar looks at the "naked ugliness of the scaffolding" he also realizes that the symmetry of the construction apparent to the onlooker in front conceals a chaos within. This dichotomy is a leitmotif in the entire chapter: order versus chaos. The apparent order of fascism is highly vulnerable to being toppled by the forces of chaos because the two principles cannot be separated from one another. The fatal union of the rational and the irrational in German fascism reveals itself in this subversion of external order through the chaos inside, a chaos already contained in the internal architecture of the ideology, here represented through the labyrinthine scaffolding of the rostrum, and brought to the fore by the trickster. Two types of music correspond to this dichotomy of the outward symmetry of the rostrum and its labyrinthine interior: Oskar's wild drumming displaces the "gradlinige Marschmusik" (*B*, 97), the rectilinear march music played during the party rally. Although Oskar initially takes up the rhythm that Bebra the clown had drummed in the circus, he soon finds his own rhythm infecting all the party musicians around him, whose music ends in pure chaos. Oskar finds his true nature, he becomes the trickster who creates chaos where there is order, thus distancing himself from Bebra in his political stance. While Bebra immediately sides with the Nazis, Oskar initially drums resistance. Hyde argues that tricksters "are regularly honored as the creators of culture. They are imagined not only to have stolen certain essential goods from heaven and given them to the race but to have gone on and helped shape this world so as to make it a hospitable place for human life" (*TMW*, 8). Although Oskar's drumming can be read as a relic of the charivari tradition in which pots and pans were struck with as much clamor as possible to announce the devil to the community and drive it away, his secret performance primarily creates a culture opposed to the official Nazi culture. Oskar temporarily displaces a music that in Wolbert's words is classical and Prussian,[32] replacing it with a Charleston, which belongs to the discursive norms of the grotesque body, the body that gives up its rigidity.

Since the grotesque had over the centuries been a component of folk culture it is this chaotic drumming that also has the purpose of returning folk humor to the *Volk*, a humor that Nazism was eager to crush along with the grotesque body. This tendency of Nazi ideology to suppress humor or merely use it for political purposes would support Adorno's and Horkheimer's notion of the inherent cruelty of Enlightenment, since it was this period that dealt the most serious blow to laughter and its embodiment, the fool. Oskar's deflation of the ruling group's power and consequent empowerment of the folk corresponds to the traditional function of the historical fool, who was to remind the King of his limitations as a human and of the presence of his inferior subjects, to whom he was responsible. This was also the objective of the Feast of Fools, a church ritual, both "parody and travesty of the official cult, with masquerades and improper dances" (*RW*, 74), meant to empower temporarily those officials in the church who normally had little say. Oskar's subversion of the Nazi dance and later desecration of the Church of the Sacred Heart can be seen as a twentieth-century renewal of medieval and Renaissance mirth. Oskar's music is carnivalesque in the sense that carnival has the same function of unleashing folk humor, which temporarily replaces the official seriousness of church and state. "Gesetz ging flöten und Ordnungssinn. Wer aber mehr die Kultur liebte, konnte auf den breiten, gepflegten Promenaden jener Hindenburgallee, die während des achtzehnten Jahrhunderts erstmals angepflanzt, bei der Belagerung durch Napoleons Truppen achtzehnhundertsieben abgeholzt und achtzehnhundertzehn zu Ehren Napoleons wieder angepflanzt wurde . . . meine Musik haben" (*B*, 98; "Gone were law and order. The more culture-minded element repaired to the Hindenburg-Allee, where trees had first been planted in the eighteenth century, where these same trees had been cut down in 1807 when the city was besieged by Napoleon's troops, and a fresh set had been planted in 1810 in honor of Napoleon": *TD*, 122). As the *tambour-major* in Heine's *Ideen, Das Buch Le Grand* drums to the spirit of Napoleon's renewal of Germany, Oskar's drumming carries as far as the rectilinear set of the trees on Hindenburg Allee, dissolving Prussian rigidity through his liberating rhythms. As the Prussians had once looked for his grandfather, the arsonist, while he was hiding under the skirts of Anna Koljaiczek, the Nazis are now looking for Oskar round the rostrum, poking into crannies. Like his grandfather, Oskar waits out the danger inside his place of hiding, happy that his stature allows him to escape unnoticed. He compares the rostrum with the proportions of the prophet-swallowing whale, compares himself with Jonah in the whale. This scene in which Oskar destroys the work of the official culture points to the still distant end of fascism. At this moment in the book, Oskar is therefore articulating a hope that can be compared with Albert Bloch's vision of the end of fascism in his painting *March of the Clowns,* where a cortège of carnival figures is seen walking around a circus arena, carrying an effigy of Hitler hanging from a swastika.

Grass's rostrum scene evokes the grotesque marketplace spectacles of the Middle Ages and the Renaissance with their theater scaffoldings, an atmosphere that Rabelais had recreated lavishly in the Chronicles of Gargantua "in which the exalted and the lowly, the sacred and the profane are leveled and are all drawn into the same dance" (*RW,* 160). Bakhtin's categories of the marketplace, the language of oaths and curses and images of the lower bodily stratum, all conjoin in this scene. As Bakhtin argues, the medieval mystery is an important source of the grotesque concept. He explains that "in these plays the stage reflected the medieval idea of the world's position in space. The front of the stage presented a platform that occupied the entire first floor of the structure and symbolized the earth. The backdrop was formed by an elevated set that represented heaven or paradise. Beneath the platform representing the earth there was a large opening, indicating hell, covered by a broad curtain decorated with a huge mask of the devil (Harlequin)" (*RW,* 348). It was from this opening that Satan's devils would spring into the world. This performance image of Satan springing from a box has made its way into literature. There is a scene in Grimmelshausen's picaresque novel *Simplicius Simplicissimus,* for example, in which Simplicius opens a kneading trough from which rises a black man: "[ich] fand aber nichts als ein leer Bett darinnen und einen beschlossenen Trog, den hämmert ich auf in Hoffnung etwas Kostbares zu finden, aber da ich den Deckel auftat, richtet' sich ein kohlschwarzes Ding gegen mich auf, welches ich für den Luzifer selbst ansah" (I found nothing but an empty bed and a kneading-trough with the lid fixed down. I prized it off, hoping to find something valuable inside, but as I lifted the lid some coal-black thing rose up towards me which I took to be Lucifer himself.)[33] This moment is undoubtedly a relic of the medieval mystery plays. In these plays hell was often represented in the form of huge jaws, an image that can also be detected in the horse's head releasing the swarm of eels that eventually cause Agnes's death in *Die Blechtrommel.* Like Rabelais's novels, *Die Blechtrommel* frequently displays the two related folk cultural images of the gaping mouth and the act of swallowing. The giant versus the dwarf, the gigantic swallowing the small, this is a lower bodily image the carnival has made use of throughout the ages. In the rostrum scene Oskar sits in the spot the devil/Harlequin used to occupy in the medieval mystery play, under the stage, one of the many allusions to Oskar's satanic nature. This is where his similarity with Hermes truly shows; he is a messenger of the gods, in that he tries to disrupt the satanic event, but he is also to be found in the underworld. Sitting inside the rostrum, Oskar is

located at the very center of the hell created by the Nazi party, which ema-
nates from the center, the rostrum, to the periphery, thus trying to draw in
the whole population. The gullible Germans outside, who fall for the satanic
charm of the Nazis, do not have the same insight made possible by Oskar's
central position. Jonah in the whale arrives at the same sort of clairvoyance
about his life, a perspective he would not receive in the outside world. By
adding to the sinister event his comic disruptive diablerie, Oskar is playing
the role of the typical Harlequin, who developed from the specter-devils and
the clown-devils of the early Middle Ages into a predominantly clownish
character in the *commedia dell'arte* of the Italian Renaissance.

Harlequin Institutionalized

Oskar's carnivalesque activities move Grass's text into the vicinity of the
commedia, which arose in the late Renaissance, was performed until the
eighteenth century, and still leaves its mark on the culture of the twentieth
century, in literature as well as in the performing and the visual arts. Around
the beginning of the twentieth century the avant-garde in Germany and
Russia became very interested in the *commedia*. In Russia its motifs were
adapted for their anti-bourgeois theater, and in America Charlie Chaplin
became a reincarnation of Harlequin. In *The Great Dictator* (1940), for
example, fascism is represented through imagery derived from the *commedia*.
In this film fascism itself is displayed as comedy, unlike Albert Bloch's painting *March of the Clowns,* which uses the comic as relief from fascism, and
serves as an incantation of the end of fascism. Like the *commedia, Die Blechtrommel* makes use of certain stock characters, like the doctor (Hollatz), or
the courtesan (Raguna). As *Die Blechtrommel* tries to subvert the rationalism
of its time, the *commedia dell'arte* satirized its own counterpart, the *commedia sostenuta,* or learned drama, performed from a written text. The *commedia dell'arte* too was rich in heteroglossia, Italy's regional dialects and their
"wit of words tumbling over one another in rapid succession, of macaronic
Latin, of non sequiturs, equivocations, word games, and puns" (*HM,* 9),
from the Venetian merchant's dialect to the elegant Tuscan and to low
vernacular. It was a satire of the upper and lower strata of society, one of
whose favorite themes was adultery, an endless source of ridicule and shame,
and featured lecherous old men. The most common plot, however, was
based upon a threat posed to two young sweethearts by an overly protective
parent. Only a servant could bring about their union, which entailed a carnivalesque reversal of high and low, of servant over master.

    In *Die Blechtrommel* the lowly is centralized in the figure of Oskar him-
self, his perspective from the bottom. Grass's novel is not exclusively a love
story but, as we have seen, the low also uncrowns the powerful (for example,
Oskar destroys Matzerath). Moreover, madness is a key theme in the *com-*

media, madness as a form of travel. The figures of the *commedia* were all tricksters, *arte* standing for the talents and skills of the actors but also for commercially profitable trade. They were tricksters traveling to exotic and imaginary lands, sometimes off the Earth altogether and into the cosmos (*HM,* 25). This is a motif that seeped into literature in the seventeenth and eighteenth centuries, as becomes evident when we look at Simplicius's trip to the center of the Earth or Baron von Münchhausen's journey to the moon. *Commedia* intends to alienate its audiences through its exotic elements and its shape-shifting characters with their fluid nature, like Mercury. Harlequin is mercurial and lunatic, as is indicated, for example, by Nolant de Fatouville's play *Harlequin, Emperor of the Moon,* of 1684 (*HM,* 25). In the French *commedia,* the lunar and lunatic Harlequin and his fellow clown Pulcinella became the subversive counterparts to absolutism and its ruler Louis XIV, the *Roi-Soleil,* who finally banned the *commedia* in France. As fellow clowns, Bebra and Oskar are Grass's version of Harlequin and Pulcinella. In the role of Harlequin, Bebra, who is descended from Prince Eugene, the son of Louis XIV, is a representation of the wise fool joined to the ruler, Hitler. This corresponds to the traditional courtly pattern in which Harlequin on the Moon is the counterpart to the Sun King. Oskar, who also has much in common with Harlequin, has, however, a stronger likeness with the Neapolitan *commedia* trickster Pulcinella. Hunchbacked with a phallic nose, Pulcinella was usually associated with sticks in his hands, either a dagger or macaroni, and was "a great beater of others and much beaten himself."[34] We see him, a peasant from the region around Naples, come back to life in Oskar, who forges his papers, changing his identity to "Oskarnello Raguna, geboren am einundzwanzigsten Oktober neunzehnhundertzwölf in Neapel (born on October 21, 1912 in Naples, *B,* 268), when he joins the theater at the front. By screaming glassware from the reign of Louis XIV to pieces, Oskar not only offers his services to Nazi rule, participating in the German destruction of France, but unconsciously also engages in a subversive act opposed to the official culture of absolutism and the reign of the Sun King. Oskar's girlfriend Roswitha Raguna, herself from Naples, is the great *somnambulist,* which also evokes the French tradition of the *commedia,* the *Théatre des Funambules* (Theater of the High Wire) and its very own Harlequin, Pierrot, a central image of the artist and as such much abused by society. Pulcinella became increasingly unpopular in the Age of Enlightenment; in 1760 the Neapolitan authorities considered banishing Pulcinella because they considered his obscenities to be dangerous for noblewomen and regarded him as politically too subversive (*HM,* 60). Pulcinella was ultimately deprived of any political danger he might pose to official culture when he was reduced to a mere marionette, like the German *Hanswurst* in puppet theaters.

The disappearance of Harlequin and Pulcinella parallels the decline of the carnival and its grotesque images in the eighteenth century. Due to the

Enlightenment's insistence on reason and the bourgeoisie's quest of fulfillment here on Earth rather than in the after-life, the notion of hell and its iconography was regarded with increasing skepticism. If the origin of the term carnival is a holy site (karne) to which the dead (val, wal) are led, there is a proximity between carnival and the idea of hell.[35] The image of being swallowed so abundant in carnival would then imply being swallowed by hell, and indeed carnival hell was seen in various forms: a giant devouring children, as we can see in many folk-tales, or an oven for the baking of fools (*RW*, 393). If we apply these images to the context of Nazi atrocities, as Grass's novel suggests, this approximation becomes so macabre that it stifles the folk laughter that these carnival images originally provoked with the intention of defeating the fear of hell. As we know from Terrence Des Pres, however, in the midst of that hell called Auschwitz, at times laughter was the only means to survive. In the Middle Ages laughter lay outside of officialdom and since carnival laughter was in opposition to the seriousness of the church, European cultures associated it with the devil. Yet as long as the carnival kept the image of the devil in everyone's consciousness, the presence of evil in daily life was ubiquitous and could not be forgotten.

After the Age of Enlightenment, the iconography of hell faded into oblivion and with it the laughter of the oppressed lower classes that had had the function of liberating them from their fear of hell. That the bourgeoisie of the nineteenth century considered folk humor as inappropriate led to an increasing intolerance towards the impurities of the grotesque, an intolerance that climaxed in the deadly seriousness of Nazi genocide. As images of the Holocaust became known after the war, they initially commanded general silence. To break the spell of this seriousness with laughter would by most people's common sense be a major affront towards the victims, and yet to those struggling for survival in the camps and those who did survive, humor often remained their only weapon. As Des Pres argued in defending artistic responses to the Holocaust that employ a sense of humor, "it's not fear and sorrow we need more of, but undaunted vision. The paradox of the comic approach is that by setting things at a distance it permits us a tougher, more *active* response. We are not wholly, as in the high seriousness of tragedy, forced to a standstill by the matter we behold."[36] As Nietzsche once put it, "even if nothing else today has any future, our *laughter* may yet have a future."[37] Oskar's final reaction to his life and the German past is one of liberating laughter as he flees westward. In Grass's novel we hear the mad laughter of the perpetrators, the madness of Rasputin, of Dionysian excess, as the death of four thousand children in the gas chambers is evoked by the daunting image of the merry-go-round in the chapter "Desinfektionsmittel" (Disinfectant) and we hear the laughter of persecuted Oskar. Although his laughter functions as comic relief it also contains a certain madness, which contributes to his institutionalization in a mental asylum, as a new officialdom disciplines those who laugh: "Mich [Gottfried von Vittlar] kränkte das Gelächter des Herrn Matzerath. Er lag auf dem Rücken, wühlte seinen Buckel in die lockere Erde, rupfte mit beiden Händen Gras aus, warf die Büschel hoch und lachte wie ein unmenschlicher Gott, der alles kann" (*B*, 481; "I was offended at Mr. Matzerath's laughter. He lay on his back, rolling his hump in the loose earth, pulling out clumps of grass with both hands, tossing them up in the air, and laughing like an inhuman god who can do anything he pleases": *TD*, 576).

Although Oskar is aware that his healing is successful in the secular sphere, his relationship with the church remains forever tainted: "der Erfolg meiner Stimme dem Profanen gegenüber [machte mich] fortan auf meine Mißerfolge im sakralen Sektor aufmerksam"(*B*, 118; "the triumph of my voice over profane targets made me painfully aware of my failures in the sacred sector": *TD*, 146). He realizes that he is at home neither in the sacred nor the profane realm but dwells on the fringes, in a mental hospital. It is here that he therefore finds himself more than ever in that liminal space of the trickster's threshold existence. His ultimate institutionalization in the Federal Republic takes place after three failed attempts during the Third Reich, which would have killed him. The first appeal for Oskar's internment follows his transient lifestyle in Bebra's circus on the front, the second one comes after his criminal acts with the Dusters, who loot churches and party treasuries, and the third one, which Matzerath ultimately signs, follows upon the complete desecration of the Church of the Sacred Heart. What saves him from the killing institution is the end of the war.

Oskar is institutionalized for the murder of Sister Dorothea, although it is not quite clear whether he can be accounted responsible for such a crime, since he is clearly insane. When he is arrested at the top of the escalator in a Paris metro station, he still insists that he is Jesus. Oskar's institutionalization fulfills both his own desire for a refuge from the surrounding world and the desire of his contemporaries who are put to shame by his shameless trickster work in church and other sacred grounds. Oskar's function as healer is completely ironical.[38] In Jungian terms Oskar is the Germans' shadow, both in the form of Hitler (as drummer boy he not only replaces the passive Jesus but also stands for Hitler drumming up the Germans), who represents the Germans' subconscious desires, and after the war as an incarnation of the Germans' repressed guilt and disruptor of collective amnesia.[39] That Jung thought of Hitler when he wrote about the trickster can be seen in that elucidating passage in which he points out that the trickster can always surface from the collective unconscious, "even on the highest plane of civilization" and that his "monkey tricks" can be found primarily in politics: "the so-called civilized man has forgotten the trickster. . . . He never suspects that his own hidden and apparently harmless shadow has qualities whose dangerousness exceeds his wildest dreams. As soon as people get together in masses and submerge the individual, the shadow is mobilized, and, as history shows, may even be personified and incarnated."[40] It becomes clear that Oskar embodies both the madness of the persecuted and that of the persecutors. As Oskar unites these conflicting roles of victim and perpetrator within himself, he fulfills one of the central functions of the trickster, who is a figure on the threshold uniting all dichotomies. Through this function he forms a counter-culture to postwar German society and its one-sided interpretation of the Third Reich as a purely irrational phenomenon. While in the Middle Ages reason and unreason were allowed to coexist in public life, the bourgeois age experienced an increasing segregation of unreason. The carnival and its cultural phenomena, like the fool and the marketplace, were rapidly losing their original functions in the nineteenth century, the age of science, industrialization and urbanization that was deeply hostile to ritual.[41] Stallybrass and White discuss Freud's case studies of hysteria, which show that as carnival activity gradually diminished in the course of the nineteenth century, the individual became increasingly vulnerable to the effects of isolation, a sort of internalized private terror that could no longer be acted out the way it was in communal ritual in the marketplace. The bourgeois rejection of the carnival, of traditional marketplace activities and such institutions as the ass-eared fool, was a part of what Norbert Elias called the "civilizing process," an increasing insistence on civility that would no longer allow for carnival's allusions to the bodily substratum. Grass seems to understand that Germany's flight into rationalism after 1945 was no solution for the healing of the German wound, but was bound to worsen the neuroses for which folk humor had always functioned as a valve. Along with Arno Schmidt, Edgar Hilsenrath and others, Grass must have understood that when the grotesque and the irrational are outlawed, mass hysteria is the consequence. Guidry sees in Oskar a culture-hero, who like Jesus takes the guilt of his contemporaries upon his shoulders. At the same time, he is an unwelcome figure in Germany because he reminds this society of its own only all-too-recent infantilism. His institutionalization shows that there is no place for him in a country that was skeptical of all forms of irrationalism well into the 1960s. The lesson of this book is that only by admitting the irrational in the shape of the grotesque, and as a *modus vivendi* far from the dictates of bourgeois respectability, can there be a truly liberal and liberated society, a message that at the time of *Die Blechtrommel*'s publication anticipates the emergence of German liberalism by at least ten years.

Notes

[1] Wolfgang Zucker, "The Clown as the Lord of Disorder," in *Theology Today* 24.3 (1967): 306.

[2] Ernst Klee, ed., *"Euthanasie" im NS-Staat: Die "Vernichtung unwerten Lebens"* (Frankfurt/Main: Fischer, 1989), 55: "Als 'asozial' gelten Bettler, Landstreicher, Zigeuner, Landfahrer, Arbeitsscheue, Müßiggänger, Prostituierte, Querulanten, Gewohnheitstrinker, Raufbolde, Verkehrssünder, Psychopathen und Geisteskranke." (The Nazis considered as anti-social beggars, drifters, gypsies, vagrants, those shying away from work, the lazy, prostitutes, the quarrelsome, alcoholics (habitual drinkers), those engaging in fights in public places, traffic violators, psychopaths and the mentally disabled.)

[3] Cf. Klee, *"Euthanasie,"* 38 and Ulrike Schulz, *Gene mene muh raus mußt du: Eugenik von der Rassenhygiene zu den Gen- und Reproduktionstechnologien* (Munich: AG SPAK, 1992), 37: "Die Sterilisationen wegen 'Schwachsinns' stellten den höchsten Anteil, sie stiegen von 1934 mit 53% auf 1935 mit 60% an. An zweiter Stelle stand die 'Schizophrenie' mit mindestens 20%." (Of all people sterilized the largest part consisted of those with dementia; their number increased from 53% in 1934 to 60% in 1935).

[4] Klee, *"Euthanasie,"* 37: "Wer selbständig einen Beruf ausfüllen kann, ist nicht schwachsinnig. Wer aber nicht fähig ist, 'in einem geordneten Berufsleben seinen eigenen Unterhalt zu verdienen, noch sonst sich sozial einzufügen,' ist es mit großer Wahrscheinlichkeit." (Those who are able to have a profession which they perform independently do not suffer from dementia, but those who are not able to earn their own living or to integrate themselves into society in any other way probably do.)

[5] Schulz, *Gene mene muh*, 39: "Seit 1936 kam unter der Diagnose 'Lebensbewährung' die *fehlende Leistungssteigerung* als Sterilisationsgrund hinzu." (As of 1936 the diagnosis that a person could not increase his/her performance became a reason to sterilize that person.) Those who escaped sterilization "mußten nicht nur fleißig sein, entscheidend war, ob sie sich aus eigener Kraft *emporgearbeitet* hatten. Denn der Normale hat meist Wünsche, die ihm eine rein monotone Tätigkeit auf Dauer unerträglich werden lassen, während der Schwachsinnige solche Mißempfindungen meist nicht hat." (not only had to be diligent, they also had to have worked their way up through their own strength. The "normal" person is usually unable to bear a purely monotonous activity for a long time, while the weak-minded do not suffer from this sense of boredom.)

[6] Dr. Thomas Röder, Volker Kubillus, and Anthony Burwell, *Psychiatrists: The Men behind Hitler: The Architects of Horror* (Los Angeles: Freedom Publishing, 1995), 177.

[7] Simon Mawer, *Mendel's Dwarf* (New York: Harmony Books, 1998), 270: "The old eugenics died with the Third Reich, but make no mistake, the new eugenics is with us. It isn't in the future, it is here and now."

[8] Mikhail Bakhtin, *The Dialogic Imagination: Four Essays by M. M. Bakhtin*, ed. Caryl Emerson and Michael Holquist (Austin: U of Texas P, 1981), 159.

[9] Another excellent study of the fool is Vicki K. Janik, ed., *Fools and Jesters in Literature, Art, and History: A Bio-Bibliographical Sourcebook* (Westport: Greenwood, 1998).

[10] Cf. Paul Williams, ed., *The Fool and the Trickster: Studies in Honor of Enid Welsford* (Totowa: Rowman & Littlefield, 1979), 32.

[11] Williams, *The Fool and the Trickster*, 18.

[12] According to C. G. Jung, *The Archetypes and the Collective Unconscious* (Princeton: Princeton UP, 1969), 255, one of this figure's features is his "approximation to the figure of the savior."

[13] Glenn Guidry, "Theoretical Reflections on the Ideological and Social Implications of Mythic Form in Grass' *Die Blechtrommel*," in *Monatshefte* 83.2 (1991): 130: "Yo, the Dahomean trickster, is portrayed as a singer whose voice has magical powers over others," while for the Doga tribe in West Africa "Ogo-Yurugu plays his drum so compellingly that others are placed in thrall."

[14] C. G. Jung, "On the Psychology of the Trickster Figure," in Paul Radin, *The Trickster: A Study in American Indian Mythology* (New York: Schocken Books, 1972), 203.

[15] Jung, "Psychology of the Trickster Figure," in Radin, 195.

[16] Cf. Peter Aley, *Jugendliteratur im Dritten Reich: Dokumente und Kommentare* (Hamburg: Verlag für Buchmarktforschung, 1967), 103–5.

[17] Richard Erdoes and Alfonso Ortiz, ed., *American Indian Trickster Tales* (Harmondsworth: Penguin, 1999), xix.

[18] Peter Stallybrass and Allon White, *The Politics & Poetics of Transgression* (Ithaca: Cornell UP, 1986), 22–23.

[19] Barry Sanders, *Sudden Glory: Laughter as Subversive History* (Boston: Beacon, 1995), 243.

[20] John Money, *The Kaspar Hauser Syndrome of Psychosocial Dwarfism* (Buffalo: Prometheus Books, 1992), 40.

[21] *Psychopath* was a favorite term of the Nazis to categorize the nature of some criminals. The term sufficed to justify someone's internment in a concentration camp.

[22] William J. Hynes and William G. Doty, ed., *Mythical Trickster Figures: Contours, Contexts, and Criticisms* (Tuscaloosa: U of Alabama P, 1992), 37.

[23] Mockery, abuse, and embarrassment in the marketplace seem to be European phenomena. By comparison, in Native American cultures like that of the Hopi, laughter itself is often sacred and lacks cynical undertones, a fact that is confirmed by their rituals in the plaza, the center of the pueblo. Here rituals in which clowns allude to the sexual act and the process of defecation are performed without embarrassment and accompanied by laughter that contains no derision. Cf. Richard Erdoes and Alfonso Ortiz, *Trickster Tales*, xxi.

[24] Stallybrass and White, *Politics & Poetics*, 36.

[25] Stallybrass and White, *Politics & Poetics*, 42.

[26] Jack Zipes ed., *The Complete Fairy Tales of the Brothers Grimm* (New York: Bantam, 1987), 659.

[27] Günter Lewy, *Nazi Germany and the Catholic Church* (New York: Da Capo, 2000, originally published in 1964), 292.

[28] Cf. Lewy, *Nazi Germany and the Catholic Church*, 279, for example: "the veteran National Socialist priest Father Senn . . . in 1934 hailed Hitler as the tool of God, called upon to overcome Judaism."

[29] Cf. Lewy, *Nazi Germany and the Catholic Church*, 279.

[30] Jung, "Psychology of the Trickster Figure," quoted in Radin, 198.

[31] Victor Turner, *The Forest of Symbols: Aspects of Ndembu Ritual* (Ithaca: Cornell UP, 1967), 128.

[32] Klaus Wolbert, *Die Nackten und die Toten des Dritten Reiches* (Gießen: Anabas Verlag, 1982), 148: "das Klassische ist sogar dem Preußischen und, in gewissem Sinne, dem Parademäßigen verwandt." (the classical has Prussian and in a way parade-like qualities.)

[33] Johann Grimmelshausen, *Der abenteuerliche Simplicissimus* (Frankfurt am Main: Fischer, 1962), 186; Johann Grimmelshausen, *Simplicissimus,* trans. Mike Mitchell (Sawtry, UK: Dedalus, 1999), 222.

[34] Giacomo Oreglia, *The Commedia dell'Arte* (New York: Hill & Wang, 1968), 93.

[35] Bakhtin, *Rabelais and his World,* 392. There are other speculations as to the origin of the word *carnival,* cf. Stallybrass and White, *Politics & Poetics,* 184: *carne levare,* the roasting and taking up of meat; or Sanders, *Sudden Glory,* 155: *carnis,* flesh, *vale,* farewell, a farewell to flesh.

[36] Terrence Des Pres, *Writing into the World: Essays, 1973–1987* (New York: Viking Penguin, 1991), 282.

[37] Friedrich Nietzsche, *Beyond Good and Evil: Prelude to a Philosophy of the Future,* trans. Walter Kaufman (New York: Random House, 1966), 150.

[38] As Hynes argues (in Hynes and Doty, *Mythical Trickster Figures,* 40) the trickster's function as a cultural transformer is often subject to parody.

[39] Jung, "Psychology of the Trickster Figure," in Radin, 209: "the trickster is a collective shadow figure, a summation of all the inferior traits of character in individuals."

[40] Jung, "Psychology of the Trickster Figure," quoted in Radin, 206.

[41] Stallybrass and White, *Politics & Poetics,* 172.

6: Gypsies, the Picaresque Novel, and the Politics of Social Integration

ABEL WAS A KEEPER OF THE SHEEP, Cain a tiller of the ground. That is, the first was a nomad and the second was sedentary. The quarrel of Cain and Abel has gone on from generation to generation, from the beginning of time down to our own day, as the atavistic opposition between nomads and the sedentary, or more exactly as the persistent persecution of the first by the second. And this hatred is far from extinct. It survives in the infamous and degrading regulations imposed on the Gypsies, treated as if they were criminals, and flaunts itself on the outskirts of villages with the sign telling them to "move on."[1]

Persecuted Transients

Michel Tournier's *Le Roi des Aulnes* (1970; translated as *The Ogre*, 1972) displays the international appeal that fascism's exclusion of the poor, transients, and the Gypsies had and still has for the bourgeois mind. In France the persecution of Gypsies, the attempt to make them settle down and give up their nomadic way of life, and the desire to educate them and turn them into useful citizens arose in the Age of Absolutism, under Louis XIV. This policy was an improvement vis à vis what Foucault describes in connection with the poor and transients in the age of the great confinement, the Early modern Age, with its "imperative of labor" resulting in arrests of beggars roaming the streets of Paris (1532), who were then forced to work in the "sewers of the city, chained in pairs" (*MC,* 47). Transients and the unemployed were treated like criminals. They were no longer driven away or punished but imprisoned, at the expense of the nation and of individual liberty (*MC,* 48). The poor were confined, since they were neither producers nor consumers: "Idle, vagabond, unemployed, he belonged only to confinement, a measure by which he was exiled and as it were abstracted from society. With the nascent industry which needs manpower, he once again plays a part in the body of the nation" (*MC,* 230). Not until 1789 and the "Declaration of the Rights of Man" was there a relaxation of these practices of confinement in France.

Likewise, in Austria, under Maria Theresia and Joseph II, there were repeated attempts to turn the Gypsies into better people by forbidding them to change their names and to wander through the woods, and forcing them to live in houses and take to agriculture, all this an improvement over the situation before 1783, when it was still possible to kill any Gypsy as an outlaw.[2] Their vagrant way of life was widely associated with the notion that they were prone to a criminal mentality and likely to elude the regular performance of work, while the respectable citizen, who was settled, could be more easily controlled by the state as to his whereabouts and work ethic. From the eighteenth century on, the Gypsies' lack of roots was linked to the impossibility of educating them. The politics of social integration, propagating a sedentary way of life, were thus inseparably linked to the politics of education, of *Bildung*. Apart from this distinction between the bourgeoisie's desire to settle down and an asocial nomadic life, certain myths were attached to the Gypsies, such as their cult of the Virgin Mary, the fear that they would gang up with other criminals, and the fear that they would steal children and make food out of them, a common myth also applied to Jews.[3] Through his profession of stealing children from their parents for recruitment to the Russian front, Tournier's protagonist Abel Tiffauges is an incarnation of this myth, but here it is the Nazis who steal children. Tournier debunks the myth by inverting the positions of the respectable citizen versus the asocial nomad. Abel is a nomad who protects himself from being persecuted by the Nazis by using the very myth that would make him a victim of persecution as a service to his persecutors. In this he resembles Oskar Matzerath and the Tom Thumb figures, who offer the very qualities through which they are endangered to those who threaten them: Oskar becomes a fool for the Nazis and the Tom Thumbs of the Grimm Brothers offer the advantages of their size to thieves.

The Nazis no longer believed in the educability of the Gypsies and other transients, or in the probability of turning them into respectable citizens. In the Third Reich the practice of confining transients and the poor reaches a fatal perversion; the expense that the unemployed caused the nation led to the nation's desire to get rid of them by working them to death. The question of expense caused by the so-called useless members of society gained particular significance during the war years, while throughout the Nazi period criminality, insanity, and the reluctance to work were consistently seen as congenital conditions, which makes it clear that the Nazis' racist ideology also stood behind the extermination of these groups of people. When it came to the distinction between good and bad blood there was ultimately little distinction among Jews, the insane, Gypsies or *nach Zigeunerart umherziehenden Personen,* people roaming in gypsy fashion, nomads without tradition or race, rootless urban cosmopolitans. Nazism was "a doctrine of farmers and sedentaries strongly rooted in the ancient soil of Germany. . . . For us," Doctor Blättchen tells Abel, "everything is in the hereditary equipment handed down to us from generation to generation according to known and inflexible laws. Bad blood is neither treatable nor educable: the only way of dealing with it is destruction pure and simple."[4] A rootless way of life seems to be irreconcilable with nationalism and in the Third Reich became a threat to *völkische* stability. While in the nineteenth century foreigners were one embodiment of the threat to national unity, the migratory urban proletariat and the Jews were others. As Baigent and Leigh argue, in *"völkische* ideology the Jew was the very incarnation of rootlessness. The "Wandering Jew" could only too easily be identified as the natural adversary of *das Volk,* the inimical outsider and stranger, the unwelcome intruder."[5] Yet to the Nazis the so-called *Landstreicher,* people who were aimlessly roaming across the land, were also subhuman, degenerate (*entartet*), and "morally sick" (*sittlich-krank*).[6] It was the ideologues' conviction that these people do not participate in the fight for survival but are full of self-pity and hatred for others who are better off.[7] What in the Weimar republic the reactionary modernist Werner Sombart had criticized as Jewish Saharism, rootless nomadism, Nazi ideology rejected as asocial and dangerous.[8] The Nazis distinguished between good and bad wanderers, wanderers who were willing and able to work and those who were not.[9] The nation of hikers and wanderers categorized among those wanderers, healthy men who were looking for work as well as wandering apprentices of a trade on the one hand and, on the other hand, those wanderers who were to be persecuted: professional beggars, obsessive hikers, and notorious drinkers. These were no longer to have the right to wander but were to be sterilized and taken to concentration camps.[10]

In 1938 a law was issued that classified the so-called *Landfahrer* (Gypsies) as asocial and made it possible to deport them to concentration camps. Several charges were laid against these aimless wanderers to facilitate their persecution. One of the principal fears was the wanderer's reluctance to work. The Nazis wanted to make sure that whoever could not or did not want to work had no right to reproduce. The aimless wanderer was considered an active parasite attacking the *Volkskörper,* as opposed to the passive parasites, the physically and mentally handicapped. It becomes clear how contradictory the Nazis' concerted effort in stigmatizing certain people was if we consider that these wanderers' "dämonische Anlage des Wandernmüssens" (demonic compulsiveness to roam) was seen as a pathological disorder, which would make them passive rather than active parasites. Aimless wandering in the bourgeois age implied a displacement from one's home, hence a form of insanity. Yet there was another reason for persecuting these insane wanderers. Not only were they seen as a "reserve army of communism"[11] but, like the Nazis' perception of Jews as disease carriers, the aimless wanderer's Gypsy-like lifestyle was associated with a dissemination of bacilli.[12] Contempt for the aimless wanderer was thus determined by these people's unwillingness to work, a fear of the contagious impact this mentality could have on the good members of society, and also the wanderer's proneness to transmit infectious diseases. Wandering and a lack of roots, — that is, an individual's elusiveness to the grasp of the state's forces of control — were also associated with a criminal nature. In National Socialist stereotyping it was only a step from the *Landstreicher*, people whose poverty forces them to furtively roam the land, to the thief. Unlike the insane, criminals were classified as active social parasites, a form of *Untermensch* that ranked high on the list of people the Nazis tried to eliminate.

To what extent does Oskar Matzerath become a victim of this ideology? As we have seen, the practice of euthanasia was determined by both racial and economic motivations. Oskar is a victim of both. Günter Grass creates a character who at the time in which he lives is considered racially inadequate and an economic burden to his society. He is, of course, ethnically neither a nomadic Gypsy nor a cosmopolitan Jew, but during the war years he roams in Gypsy-like fashion. Thus the motives for the persecution of Gypsies also apply to Oskar's persecution. Oskar's lack of a school education, his resistance to being educated and socially integrated, his ganging up with the Dusters, with whom he roams the streets at night and whom the Nazis would label as *Straßengesindel* (scum living in the streets) or *nach Zigeunerart umherziehende Personen* (people who move around like gypsies), and his questionable usefulness to society all mark him as asocial and make him highly suspicious in the eyes of the Gestapo. Forever concerned that Oskar is a drain on the Matzeraths' budget, his stepmother Maria is wary of the general lack of orientation in Oskar's life, and upon his return from France she immediately thinks of his institutionalization. Now that he has left the theater at the front, he is in particular danger because he is no longer useful to the Nazis. Although Oskar's entry into the circus world temporarily makes him a useful member of society, this association with a Gypsy-like way of life also makes him suspicious to the authorities. His girlfriend Raguna, for example, fits perfectly into the stereotype of Gypsies as soothsayers, since she is a *clairvoyante* who can see into the hearts of men, revealing personal data from the soldiers' lives during the performances at the front. After his return to Danzig, Oskar becomes the leader of the Duster gang and begins to engage in a series of criminal activities. After desecrating the Church of the Sacred Heart he has to stand trial, and Matzerath is once again approached by an official in civilian clothes, who hands him a paper saying that considering how helpless and gullible Oskar is and because he is always ready to be taken in by disreputable elements, Matzerath ought to get the child off the streets and put him in an institution. The official's comment is a reference to Oskar's purported mental deadness and it echoes Maria's earlier words that "he's always being pushed around" by others, that he does not have a will of his own. Both are wrong since we know that Oskar is the leader of the gang, the brain behind all of the gang's activities. Yet the authorities now have yet another reason to institutionalize Oskar and get rid of him, since he also falls under the category of criminal, an active social parasite.

What happened to the asocial victims, the wanderers, petty thieves, and the lazy? They were interned in concentration camps where they had to break granite out of a hill, material for Albert Speer's colossal buildings and auto-bahn bridges.[13] The idea was to get rid of them by working them to death, the so-called *Vernichtung durch Arbeit*. The timeless granite and the fragility of the persecuted are a contrast that Grass exploits as a theme in the scene in which Oskar wants to work for Korneff the stonemason in the early years of the Federal Republic. It is an interesting detail that Oskar tries to do the kind of work that he would have done in a labor camp only a few years earlier had he been interned, work that surely would have killed him: "Schon nach einer Woche zeigte sich, daß meine Kräfte für grobe Steinmetzarbeiten nicht reich-ten. Ich sollte eine bruchfrische Wand Belgisch Granit für ein vierstelliges Grab bossieren und konnte nach einer knappen Stunde kaum noch das Eisen und nur noch gefühllos den Bossierschlägel halten" (*B*, 367; "It was clear by the end of the first week that I was not strong enough for the heavy work. I had been given the job of embossing a slab of Belgian granite, fresh from the quarry, for a family vault. In an hour's time I could scarcely hold the chisel and my mallet hand was numb": *TD*, 443). The mention of granite is likewise interesting in the context of National Socialism because wood and granite, in which the Nazis saw inscribed the German character, were the preferred materials for their monumental statues displaying the perfect Aryan body (*NT*, 100–104). Consequently, Oskar works with the very material that not only would have killed him during the war but was also used for the display of the body that is the very antithesis of his own. Working in labor camps implied a lot of bullying suffered by the inmates. They were, for example, forced into ice-cold water barrels in the winter, which usually killed them,[14] another his-torical detail that is interesting in light of Greff's bathing routine in the icy waters of the Baltic Sea, by which he tries to compensate for his "softness," his homosexuality. He literally freezes his sexuality, which to him and society seems threatening, and suppresses it under the ideal of the "soldatischen Mann," the military man.[15] While for Greff, swimming in ice-cold water is a form of self-flagellation, the image of a hunchbacked dwarf working with granite serves as a macabre parody for the torture the so-called *Untermenschen* were forced to endure in the labor camps.

Transients and the Question of Genre

This historical phenomenon, the exclusion and persecution of transients, who were believed to have a criminal nature, is inseparably linked to the question of genre in *Die Blechtrommel*. That this text is a picaresque novel written in opposition to the nineteenth-century Bildungsroman adds another dimension of popular culture, subverting learned culture and contrasting the asocial outsider with the bourgeois order. Unlike the Bildungsroman and its teleology of social integration, the picaresque novel is the ideal genre to represent the principles of homelessness and social marginalization that Bakhtin saw as key factors for the modern novel in general with its key figures, which he called life's maskers: the clown, the fool, and the rogue.[16] The latter corresponds to the German *Schelm*, who is both the mythological trickster and the picaro of the *Schelmenroman* (picaresque novel).[17] The German tradition of the picaresque novel is rooted in written as well as oral culture, since it harks back not only to the Spanish tradition but also to the German *Schwank*,[18] such lore as *Till Eulenspiegel* (1515), the story of a North German peasant clown from the fourteenth century. The picaro could be conceived as the literary cousin of the trickster populating orally trans- mitted myths. What Paul Radin says of the Native American trickster, that he knows neither good nor evil and possesses no moral or social values,[19] can also be said of the picaro. The rogue in *Lazarillo de Tormes* of 1554, for example, is without home, family, or possession.[20] With the picaresque novel the trickster myths share the focus on aimless roaming rather than on social integration, the telos of the nineteenth-century German Bildungsroman. As aimless wanderers seeking opportunities, the trickster and the picaro are Proteus-like characters, shape-shifters, who engage in criminal activities. The disappearance of the picaresque novel for the duration of the eighteenth and nineteenth centuries was a result of the antipathy that bourgeois authors and readers shared for the figure of the rogue, whose parasitic and criminal way of life contrasted starkly with the notions of order of a rising bourgeoisie that could no longer identify with the picaro. Foucault pointed out that in the age of bourgeoisie, which was characterized by its search for national unity, "the law of nations" no longer countenanced "the disorder of hearts" (*MC*, 60), and the rising bourgeoisie's great dream was that "the laws of the State and the laws of the heart [were] at last identical" (*MC*, 63). This was a sociopolitical development for which the Bildungsroman, with its dismissal of the hero's youthful dreams and ambitions and his final acceptance of social reality, was an adequate literary representation. Instead of a mischie- vous social outsider who was forever fighting against a pitiless society, pref- erence was given to a literary hero who was willing to find his way into society, and who would aspire to reconciliation between his ego and the world. This optimism disappeared again in the Naturalist period at the end of the nineteenth century. There was a renewed interest in the Bildungsro- man during the Third Reich, while the picaresque novel, due to its parasitic protagonist who remained outside the pale of society was, like the allegedly degenerate literary fairy tale, hard to fit into Nazi ideology. The picaro's main qualities, his flight from conformism, his cosmopolitanism, and his Proteus-like manner, were irreconcilable with Nazi politics, which aimed at eradicating individualism, (Jewish) cosmopolitanism, and nonconformism.[21] It is therefore precisely because of the picaro's reluctance to become part of the established bourgeois world that after 1945 the picaresque novel experienced a revival, while the teleology of the Bildungsroman has become highly questionable to this day.

The Bildungsroman of the nineteenth century represented the interests of the bourgeois class. It was a genre in the interests of the new bourgeois work ethic, while the picaresque novel corresponds to what Bakhtin called the travel novel, a genre that[22] shows the hero's aimless wanderings. Unlike the theme of man's emergence in the Bildungsroman, the development of the travel novel's protagonist is nonexistent. The picaro's status may change but there is no inner development. Yet this development of the protagonist into a responsible citizen is at the core of the Bildungsroman. Johann Grimmelshausen's *Der abenteuerliche Simplicissimus* is mentioned by Bakhtin as a Bildungsroman because the protagonist undergoes some change.[23] He climbs the social ladder and changes from a completely undeveloped character, a fool in the best sense of the word, to a fool who displays wisdom. The ending in this novel, however, contains a sort of anti-*Bildung* in that Simplicius withdraws from society and becomes a hermit, a development that eludes the teleology of the nineteenth-century Bildungsroman. Emrich detects three phases for Simplicius's development, (1) his appearance in the world as fully developed because of his innocence and purity, (2) the loss of this purity on account of the world's evil,[24] and (3) his withdrawal from this corrupt world.[25] He argues that in Grimmelshausen's novel there is a clash between the corrupt world and the human soul, which is of divine origin and therefore needs no development, since it is fully developed from the start. We can observe the same three phases in Grass's novel: Oskar argues that his development is completed at birth, and his immediate desire to return to the mother's womb stems from his fear that the world will corrupt him (and indeed it does!). Like Simplicius, Oskar becomes guilty in the course of his life and finally withdraws from the world to his hermitage, the mental institution.[26] Is there *Bildung* in these two novels? According to Bakhtin's theory, there definitely is. He distinguishes several types of novels of emergence, among which the fifth type is the one that corresponds to Grimmelshausen's and Grass's texts and to what Gerhard Mayer called the anti-Bildungsroman.[27] In this type, Bakhtin argues, "man's individual emergence is inseparably linked to historical emergence,"[28] by which he means the transition from one epoch to another, a transition that is reflected in the development of the protagonist. This cannot be said for the nineteenth-century Bildungsroman of poetic realism, which does not contain historical movement from one epoch to another, but it nonetheless holds true for *Simplicissimus,* which reflects the dawn of the bourgeois age, and for *Die Blechtrommel.* In the latter the two epochs are the Third Reich and the early Federal Republic and the transition from one to the other is reflected in Oskar's change from a boy who wants no development to one who becomes misshapen as a reflection of Germany's crippled self-image. This is the ultimate parody of Bakhtin's fifth type of Bildungsroman: that it literally becomes a *Missbildungsroman* (deformation novel).

Grimmelshausen's novel is primarily a picaresque novel, much like Grass's book. Both are hybrids uniting the picaresque with anti-*Bildung*, which makes *Simplicissimus* so attractive to an author after 1945. In its recognition of the fragmentary nature of the world, Grimmelshausen's book is closer to postmodernity than the futile attempts of the nineteenth-century Bildungsromane to mend the rupture in the world. The fact that the picaro's very nature was irreconcilable with Nazi ideology does not imply, however, that Grimmelshausen was banned by the Nazis. On the contrary, as with much literature that was not Jewish or did not display an immediately obvious degeneracy, *Simplicissimus* was appropriated by the Nazis and misinterpreted until it fit perfectly into the construct of *völkisch* ideology. Nazi critics focused on such aspects as Grimmelshausen's adaptation of the Spanish picaro, that he stripped the Spanish picaro of his proletarian origin and gave him good German blood, and the camaraderie of the *Fronterlebnis*, the experience at the front. They celebrated the novel's regionalism, its closeness to the *Volk*, and Grimmelshausen's alleged hatred of Germany's lack of unity.[29] They must have completely ignored Simplicius's thievish nature and Gypsy-like lifestyle — "führte ich wieder überall ein einsiedlerisch Leben . . . ohne daß ich sehr viel stahl . . . auch keine stetige Wohnung hatte, sondern bald hie bald dorthin schweifte" (*AS*, 116; "I led the life of a hermit . . . except that I stole a lot. . . . Nor did I live in one place alone, but roamed here and there": *S*, 144), as well as the novel's subversive carnivalesque atmosphere and its inherent social criticism, while its impact on *Die Blechtrommel* shows that Grass must have been interested in precisely these subversive carnivalesque elements. To Grass, Grimmelshausen's novel, whose protagonist remains a social outsider, offers a way to attack the bourgeois order. The Nazis' interpretation of the novel completely misses its anti-social message. In fact, one of the major Grimmelshausen critics during the Third Reich, Hermann Eris Busse, also the author of *Zum silbernen Stern*, a narrative about Grimmelshausen, denied that the novel teaches *Weltflucht* (escape from the world and society), interpreting it instead as promoting self-control, spiritual fortification, and heroism.[30]

If one takes a closer look at Grimmelshausen's book it becomes clear to what extent it is grounded in popular culture. The author sides with the lowest in society, not, as the Nazis thought, in celebration of the peasant class and their camaraderie at the front. He empathizes with the victims of the Thirty Years' War (1618–48), with the poor who died either as soldiers, from starvation, or from diseases like the plague and smallpox. In opposition to the Nazis' view of Grimmelshausen as an advocate of camaraderie at the front, he sees in war an inexhaustible source of vice. That the text is a satire becomes clear as soon as one looks at the cover illustration of the 1668 version. It shows a satyr with a misshapen, grotesque body consisting of the face of a devil, a human chest and arms, and various other animal parts. The satyrs were creatures that, according to baroque understanding, would tell any person unabashedly what they thought of them, and would do so with mocking gestures and under great laughter with their mouths wide open.[31] The satirical novel harks back to the medieval saturnalia as well as to these creatures, which display all the features of Bakhtin's "grotesque body." Grimmelshausen's satyr is also an allusion to the mythical creature that Horace (65–8 B.C.) describes at the beginning of his *Ars Poetica* (c. 20 B.C.), which has the head of a beautiful woman and the lower body of a fish, and which serves him as a deterrent against violations of the Classicist rules governing art. The mishmash of body parts coming from various species in Horace's fantastic creature implies that art should stay away from too much fantasy but that instead it should imitate nature (*imitation, mimesis*) and not violate the laws of probability (*verisimilitudo*), requirements that Horace shares with Aristotle. According to this Classicist perception of art, which had its validity well into the eighteenth century (for drama it resurfaces in French Classicism and under Gottsched, for example), a *roman comique* like Grimmelshausen's was considered of low genre as opposed to the high genre of the Bildungsroman, which reflects bourgeois seriousness and contains no satire and fantastic elements. Grimmelshausen's novel is social satire targeting the corruption of society. Primarily through its utopian passages, such as Simplicius's journey to the kingdom of the Sylphs at the center of the Earth or his journey to the Hungarian Anabaptists, the text reveals the corruption of humanity during the seventeenth century. These segments display an ideal vision of society and, since they are utopian, one that would be impossible to realize. When, for example, Simplicius tells the King of the Sylphs about life on Earth, he describes it as the opposite of what it actually is, thus sketching an ideal vision of life on Earth, which satirically reveals life as it is.

The satire and its carnivalesque features place Grimmelshausen's novel in line with Rabelais and Grass. Like Oskar, Simplicius is a mirror reflecting the rottenness of the times he lives in. Both novels insist that their heroes' lack of morals is not a result of their inherent nature but the fault of a society that corrupts them. Simplicius is a fool and a trickster figure: "alle Tag war mirs Martinsabend oder Fasnacht" (*AS*, 288; "Every day was a feast day or carnival to me": *S*, 336). One of the traditional tasks of the courtly fool of the Renaissance, as opposed to the dim-witted fool of the Middle Ages, was to comment on his times with foolish wisdom, and this is something we do see in both Oskar, whose folly disrupts officialdom, and Simplicius, whose conversation and behavior are simple but "mehr sinnreich als närrisch" (*AS*, 129; "tended to make people think rather than laugh": *S*, 158). Like Hauff's Muck, Simplicius develops from a naive fool to a wise one, thus reflecting the changing functions of the court fool from the Middle Ages to the Renaissance. Like

Oskar he appears on stage in France, where he is a "parasite" at Monsieur Canard's table and, and, like Hermes the trickster, he plays the lute. This is quite possibly a segment that also inspired Thomas Mann's Felix Krull, another *bel allemand,* who evolves into a trickster and thief while in France and who is also compared with Hermes in regard to his thievishness as well as his beauty.[32] Despite his physical beauty, Simplicius is an oddball steeped in the carnival tradition and as such also displays images relating to Bakhtin's "grotesque body." He shares his obsession with fecal matter with Hermann Goering, one of Michel Tournier's ogres in *Le Roi des Aulnes,* and, with the mythological trickster, in truly Rabelaisian fashion he relishes in emissions of the lower bodily stratum. The famous Hanau banquet at Governor Ramsey's court, which is served at the expense of hundreds of starving war victims, is teeming with Rabelaisian images. Simplicius is tied to a pig's trough, is mocked by the guests and, since he is not used to the rich food, reacts violently against its abundance. He breaks wind and "spoils the dance" by losing control of his bowels: "es entwischte mir auch ohngefähr etwas in die Hosen, so einen über alle Maßen üblen Geruch von sich gab, dergleichen meine Nase lange nicht empfunden (*AS,* 76; "something slipped out into my trousers which gave off an awful stench, the like of which I had not smelt for a long time": *S,* 97). As Anne Leblans convincingly argues, his "protest comes literally from below and debases everything that is high."[33]

Like Hauff's Zwerg Nase, his insanity is displayed in the marketplace. Simplicius's insanity, obscenity, and profanity in the sacred realm are typical features that mark this novel as part of the kind of low genre, the *roman comique,* to which such authors as Rabelais, Bulgakov, and Grass have contributed. One of the main purposes of this genre is precisely what Simplicius does time and again, namely to debase that which is high, an objective that the Nazis simply ignored in this novel. Simplicius is the carnival king, who, like Oskar when he disrupts the Nazi party rally, protests against a higher authority. Like all tricksters, Simplicius shows a lack of morals. He cheats on his wife while in France and as an "itinerant quack" tricks a group of peasants with fake medicine. Like all tricksters he has a voracious appetite, "wie ein Drescher (*AS,* 259; "like a gannet": *S,* 303). He is taken for Mercury, who is identical with Hermes,[34] and he becomes a consummate thief who in one instance, like the North American trickster, tries to steal food and gets caught in his own trap. In this carnivalesque scene (book 2, chapter 31) Simplicius enters a priest's kitchen through the chimney in order to steal typical carnival food, ham and sausages. Like Tom Thumb, who ends up in the inside of a sausage, Simplicius is associated with carnival food, which goes to show how close the picaresque can be to the fairy-tale world. Simplicius gets trapped and, full of soot, reveals himself as the devil. This scene is particularly close to Grass's chapter "Auf dem Kokosteppich" (On the Fiber Rug), in which Oskar cures his ravenous hunger with blood sausage and frightens Sister Dorothea. Her reaction to Oskar in the dark, hiding in a coconut fiber rug, is like Grimmelshausen's priest when he sees Simplicius. She takes Oskar for the devil, who then replies that he is Satan who has come to call on her. We can see how dense the intertextuality between the two novels has become in this scene that reveals the satanic side of the trick-ster figure, the duplicity of their harlequinades. This episode, in which Sim-plicius has turned from a jester with donkey's ears into Satan, is a literary representation of the satyr in the cover illustration. The carnivalesque images of the fool/devil garments, the jester's donkey's ears and the devil's goat's ears, are a leitmotif, and in carnival fashion the text conflates the jovial with the sinister, death with laughter, satanic laughter, the kind of mad laughter that also reverberates through the end of Grass's novel and helps Oskar allay his fear of persecution: "davon soff sie ihrem Kind zeitlich das Leben ab, und entzündet' sich selbsten das Gehäng dergestalt, daß es ihr auch bald hernach entfiel, und mich wiederum zu einem Witwer machte, welches mir so zu Herzen ging, daß ich mich fast krank hierüber gelacht hätte" (*AS*, 334; "her drunkenness quickly sucked the life out of her child and so inflamed her own innards that soon after they dropped out and made me a widower for the second time, at which I almost died laughing": *S*, 384).

The carnival world in Grimmelshausen's novel forms a stark contrast to the grim reality of the Thirty Years' War. In *Die Blechtrommel*, too, laughter in the face of death seems to be the only weapon left to man. Simplicius and Oskar are comic monsters, satyrs, who can temporarily defeat terror. Despite its grotesque features, Grimmelshausen's novel also advocates certain Chris-tian virtues. Although it directs its criticism at the church,[35] it does on the whole not question the idea of salvation and does not contain the kind of mockery of the church that we find in Grass's text. Unlike *Die Blechtrommel*, which rules out any hope for an after-life, this baroque novel concludes that all worldly existence is *vanitas*, both vain and in vain. Whatever we do is ultimately in vain due to the evanescence of all terrestrial things, and the only hope for man lies in the *jenseits*, after death. Although it seems torn between the advocacy of Christian virtues and the concept that all is *vanitas*, Grimmelshausen's novel heralds the coming bourgeois age by condemning such vices as slothfulness and abstention from a rigid work ethic. Simplicius's aimless wandering all over Germany, for example, is regarded with skepti-cism by some citizens, who consider him a Gypsy after he returns from the center of the Earth, because they do not think a respectable citizen would be wandering through the depths of the forest at such a late hour (*AS*, 360; *S*, 411). Their attitude reflects the dawn of the bourgeois order. The novel appeared at a time far from the height of the bourgeois age, but the carnival and such figures as the court fool were already increasingly in decline. The picaresque novel with its carnivalesque atmosphere was a substitute for the disappearing street carnival, the picaro a substitute for the vanishing fool.

Die Blechtrommel revives the picaresque tradition in its original carnivalesque atmosphere while parodying the Bildungsroman, a genre that the Nazis did not have to twist as much as they had to twist Grimmelshausen to make it fit their ideology. Representative authors of this genre, such as Goethe, Gustav Freytag, and Wilhelm Raabe, were extremely popular among Nazi ideologues and educators. As for Raabe, Nazi-*Germanistik* (German Studies) exploited him for his love of *Heimat,* the homeland, for his philosophy supporting a sedentary way of life, for his closeness to the German folk soul, for his portrayal of German peasantry, for his concern with *Bildung* and education — Bildung in the sense of personal development into a socially integrated being — and ultimately for his portrayal of Jewish characters, which easily lent itself to the Nazis' racist ideology.[36] About Raabe's purported anti-Semitism in *Der Hungerpastor,* Köttgen says that the author saw in Hans Unwirsch a German and in Moses Freudenstein an anti-German nature, and that through this natural view he stands closer to contemporary, that is, Third Reich perceptions than many others who provide only Jewish caricatures.[37] The Nazis perverted Raabe into one of the foremost precursors of fascism among German authors of the nineteenth century and the Raabe Society became an eager accomplice to the Nazi cause.[38] One consequence of this complicity was that Jews were expelled from the Society, the historian Heinrich Spiero being the most prominent victim of this expulsion.[39] That Raabe himself was not the kind of anti-Semite that the Nazis liked to see in him has been shown time and again. Horst Denkler even goes so far as to contend that the anti-Semitic passages in Raabe's novel *Der Hungerpastor* and the portrayal of the Jewish antagonist Moses Freudenstein were created not from anti-Semitic prejudice but as social criticism of the anti-Semitic times that Raabe lived in.[40]

Parodying Goethe

Goethe too was appropriated as a cultural hero. German Studies scholars like Julius Petersen, Gerhard Fricke, Franz Koch, and Wilhelm Emrich perverted his elevated goals for the enlightenment of humanity into their racist and misanthropic ideology.[41] They celebrated the Nordic character of the storm-and-stress period and of Faust, his eternal striving to ever higher levels of awareness, thus adopting Classical *Bildung* and the German tradition of idealism, Goethe's telos of the individual's unconditional surrender to the demands of the world and society,[42] for their own telos of *völkisch* determination. Koch interpreted Wilhelm Meister's craving for eternity and immortality as Goethe's conviction that the individual needs to be accommodated by institutions that transcend individualism, such as the family, the people, and the state, and concludes from this that Goethe must have had a deeper knowledge of man's determination through his congenital instincts and blood ties.[43] Koch even went so far as to turn Goethe into a fierce anti-Semite, but as in the case of Raabe's critics and his alleged anti-Semitism, Koch failed to distinguish between the author's perception of Jews and his criticism of the anti-Semitism of his time. Like the Raabe Society, the Goethe Society got rid of its Jewish members. In his speech for the fiftieth anniversary of the Goethe Society in 1935, its president Julius Petersen emphasized that Goethe would have embraced National Socialism, and just as he gave his blessing to the Prussian soldiers in 1813, he would have supported the Nazi troops.[44] This appropriation of Goethe for the rhetoric of war and the idea of camaraderie reminds us of the manipulation of Grimmelshausen by Nazi critics. In the war years, Goethe and Weimar Classicism had the specific function of arming German soldiers spiritually (*geistige Aufrüstung*) for the *Endsieg*, the final victory. Goethe came to be used for German imperialist aspirations, not only Goethe, the Classicist, but also the Goethe of the storm-and-stress period standing by the cathedral of Strasburg and praising German genius. By placing a German folk-tale gnome under the French Eiffel Tower in his fictional rendering of the Nazi occupation of France, Grass seems to poke fun at this historical moment, in which the genius of Goethe is in awe of the Promethean spirit behind the construction of the Alsatian cathedral. In merging the positions of Oskar and Goethe, Grass dwarfs the latter. He dwarfs German high culture in the face of French cultural achievements, thus deflating the Nazis' vision of Goethe, whom they had used for their imperialist aim of making Alsace-Lorraine a part of Germany.

Although the Nazis' discriminatory politics were far removed from Goethe's high aims for all humans, there seems to be something in his obsession with form and formation, the perfectibility of man, that makes Oskar say that he fears the intolerance of this man of the Enlightenment because of a suspicion that if he had lived and drummed at his time, Goethe would have thought him unnatural and would have hit him over the head with *Faust* or a big heavy volume of his *Theory of Colors*. The dwarf's soul and his search for happiness were surely not as much a concern of Classicism as they were of Romanticism. "Who knows what I, the dwarf, have abrewing in my innermost being, to which none has access? Who knows anything about the dwarf soul, the most enclosed of all, where their fate is determined? Who can guess my true identity?" says Lagerkvist's Piccoline (*D*, 139). The fairy-tale dwarf displays a quest of happiness, an inner formation that contrasts with his external deformation. While in the folk-tales the quest of happiness and the hero's growth of wisdom are outlined in simple form, these concepts are developed more elaborately in the literary tales. The themes of education, wandering into the world, apprenticeship, recognition of mistakes, and the eventual homecoming are typical of the Bildungsroman but they also do occur in these tales. Oskar as a searching individual with the potential of development accentuates the monstrosity of the Nazis' denial of *Bildung* to so-called unworthy life. A character who does not embark on a search for happiness would be quite unthinkable, and Oskar's quest is important in light of the Nazi euthanasia that is being attacked, since it implies the complete lack of mental progress of the disabled (*tote Seelen*), and is thus based on the denial of the pursuit of happiness in its victims.

In contrast to the Romantics' view of *Bildung*, which makes room for aberrations, Grass views the more idealist tradition of Classical *Bildung*, and primarily Goethe, as already inherently discriminatory, which results in his parody of the Bildungsroman genre. His attack on Goethe as a cultural hero is echoed by other postwar German writers, such as Arno Schmidt. Schmidt, who criticizes Goethe "for the conveyor belt of his shit verses,"[45] was fond of the Romantics because they were able to parody Metternich's restorative system through a deliberately oppositional art.[46] Edgar Hilsenrath too tampers with the Goethean Bildungsroman and its nineteenth-century successors. In *Der Nazi und der Friseur* the juxtaposition of the upbringing of the non-Jewish and the Jewish boy, their friendship as opposed to the prejudices of their parents, is a parody of Raabe's and Freytag's novels. Hilsenrath inverts the notions of *Übermensch* and *Untermensch* by depriving the Aryans of their *Übermensch* Goethe, that bastion of German high culture, and associating him with the Jews. They live in the Goethestraße and are civilized people as opposed to non-Jews like the butcher, who does not even know Goethe's poem about the Erlking, and that ominous Aryan character Slavitzki, who rapes his own stepson, the protagonist Max Schulz.

Although on the one hand Grass's Oskar displays a quest for happiness that he shares with the Romantic fairy-tale dwarf, from the very beginning his existence shows Goethean idealism to be an anachronism. Oskar's reluctance to grow is a protest not only against the world of adults but also against Goethe and those who would use Goethe for their own teleological politics:

[Ich] blieb der Dreijährige, aber auch Dreimalkluge, den die Erwachsenen alle überragten, der den Erwachsenen so überlegen sein sollte, der seinen Schatten nicht mit ihrem Schatten messen wollte, der innerlich und äußerlich vollkommen fertig war, während jene noch bis ins Greisenalter von Entwicklung faseln mußten, der sich bestätigen ließ, was jene mühsam genug und oftmals unter Schmerzen in Erfahrung brachten, der es nicht nötig hatte, von Jahr zu Jahr größere Schuhe und Hosen zu tragen, nur um beweisen zu können, daß etwas im Wachsen sei. Dabei, und hier muß auch Oskar Entwicklung zugeben, wuchs etwas — und nicht immer zu meinem Besten — und gewann schließlich messianische Größe. (*B*, 47)

[I remained the precocious three-year-old, towered over by grownups but superior to all grownups, who refused to measure his shadow with theirs, who was complete both inside and outside, while they to the very brink of the grave, were condemned to worry their heads about "development," who had only to confirm what they were compelled to gain by hard and often painful experience, and who had no need to change his shoe and trouser size year after year just to prove that something was growing. However, and here Oskar must confess to development of a sort, something did grow — and not always to my best advantage — ultimately taking on Messianic proportions. *(TD,* 61)]

Bildung in this passage is satirically reduced to the growth of his phallus. Oskar's insistence that his mental development was completed at birth and his superiority to the adults surrounding him justifies his position of omniscient narrator and allows him to become a critical observer of his time. In light of this self-understanding it is easy to read the various stages of his ensuing *Bildung* only as irony. In its entirety, *Die Blechtrommel* is an invalidation of the teleology of the Goethean Bildungsroman, although at the surface the novel progresses along formative stages that recall those of the nineteenth-century Bildungsroman.[47] We are told of Oskar's birth, his childhood, his school experiences, the books he is exposed to, his early mentors, the experience of a theater performance, the death of his mother, his first loves, his wandering, his homecoming, his presumed fatherhood, his apprenticeship, his attempted socialization, even the motif of incest and inheritance.

The discussion that follows will focus on three areas of parody: Oskar's birth, his exposure to the theater, and the distinction between the Apollonian and the Dionysian. Grass parodies Goethe's optimism concerning his own life at the moment of his birth in *Aus meinem Leben: Dichtung und Wahrheit* (Truth and Poetry: From My Own Life, 1811–1833). He tampers with Goethe's concept of *Bildung* in the episode of the theater performance. Finally, he connects Goethe and Rasputin with Nietzsche's duality of the Apollonian versus the Dionysian, which is inseparably linked to the Nazi context.[48]

The famous passage in *Dichtung und Wahrheit* that describes the constellation of stars at the time when Goethe was born and the impact it had on his life becomes a target for Grass's irony. Let us quote Goethe first:

Am 28sten August 1749, mittags mit dem Glockenschlag zwölf, kam ich in Frankfurt am Main auf die Welt. Die Konstellation war glücklich: die Sonne stand im Zeichen der Jungfrau und kulminierte für den Tag; Jupiter und Venus blickten sie freundlich an, Merkur nicht widerwärtig; Saturn und Mars verhielten sich gleichgültig; nur der Mond, der soeben voll ward, übte die Kraft seines Gegenscheins um so mehr, als zugleich seine Planetenstunde eingetreten war. Er widersetzte sich daher meiner Geburt, die nicht eher erfolgen konnte, als bis diese Stunde vorübergegangen.[49]

[On the 28th of August, 1749, at mid-day, as the clock struck twelve, I came into the world, at Frankfort-on-the-Main. My horoscope was propitious: the sun stood in the sign of the Virgin, and had culminated for the day; Jupiter and Venus looked on him with a friendly eye, and Mercury not adversely; while Saturn and Mars kept themselves indifferent; the Moon alone, just full, exerted the power of her reflection all the more, as she had then reached her planetary hour. She opposed herself, therefore, to my birth, which could not be accomplished until this hour was passed.][50]

Grass uses this passage three times: for the birth of Oskar's mother, for Oskar's own birth, and the birth of his purported son. In particular the intertextuality in the scene of Oskar's birth shows how Goethe's self-inflated optimism is subverted:

> Es war in den ersten Septembertagen. Die Sonne stand im Zeichen der Jungfrau. Von fernher schob ein spätsommerliches Gewitter, Kisten und Schränke verrückend, durch die Nacht. Merkur machte mich kritisch, Uranus einfallsreich, Venus ließ mich ans kleine Glück glauben. Im Haus des Aszendenten stieg die Waage auf, was mich empfindlich stimmte und zu Übertreibungen verführte. Neptun bezog das zehnte, das Haus der Lebensmitte und verankerte mich zwischen Wunder und Täuschung. Saturn war es, der im dritten Haus in Opposition zu Jupiter mein Herkommen in Frage stellte. Wer aber schickte den Falter und erlaubte ihm und dem oberlehrerhaften Gepolter eines spätsommerlichen Donnerwetters, in mir die Lust zur mütterlicherseits versprochenen Blechtrommel zu steigern, mir das Instrument immer handlicher und begehrlicher zu machen? (*B*, 36)

> [It was in the first days of September. The sun was in the sign of Virgo. A late summer storm was approaching through the night, moving crates and furniture about in the distance. Mercury made me critical, Uranus ingenious, Venus made me believe in comfort and Mars in my ambition. Libra, rising up in the house of the ascendant, made me sensitive and given to exaggeration. Neptune moved into the tenth house, the house of middle life, establishing me in an attitude between faith in miracles and disillusionment. It was Saturn which, coming into opposition to Jupiter in the third house, cast doubt on my origins. But who sent the moth and allowed it, in the midst of a late-summer thunderstorm roaring like a high school principal, to make me fall in love with the drum my mother had promised me and develop my aptitude for it? (*TD*, 48)]

The first sentence about the sun announces the subtext *Dichtung und Wahrheit*. Goethe's description of his birth contains a fair amount of pompousness in declaring the planets as benevolent witnesses of his birth. Only the moon causes some complications; this, however, proves to be advantageous to his fellow citizens because the episode leads to a future reinforcement of training for midwives. In this way Goethe's birth alone bestows a service on mankind, let alone the benefits of his entire life. Goethe's passage contains a completely undisturbed optimism in the success and happiness of his life, a sense of confidence that is absent in Oskar. While the sky over Goethe's birth seems untroubled, Oskar's birth is accompanied by thunder. The success of Goethe's life is announced by the fact that the stellar constellation was a "propitious" one, by the "culmination" of the sun, which at the same time heralds the birth of his Apollonian spirit, as well as the benevolence of Jupiter, Venus, and Mercury, the latter being the trickster planet. The stars are not quite as benevolent for Oskar. His hope for happiness is only "small," as he will be in stature. Primarily, however, it is Saturn's influence that casts doubt on his origins, a reference to the doubtful origins of the picaro, specifically to Simplicius Simplicissimus, whose story is rooted in the saturnalia, as the cover illustration of Grimmelshausen's novel makes clear. It is ultimately also the little moth that deflates the Goethe quotation. In comparison with the high hopes for Goethe's success as an artist, Oskar's future exploits on the tin drum that he owes to the moth's appearance seem like a diminutive art. The failed political impact of Oskar's drumming echoes the apolitical nature of Goethe's own art. However similar these passages are, they contrast Goethe, a child of the day, with Oskar, who is born at night. This detail alone would align him with the dark Dionysian world of the Romantics, which Goethe had described as diseased. Yet even in the Romantics' representation of the night as a reflection of the mysteries of the human soul, we encounter variations between the tempestuous and the tranquil. As Jahnke and Lindemann have pointed out, the passage of Oskar's birth also recalls a passage from Joseph von Eichendorff's poem "Unstern," in which he describes a magnificent but deep, still, and clear winter's night, a passage that itself was modeled on Goethe.[51] Of the three passages that intertextually play with Goethe's birth scene, Oskar's birth during a tempestuous night is at the opposite end of Goethe's on a calm day and gives us an intimation of the "diseased" Romantic soul, the perturbed spirit that will accompany him through his life and ultimately lead him into the mental asylum.

The theater segment, which Goethe treats in all seriousness in his *Wilhelm Meister* novels, is deflated through the Tom Thumb performance in *Die Blechtrommel*. Krumme argues how insignificant Oskar's visit to the theater is compared to Wilhelm Meister's,[52] yet one could argue that the juxtaposition of the two performances that Oskar mentions, the story of Tom Thumb and Wagner's *Der fliegende Holländer* (The Flying Dutchman) that he hears in the summer of 1933, describes the world he lives in. He identifies with the vulnerability of the Tom Thumb figure at a time that favors gigantism and heroism. Goethe's puppet play of David against Goliath in the *Wilhelm Meister* novel forms a model for Grass's novel, which contrasts the microcosm represented by the fairy tale (David) with the macrocosm of the Third Reich and Wagnerian music (Goliath), the dwarf who journeys from a mouse hole through a snail's house into the cow's stomach versus the grand heroism expressed in Wagner's operas. Wagner's music is relevant in yet another respect. As "entseelte Innerlichkeit," pleasure rather than true art,[53] it supplants the soulful music of composers like Beethoven, a process that is echoed by Matzerath's replacing the Beethoven portrait with the one of Hitler. The theme of music in this novel, the contrast between Wagner and Beethoven, illustrates to what extent form replaced content in the perception of art during the Third Reich. Oskar, one of whose multiple roles is that of an anti-fascist, tries to subvert this worship of form by bringing the Wagner opera to an abrupt end in that he destroys the main light with one of his screams. As the Hitler portrait and Wagner's music replace Beethoven, Goethe overshadows Rasputin. Wagner and Goethe are both equated with the predominance of form.[54]

Apollo and Dionysus

Goethe and Rasputin are the two key figures in Oskar's education. The Apollonian order- and form-loving spirit of Goethe and the Dionysian chaotic, physical world of Rasputin are two inseparable realms. Most critics agree that although Oskar favors Rasputin over Goethe he never manages to free himself from the latter: "So kann es das Wörtchen Goethe sein, das mich aufschreien und ängstlich unter die Bettdecke flüchten läßt. So sehr ich auch von Jugend an den Dichterfürsten studierte, seine olympische Ruhe ist mir schon immer unheimlich gewesen." (*B*, 485; "Sometimes, for instance, it is the name 'Goethe' that sets me screaming and hiding under the bed-clothes. From childhood on I have done my best to study the poet prince and still his Olympian calm gives me the creeps": *TD*, 581). Oskar's fear of Goethe implies a fear of the forces of reason that are intolerant of his own Dionysian transgressions.[55] As Wolbert points out, the concept of man's dignity reflected in his body, which the Nazis tried to idealize in their statues, was derived from Goethe's view of man's beauty reflecting his spirit (*NT*, 13). In the context of fascism, the Classical becomes a problematic notion. How was it possible that a genuinely humane ideal could thrive within a decidedly inhumane system? And yet, while for German Classicism the individual was the focus of this worship of form, in National Socialism the *Volk* became the standard, and while Classicism implied that the perfect body was merely an ideal, in the Third Reich it became the object of a national quest. Not only did the Nazis' vision of racial supremacy taint the folk-tales, but it also forever left its mark on Classical idealism.

One must, however, be careful in mentioning Goethe along with Wagner and Nietzsche. For Nietzsche the statement that he was a precursor of Nazi ideology certainly has more validity. Especially when it comes to the destruction of undeserving life, Nietzsche quotations are readily used, a fact one might find ironic in view of his own madness at the end of his life, which would have qualified him too as a candidate for the Nazi euthanasia pro-gram.[56] As the principal instigator of body aesthetics in the nineteenth cen-tury, Nietzsche preached the superiority of body over spirit and saw the aim of humanity in the cultivation of its highest, most superior exemplars. Both he and Goethe, who also held the dignity of man in high esteem, saw in the Greek statue a reflection of the godlike in man. Due to this elevation of man to the status of God, it was easy for the Nazis to appropriate these two thinkers for their ideology. Nietzsche's philosophy was a reaction against the "Herdentier-Moral," the gregarious spirit of socialism. To the ideal of equality, which he despised, he opposed his vision of the *Übermensch* with his extreme physical beauty. According to Nietzsche it was insanity to believe that a misshapen person could have a beautiful soul (*NT,* 155). Nietzsche's *Übermensch,* a term he possibly derived from Goethe's *Faust,*[57] was an aes-thetic fiction and thus still far from its practical application, yet as Kalte-necker convincingly points out, it can hardly be denied that Nietzsche's philosophy influenced a wide readership of educated citizens and finally also contributed to the fascists' perception of man and art.[58] Nietzsche's radical aestheticism arose from his despair in view of the decline of *Bildung* in Germany. He contended that German *Bildung* could only prosper if the distinction between content and form were abolished, and this is where we see his proximity to Goethe, who was also convinced that someone's exterior was a reflection of his interior, that therefore there could not be a distinction between outside and inside, form and content, a radical aestheticism that links physical *Bildung* to mental and spiritual *Bildung.*

This nineteenth-century aestheticism is in stark contrast to Rabelais's advocacy of the grotesque. In his prologue to *Gargantua,* for example, he expresses the thought that something or somebody may have an ugly form but a divine content. Here Socrates is compared to a silenus, an antique pill box that is grotesquely shaped on the outside but contains rare drugs. Soc-rates' divine superhuman wisdom is contrasted with his ugly body, "his pointed nose, his bovine expression, and his idiotic face" (*GP,* 37). In the context of this comparison Rabelais warns against interpreting his books as "nothing but mockery, fooling, and pleasant fictions" (*GP,* 37) but wants the reader to "carefully weigh up its contents. You will discover then that the drug within is far more valuable than the box promised; that is to say, that the subjects here treated are not so foolish as the title on the cover sug-gested" (*GP,* 38). The same could indeed be said for Grass's novel, its gro-tesque protagonist who may fool the reader about the grave content of the book, and its historical subtext. The nineteenth-century quest of what Georg Lukács, no doubt thinking of the Greek statues, called totality, evokes Goethe's vision of the *schöne Seele,* the beautiful soul. This quest of totality implies the healing of the rupture between spirit and nature, between the soul and the body, the self and the world — that eternal dilemma of modern man.[59] While this quest was still a concern of modernism, postmodernism has finally given up any attempt to regain the totality of what Schiller called the naive man and has accepted the fragmentary nature of sentimental man, in whom the Apollonian (reason) and the Dionysian (body) are forever separated. Oskar's ultimate withdrawal into an insane asylum confirms the absurdity of his attempt to unite the two within himself.

If we view modernism versus postmodernism from a generic point of view, it becomes clear that the Bildungsroman was an artistic form that aimed at regaining the totality of the blissful times that Lukács and Goethe saw in Greek antiquity, in which man was still at harmony with himself within society.[60] Like Goethe and Nietzsche, Lukács dreamed of a time in which man was not yet torn between inside and outside, between his subjectivity and the objectivity of the surrounding world, a unity between the self and the world, which corresponds to Hegel's dictum for the Bildungsroman's teleology as a reflection of this search of totality, that its hero give up the poetry of his heart for the prose of external conditions. Yet for this very reason, that the hero has to give up the poetry of his heart, the Bildungsroman does not truly achieve this unity between the self and the world, a fact that explains why Lukács sees modern man's loneliness — which he calls "transzendentale Obdachlosigkeit" (transcendental homelessness) — reflected in the novel.[61] This notion of man's homelessness in the modern world takes us back to our discussion of the persecution of transients, thieves, and the insane, for "crime and madness are objectivations of transcendental homelessness — the homelessness of an action in the human order of social relations, the homelessness of a soul in the ideal order of a supra-personal system of values."[62] While the Bildungsromane of German Classicism and poetic realism are artistic attempts to liberate man from his homelessness through social integration — and as such are far removed from the social reality that does not become adequately represented through literature until the period of Naturalism —, the Nazis tried to achieve this teleology through violence, by ridding society of its homeless wanderers, the Jews, the Gypsies, and other transients. Integration at the artistic level becomes elimination at the political level, and yet, as we have seen, in some Bildungsromane of bourgeois realism, especially those with an anti-Semitic bent, we can already observe the seed for the Nazis' all-encompassing attempt at elimination. At the end of these novels, only the bourgeois individual is rewarded, due to his successful attempt at social integration, while sexual promiscuity, aimless wandering, and cosmopolitanism are punished. Nationalism seems to be incompatible with cosmopolitanism, for, as Julia Kristeva has pointed out, "how can one reconcile the dignity of a nation-state in the process of expansion with the diversity of the world and the universalism of the philosophy that stems from it?"[63] Nationalism emerged from that bourgeois order that had initially established itself in the city,

Foucault's "moral city of which the bourgeois conscience began to dream in the seventeenth century" (*MC*, 61). The law of the *polis* is at the root of the law of the state and is opposed to the idea of cosmopolitanism, which knows no confinement, no borders. At the end of Grimmelshausen's novel, we see Simplicius traveling obsessively in search of a meaningful society. He journeys to the center of the Earth, roams through the German forests, visits the Anabaptists in Hungary, takes an amusing little trip to Moscow, and finally withdraws from society altogether. The picaro's aimless wandering becomes an emblem for this genre's acceptance that man's totality exists only as he is born but is then in the course of his life shattered and cannot be reconstituted. While the Bildungsroman and Nazism were modernist attempts to undo this loss of totality, the picaresque novel, due to its recognition of the fragmentary status of man, is rediscovered for postmodernism, hence its rise in German culture after 1945.

In the words of Donahue, who in echoing Frizen draws a line from Goethe's *Faust* (1808/1832) to the Nazis, "Grass indicates that any teleological goal is unachievable because it is literally unreal and that striving for one may be cataclysmic in its destructiveness,"[64] because:

> in attempting to achieve abstract goals, truly human concerns and suffering are forgotten. Intolerance and an uncaring attitude are the result. In Goethe's *Faust,* both with the death of Gretchen and the deaths of Philemon and Baucis at the end of Part II, we sense the essential destructiveness of the striving individual. Grass illustrates in *Die Blechtrommel* that when this attitude becomes societal, when an entire society attempts to believe in the *Weihnachtsmann,* that is, an ideal, mythic character who offers salvation, the resulting destruction is apocalyptic. Goethe becomes the embodiment of Faustian striving but also of teleological ideologies and systems which attempt to perfect or purify society — to rid it of its unnatural elements.[65]

That Grass's novel displays an acceptance of the loss of harmony between man and his world as well as the inseparability and consequent discord between the rational, Apollonian, Goethean side and the irrational, Dionysian, Rasputinian side in man demonstrates how postmodern it is. As Oskar is haunted by Goethe and Rasputin, Nazism itself reflects the inseparability of these two realms as it is not only aligned with the rational, order-seeking Goethe, but also contains the completely irrational. In Nazism the Apollonian, extreme order and the glorification of beauty, goes hand in hand with the Dionysian, the excessive destruction of individuality, whether its drowning within the masses or literally through killing millions of individuals. Enlightenment taken to an extreme leads to tragedy. According to Foucault, extreme reason becomes unreason, *reason dazzled,* blindness, which is a thought that he shares with Georges Bataille, who argues that the

Icarus flight of Enlightenment results in Icarus's blindness because he gets too close to the sun (*MC*, 108). Tom Nairn contends "that the generic code of *all* nationalisms is simultaneously inscribed by the contradictory signals of what he calls 'health' and 'morbidity': 'forms of irrationality.'"[66] What we see best at work in National Socialism is the paradox of its nationalism, which is in a Hegelian sense forward-looking in its purely rational teleology of ever-expanding national development but at the same time regressive "by looking inwards, drawing more deeply upon [its] indigenous resources, resurrecting past folk-heroes and myths about themselves and so on."[67] Consequently, the humanity that Grass envisions in the Romantic Age is also tarnished in that Nazism contains elements of both Classicism and Romanticism. Grass's appropriation of the German fairy-tale tradition in order to reveal a connection between German Classicism and Nazism, and to portray Goethe as "one of the faces of a cosmic evil"[68] becomes problematic not only in light of Goethe's humanitarian spirit but also if one takes into consideration that the Romantic tradition with its folk-tales was itself appropriated by all sorts of nationalists. Romanticism's tolerance of physical and mental aberrations and vagrancy vis à vis its flirtation with nationalist ideology, which as we said is incompatible with cosmopolitanism, is as contradictory as Classicism's bourgeois narrow-mindedness and Goethe's intolerance of the grotesque vis à vis his universalism and cosmopolitanism, his advocacy of a *Weltliteratur*, a world literature, for example.[69] The discussion as to whether Goethe and the Grimm Brothers were inherently nationalist and advocated the superiority of the Germans remains to this day controversial.[70] No doubt, Goethe is an ambivalent figure along the road to Nazi politics. The fact remains that Grass writes against Goethean philosophy, primarily against the telos of the Classical Bildungsroman. He grounds his novel in the picaresque tradition of the baroque age and the Romantic fairy-tale tradition, both of which tolerate aimless wandering, unlike the Bildungsroman, that genre representative of the politics of social integration.

Notes

[1] Michel Tournier, *The Ogre* (Baltimore: Johns Hopkins UP, 1997), 31.

[2] Michael Zimmermann, *Rassenutopie und Genozid: Die nationalsozialistische "Lösung der Zigeunerfrage"* (Hamburg: Christians, 1996), 51.

[3] Cf. Wilhelm Raabe, *Der Hungerpastor* (Göttingen: Vandenhoeck & Ruprecht, 1966), 48. This becomes discernible, for example, in Raabe's thrift-store owner. The narrator argues that mothers were afraid of letting their kids close to Freudenstein's basement shop and warned them that innocent Christian children would be chopped into sausages. The motif occurs in other literature as well: the Jewish merchant in Charles Dickens's *David Copperfield,* who wants to eat David's lungs and liver, as well as the figure of Fagin in Dickens's *Oliver Twist,* who kidnaps young boys and makes thieves out of them.

[4] Tournier, *The Ogre,* 276.

[5] Michael Baigent and Richard Leigh, *Secret Germany: Stauffenberg and the Mystical Crusade against Hitler* (London: Penguin, 1994), 210.

[6] Hegel's discussion of the age of *Sittlichkeit* (ethics) in the *Phenomenology of Spirit* is a reflection of the endeavor of the rising bourgeoisie and its nationalism to regain that harmony between the individual and society that, it was believed, existed in Greek antiquity. Cf. Georg Wilhelm Friedrich Hegel, Phänomenoligie des Geistes (Frankfurt am Main: Suhrkamp, 1970), 324–54.

[7] Ernst Klee, ed., *"Euthanasie" im NS-Staat: Die "Vernichtung unwerten Lebens"* (Frankfurt am Main: Fischer, 1989), 30: "[Die Landstreicher] kämpfen nicht im Kampf des Daseins, sondern reagieren mit schwächlichem Selbstmitleid. Gegenüber Menschen, denen es besser geht, hegen sie bitteren Groll, und alles Höhere und Ideale, alles, was über das Gemeine hinausragt, bedenken sie mit Spott und Hohn." (Vagrants do not fight for daily survival but react through weak self-pity. They are full of hatred for people who are better off, full of scorn for all ideals, for everything that transcends the common.)

[8] Jeffrey Herf, *Reactionary Modernism: Technology, Culture, and Politics in Weimar and the Third Reich* (Cambridge: Cambridge UP, 1984), 130–51. Sombart links Jewish wandering to a pernicious capitalism, which in the long run would make the Jews masters of the world. Their rootless mentality he saw as an alien and destructive element for the rooted, soil-loving German people.

[9] Klee, *"Euthanasie,"* 31: "Unsere Wanderfürsorgeanstalten leiden unter der Masse der wander- und arbeitsunfähigen sowie der arbeitsscheuen vagabondierenden Wanderer. Diese Masse lastet wie ein Ballast auf unseren Wanderfürsorgeanstalten. Erst wenn wir diese Masse los sind, werden wir die arbeitsfähigen und ordentlichen Wanderer mit wirklicher Hilfe erfassen können." (Our institutions that assist wanderers are suffering from the multitude of wanderers who are unable or unwilling to work. This multitude is a major burden for these institutions. Not until we have got rid of these people can we really assist those proper wanderers who are able to work.)

[10] Klee, *"Euthanasie,"* 39: "die Wandertypen, die wir ablehnen müssen: Der berufs-mäßige Bettler, der krankhafte Wanderer und der notorische Trinker. Diese haben kein Recht auf Wanderschaft." Ultimately, these people were to be treated by "Maß-

nahmen von medizinischer Seite aus . . ., die diese Leute für das Volk unschädlich machen." (medical treatment that would render such people harmless to society.) [11] Klee, *"Euthanasie,"* 40.

[12] Klee, *"Euthanasie,"* 63: Professor Franz Exner pointed out that vagrants are "wandernde Bazillenherde, vor deren moralischer Ansteckung unser Volk geschützt werden muß." (wandering germ carriers against whose moral contagion our society has to be protected.)

[13] Klee, *"Euthanasie,"* 65.

[14] Klee, *"Euthanasie,"* 66.

[15] Ulrike Schulz, *Gene mene muh raus mußt du: Eugenik von der Rassenhygiene zu den Gen- und Reproduktionstechnologien* (Munich: AG SPAK, 1992), 60.

[16] Mikhail Bakhtin, *The Dialogic Imagination: Four Essays by M. M. Bakhtin,* ed., Caryl Emerson and Michael Holquist (Austin: U of Texas P, 1981), 159.

[17] Cf. Claudio Guillén, "Toward a Definition of the Picaresque," in *Literature as System* (Princeton: Princeton UP, 1971), 18, "als ein in Spanien während der zweiten Hälfte des 16. Jahrhunderts entstandener Romantypus, der meist in autobiographischer Erzählform die Lebensgeschichte eines bindungslosen, vagabundierenden Außenseiters schildert, der sich in einer locker gefügten Folge von Episoden mit Gewitztheit und moralisch nicht unbedenklichen Mitteln gegen eine feindliche und korrupte Welt behauptet, wobei von dieser Welt ein satirisch gezeichnetes Panorama entworfen wird. Der Bildungsroman dagegen wäre zu bestimmen als eine im letzten Drittel des 18. Jahrhunderts entstandene und vor allem in Deutschland florierende Form, die mit psychologisch-moralischem Interesse den Werdegang einer zentralen Figur erzählt, der über Irrtümer und Krisen und durch die produktive Verarbeitung von Welterfahrung zur Selbstfindung und zur tätigen Integration in die Gesellschaft führt." (a type of novel that arose in Spain during the second half of the sixteenth century. Written mostly in autobiographical form it describes the life of a vagabond and social outsider. In a loosely structured sequence of episodes he is seen to assert himself against a hostile and corrupt environment by using his wit as well as morally questionable means. The world in which he lives is portrayed satirically. On the other hand, the Bildungsroman arose in the last third of the eighteenth century and flourished primarily in Germany. It is a type of novel that describes the psychological and ethical development of the protagonist, who after many mistakes and crises ultimately finds himself thanks to a deeper understanding of his experiences, and he succeeds in becoming integrated into society.)

[18] A type of short comical narrative from the late Middle Ages. It contained pranks and was greatly influenced by the lyrics of Neidhart von Reuental (c. 1180–c. 1245), who parodied the *Minnesang* (courtly songs) by giving it a peasant background.

[19] Paul Radin, *The Trickster: A Study in American Indian Mythology* (New York: Schocken Books, 1972), xxiii.

[20] Wilhelm Emrich, *Deutsche Literatur der Barockzeit* (Königstein: Athenäum, 1981), 229.

[21] Gerhardt Hoffmeister, ed., *Der moderne deutsche Schelmenroman: Interpretationen* (Amsterdam: Rodopi, 1985/86), 3: "gegenüber der verwalteten Welt mit ihrem Konformismus und ihrer Rubrizierungstendenz behauptet er [der Schelm] seine

derb-drastische Art in Lebensweise und Erzählstil. Seine Bindungslosigkeit in Liebes-
dingen, sein Berufs- und Ortswechsel entsprechen dem Freiheitsdrang des kosmopo-
litischen Helden. Proteusartig schlüpft er häufig in eine andere Haut, aus 'Freude am
theatralischen Spiel' (Van der Will), aber auch aus dem barocken und wiederum
modernen Bewußtsein: 'Alle Menschen sind Schauspieler in dem Sinne, daß sie
Masken tragen und Betrüger sind' (Camus)." (The picaro asserts his radical way of
life and style of narration vis à vis the bureaucratic world with its conformism and
tendency to categorize. His promiscuity and constant change of profession and place
of residence reflect the cosmopolitan hero's urge for freedom. Like Proteus, he
frequently slips into another skin because he enjoys theater [Van der Will], but also
because of his baroque and at the same time modern understanding that "all men are
actors and con-artists wearing masks" [Camus].)

[22] Mikhail Bakhtin, "The *Bildungsroman* and Its Significance in the History of Realism (Toward a Historical Typology of the Novel)," in *Speech Genres and Other Late
Essays*, ed., Caryl Emerson and Michael Holquist (Austin: U of Texas P, 1986), 10.

[23] Bakhtin, The *Bildungsroman*, 20.

[24] Claudio Guillén, "Toward a Definition of the Picaresque," 13, "Die Welt, durch die
sich der Pikaro bewegt, ist korrupt und zwingt dem einzelnen ihre Schlechtigkeit auf.
Das Gute hat in ihr . . . keine Stelle. . . . In einer solchen Welt herrschen Bosheit und
Gaunerei." (The world through which the picaro moves is corrupt and forces its evil
upon the individual. Good has no place in such a world ruled by evil and corruption.)

[25] Emrich, *Deutsche Literatur der Barockzeit*, 241.

[26] Cf. also Volker Neuhaus, *Günter Grass: Die Blechtrommel* (Munich: Oldenbourg,
1982), 35: "Wenn das Ich einerseits in seiner geistigen Entwicklung schon bei der
Geburt abgeschlossen ist und andererseits kein anderes Ziel hat, als, Distanz" von der
Welt zu halten, kommt es genau wie im Pikaroroman nicht zu einer fruchtbaren
Auseinandersetzung zwischen Ich und Welt, die das Wesen des Bildungsromans
ausmacht. . . . Durch die Blechtrommel wird Oskars Autobiographie zum Künstler-
roman, sein Instrument bezeichnet die Nahtstelle zwischen Pikarobiographie und
Künstlerbiographie." (If the self is in its mental development already complete at
birth and has no other aim than to keep its distance from the world, then as in the
picaresque novel there will not be a successful confrontation between the self and the
world, a conflict that is essential to the Bildungsroman. . . . The tin drum makes
Oskar's autobiography a novel about an emerging artist, his instrument signifies the
seam between the biography of a picaro and that of an artist.)

[27] Cf. Gerhard Mayer, "Zum deutschen Antibildungsroman," in *Jahrbuch der Raabe-
Gesellschaft* (Braunschweig, Germany, 1974), 55–64.

[28] Bakhtin, The *Bildungsroman*, 23.

[29] Volker Meid, *Grimmelshausen: Epoche, Werk, Wirkung* (München: Beck, 1984),
238–39: "echte Gemeinschaft im Soldatenleben" (true camaraderie), "Herold
deutschen Volkstums am Oberrhein" (harbinger of German folkishness on the Upper
Rhine), "jahrhundertealte Sehnsucht nach Befreiung und Führung" (a centuries-old
yearning for liberation and leadership).

[30] Hermann Eris Busse, *Grimmelshausen* (Stuttgart 1939), quoted in Meid, 242:
"Lebensbeherrschung durch die Einsatzbereitschaft für alles Lebensmögliche, Aufrü-

stung des Geistes und der selbstbewußten Persönlichkeit: So wendet sich das Leben Grimmelshausens beispielhaft als ein im Grunde heldisches Leben und heldisches Verlangen an unsere Zeit." (control of one's life through one's readiness to engage in life's many possibilities, fortification of the spirit and of the self-confident personality: in this way, Grimmelshausen's heroic life and heroic ambitions address our present age in an exemplary way.)

[31] Meid, *Grimmelshausen: Epoche, Werk, Wirkung*, 106.

[32] Thomas Mann, *Confessions of Felix Krull: Confidence Man*, trans. Denver Lindley (New York: Alfred A. Knopf, 1955), 269: Felix as Hermes, "the golden mean of human stature . . . the god in human form" is the very opposite of Oskar.

[33] Anne Leblans, "Grimmelshausen and the Carnivalesque: The Polarization of Courtly and Popular Carnival in *Der abenteuerliche Simplicissimus*," in *Modern Language Notes* 105/3 (April 1990): 500.

[34] Cf. C.G. Jung, *Psychology and Alchemy* (Princeton: Princeton UP, 1968), 344.

[35] Meid, *Grimmelshausen: Epoche, Werk, Wirkung*, 119.

[36] Cf. for example, Gerhard Köttgen, *Wilhelm Raabes Ringen um die Aufgabe des Erziehungsromans* (Berlin: Verlag Dr. Emil Ebering, 1939).

[37] Köttgen, *Wilhelm Raabes Ringen*, 82: "Es wäre ungeschichtlich gedacht, Raabe zum ausgesprochenen Judenfeind zu stempeln; aber so viel sagen wir, daß er . . . in Hans die deutsche und im Juden die gegendeutsche Natur sah, und daß er mit dieser natürlichen Betrachtungsweise unserem heutigen Empfinden näher steht als mancher andere, der nur jüdische Zerrbilder lieferte."

[38] Jeffrey L. Sammons, *The Shifting Fortunes of Wilhelm Raabe: A History of Criticism as a Cautionary Tale* (Columbia SC: Camden House, 1992), 35.

[39] Sammons, *Shifting Fortunes*, 38.

[40] Horst Denkler, "Das 'wirckliche Juda' und der 'Renegat': Moses Freudenstein als Kronzeuge für Wilhelm Raabes Verhältnis zu Juden und Judentum," in *The German Quarterly* 60.1 (Winter 1987): 5–18.

[41] Wolfgang Höppner, "'Der Kampf um das neue Goethe-Bild.' Zur Goethe-Rezeption in der Berliner Germanistik des Dritten Reiches," in *Goethe: Vorgaben: Zugänge: Wirkungen*, ed. Wolfgang Stellmacher and László Tarnói (Frankfurt am Main: Peter Lang, 2000), 373–90.

[42] Höppner, "Kampf um das neue Goethe-Bild," 379.

[43] Höppner, "Kampf um das neue Goethe-Bild," 379.

[44] Höppner, "Kampf um das neue Goethe-Bild," 383.

[45] Arno Schmidt, *Das steinerne Herz* (Zürich: Haffmans, 1986), 84: "[d]as Fließband seiner Scheißverse: da karrt der Schüdderump voll abgemurkster Idyllen, im immer gleichen grobschlächtigen Pumpertakt: pfui Deubel, der Bube!" (the conveyor belt of his shit verses: there goes the corpses' cart full of killed idylls, in coarse and ever-monotonous beat: yuk, the devil!)

[46] Jörg Petzel, "E.T.A. Hoffmann und Arno Schmidt," in *Mitteilungen der E.T.A. Hoffmann Gesellschaft* 26 (1980): 89.

[47] Grass himself acknowledged this in an interview. Cf. Günter Grass and Harro Zimmermann, *Vom Abenteuer der Aufklärung: Werkstattgespräche* (Göttingen: Steidl, 1999), 53–54: "Aber für mich war 'Die Blechtrommel' auch eine spöttisch-spielerische Auseinandersetzung mit dem, was man in Deutschland 'Entwicklungsroman' nennt." (But for me 'Die Blechtrommel' was also a playful parody of what in Germany is called the 'novel of development'). Cf. also Helmut Koopmann in Gerhardt Hoffmeister, ed., *Der moderne deutsche Schelmenroman*, 37: "Pikarisches Erzählen ist im Prinzip . . . überall dort möglich, wo ein Roman gegen den Bildungsroman Goethes angeschrieben worden ist." (The picaresque style of narration is possible wherever a novel is written against the grain of Goethe's Bildungsroman.)

[48] On the phenomenon of Goethe in *Die Blechtrommel* see also: Bruce Donahue, "The Alternative to Goethe: Markus and Fajngold in 'Die Blechtrommel,'" in *The Germanic Review* 58, 3 (1983): 115–20; Frank-Raymund Richter, *Günter Grass: Die Vergangenheitsbewältigung in der Danzig-Trilogie* (Bonn: Bouvier, 1979), esp. 95–97; Walter Jahnke and Klaus Lindemann, *Günter Grass: Die Blechtrommel* (Paderborn, München, Wien, Zürich: Schöningh, 1993), 41–49; and Detlef Krumme, *Günter Grass: Die Blechtrommel* (München: Hanser, 1986), 71–74.

[49] Johann Wolfgang Goethe, *Dichtung und Wahrheit* 1 (Frankfurt am Main: Insel, 1975), 15.

[50] Johann Wolfgang Goethe, *The Auto-Biography of Goethe: Truth and Poetry: From My Own Life*, trans. John Oxenford (London: Bell & Daldy, 1867), 1.

[51] Jahnke and Lindemann, *Günter Grass: Die Blechtrommel*, 41.

[52] Krumme, *Günter Grass: Die Blechtrommel*, 73.

[53] Richter, *Günter Grass: Die Vergangenheitsbewältigung*, 98.

[54] Richter, *Günter Grass: Die Vergangenheitsbewältigung*, 97: "Nun bedeutet zwar die Klassik nicht reine Form, aber doch Dominanz der Form." (Although Classicism does not mean pure form, it shows a predominance of form.)

[55] Friedrich Nietzsche, *The Birth of Tragedy and Other Writings*, ed. Raymond Geuss and Ronald Speirs (Cambridge: Cambridge UP, 1999), xi: while the "Apolline artist glorifies individuality by presenting attractive images of individual persons, things, and events . . . the Dionysiac is the drive towards the transgression of limits, the dissolution of boundaries, the destruction of individuality, and excess."

[56] In the chapter on suicide ("Vom freien Tode") in *Also sprach Zarathustra* (Thus spake Zarathustra, 1883–85), for example, we find the following passage, quoted in Klee, *"Euthanasie,"* 17: "Mancher wird nie süß, er fault im Sommer schon. Feigheit ist es, die ihn an seinem Aste festhält. Viel zu viele leben und viel zu lange hängen sie an ihren Ästen. Möchte ein Sturm kommen, der all dies Faule und Wurmfreßne vom Baume schüttelt! Möchten Prediger kommen des *schnellen* Todes! Das wären mir die rechten Stürme und Schüttler an Lebensbäumen! Aber ich höre nur den langsamen Tod predigen und Geduld mit allem 'Irdischen.'" (Some people never get ripe, they already rot in the summer. Cowardice keeps them on their branches. Too many live and too many hang from their branches. Let there be a storm that shakes all these lazy and rotten ones from their trees! Let there be preachers of the quick death! Those would be my preferred storms and shakers of the life trees! But I only hear the preachers of the slow death, of patience with everything terrestrial.)

[57] See Hans Erhard Gerber, *Nietzsche und Goethe: Studien zu einem Vergleich* (Bern: Paul Haupt, 1970), 99.

[58] Siegfried Kaltenecker, "Weil aber die vergessenste Fremde unser Körper ist: Über Männer-Körper Repräsentationen und Faschismus," in Marie-Luise Angerer, ed., *The Body of Gender, Körper, Geschlechter, Identitäten* (Wien: Passagen, 1995), 159: "dass in seinem Werk Gedanken zusammengefasst wurden, die aus der hoffärtigen Distanzierung gegenüber dem Sozialismus erst ihre radikale Form erhielten, dass diese inhumanen Gedanken als Gemeingut elitärer Bildungszirkel sich ausbreiteten und schließlich auch zum Bewusstsein der Faschisten über Mensch und Kunst beitrugen." (that his work summarizes thoughts that receive their radical form from his arrogance towards socialism, that these inhumane thoughts spread throughout the elite educated classes, and finally contributed to the fascists' understanding of man and art.)

[59] Georg Lukács, *Theorie des Romans* (Neuwied am Rhein: Luchterhand, 1963), 28: "Totalität des Seins ist nur möglich, . . . wo die Schönheit den Weltsinn sichtbar macht." (The totality of all essence is only possible where beauty illustrates the meaning of the world.)

[60] Lukács, *Theorie des Romans*, 22: "Selig sind die Zeiten . . ." (Blissful are the times . . .).

[61] Lukács, *Theorie des Romans*, 35.

[62] Georg Lukács, *Theory of the Novel*, trans. by Anna Bostock (Cambridge, MA: M.I.T. Press, 1971), 61–62.

[63] Julia Kristeva, *Strangers to Ourselves* (New York: Columbia UP 1991), 124.

[64] Donahue, "The Alternative to Goethe," 115.

[65] Donahue, "The Alternative to Goethe," 117–18.

[66] Quoted by Leela Gandhi, *Postcolonial Theory: A Critical Introduction* (New York: Columbia UP, 1998), 106.

[67] Tom Nairn, *The Break-Up of Britain: Crisis and Neo-Nationalism* (London: New Left Books, 1977), 348.

[68] Donahue, "The Alternative to Goethe," 117.

[69] Kristeva, *Strangers to Ourselves*, 180.

[70] Baigent and Leigh, *Secret Germany*, (208) have argued, for example, that "if Herder accorded no intrinsic superiority to the German folk soul, other people could — and the War of Liberation offered grounds on which to do so. Herder was dead by that time, and in no position to object when his conception was appropriated and conscripted on behalf of nationalism, chauvinism and a xenophobia hostile to anything foreign. When it was yoked to these things, the conception of the folk soul provided a seemingly respectable philosophical foundation for theories of racial supremacy. Goethe's ideas were vulnerable in the same way. Despite his insistence on the universality of culture, he himself could be cited as proof of the supremacy of Germanic culture. With the nationalistic self-confidence engendered by the War of Liberation, Germanic culture, as a manifestation of the Germanic folk soul, was soon being trumpeted as superior to others. And if, as Goethe maintained, the Germans were a people uniquely qualified to reflect or represent culture and the spirit, that too constituted a claim to superiority."

Epilogue: Beyond *Die Blechtrommel*: Germans as Victims in *Im Krebsgang*

THIS STUDY HAS focused on the victims of Nazi biopolitics, primarily the physically and mentally disabled targeted by the euthanasia program. In a discussion of Oskar Matzerath as a folklore dwarf and of fairy tale motifs as a vehicle for historical representation, it ought to be pointed out that Oskar is a hunchback dwarf also in the Benjaminian sense. Walter Benjamin (1892–1940) used this metaphor of the little hunchback (*das bucklicht Männlein*) throughout his work. Hannah Arendt even suggested that Benjamin's whole life could be placed under the sign of the hunchback dwarf. She contends that just before his death Benjamin stated that the little hunchback had terrified him in his early childhood and then accompanied him all through his life.[1] Benjamin was familiar with this fairy tale figure from *Des Knaben Wunderhorn* (1805–8), the famous anthology of German folk poems collected by Achim von Arnim (1781–1831) and Clemens Brentano (1778–1842), particularly from Brentano's folk rhyme "Liebes Kindlein, ach ich bitt, Bet fürs bucklicht Männlein mit" (O dear child, I beg of you, pray for the little hunchback too). In his fascinating study of Benjamin's hunchback Irving Wohlfahrt argues that Brentano's "plea for inclusion implicitly becomes that of all the excluded."[2] Yet Benjamin was thinking primarily of the plight of Jews under German fascism when he wrote of the hunchback, a figure that has all the characteristics of the trickster discussed in chapter 5 of this study. Benjamin's hunchback too creates disorder, he upsets the order of bourgeois society, and tries to resist or even subvert the tyranny of ideology. He defends the positions of both Jews and Socialists, their perspective from below, in opposition to a perspective from above, like that of the German eagle of nationalism or Goethe. Wohlfahrt's argument thus supports what I have said about the relationship between Oskar and Goethe, since in Benjamin's writing, being at the base of the German-Jewish Parnassus, not at the peak of the *Dichter und Denker,* the hunchback is likewise a direct opposite of Goethe.[3] As a hunchback in the Benjaminian sense the deformed Oskar, although not Jewish, ultimately has the function of reminding us of the six million Jews murdered in the Holocaust. The Jewish victims cannot be excluded from this study's discussion of Oskar's metaphoric and mythic implications. Oskar is emblematic for all those excluded by Nazi racist thinking and as a hunchback he therefore also carries the burden of the Holocaust upon his shoulders. He is a constant reminder of the disastrous results of organized state racism.

Die Blechtrommel is not the only work in which Grass conflates historical disasters with myth and folk culture. In much of his later work his use of fairy tale material reflects his increasing sense of doom about the possibility of German reunification and the idea of historical progress. In *Der Butt* (The Flounder, 1977), for example, Grass revisits Phillip Otto Runge's (1777– 1810) tale *Von dem Fischer und syner Fru* (The Fisherman and his Wife) about a woman's greed by arguing that it was the greed of men that led to the catastrophes of the twentieth century. Here the Faustian quest of the Nordic man that the Nazis read into the German folktales leads toward the Holocaust as the climax of modernity before the decline of mankind. In *Die Rättin* (The Rat, 1986) then, Grass develops a link between Nazi Germany and the legend of "The Pied Piper of Hamelin," with Hitler as the seductive flute player who takes rats (Jews) and children (the Germans) to their doom. In this novel the pessimism is even more pronounced. It harks back to the Nazis' perversion of folklore, primarily through the motif of the German fairy-tale forest, a chief emblem for national identity during the Third Reich, and which is now in danger of disappearing due to Germany's ecological crisis. In *Die Rättin,* not only are the German forest and German national identity about to vanish, but the fairy tales themselves are. The end of the fairy tale announces the end of mankind.

The image of the legendary Pied Piper of Hamelin, a version of the Erlking myth, occurs both in *Die Blechtrommel* and *Die Rättin.* The latter reflects Grass's habit of making characters from previous novels reappear in later ones. The narrator reminds his readers of Oskar Matzerath's duality of victim and perpetrator. Oskar has to take refuge in order not to be abducted, but at the same time he is also a seducer like Adolf Hitler, whom Grass aligns with the Pied Piper myth. It is obvious that this legend is ideal mythological material for alluding to the abduction and deportation of disabled children and Jews, their being piped out of town, and their subsequent elimination. Grass's reminder in his later novel that Oskar Matzerath like some harried rodent has sought a refuge all his life refers to the Nazis' view of him as undeserving life, even when it occurred to him to pose as a piper,[4] that is, despite his usefulness as an entertainer at the front. Oskar not only pipes for the Nazis, he also poses as a Pied Piper himself in *Die Blechtrommel* (*B,* 444). After the war he drums up a procession of remorseful Germans and leads them from the Onion Cellar to the Devil's Gulch, where they try to regain their innocence by wetting their pants like infants. This inversion of Oskar's position from nearly abducted child to an Erlking figure who abducts Germany's innocent "children" exploits the dual nature of mythological figures like the Italian harlequin and Benjamin's hunchback, who are both threatened and a threat. At the same time, these lines are a highly ironic statement on the professions of innocence so ubiquitous in Germany right after the war.

The motif of the Pied Piper's seduction through music refers not only to children in *Die Rättin,* but to the popular theory after the war of Hitler's seduction of the Germans. Hitler is both *Führer* and *Verführer.* Of particular interest is the duality this theory expresses of the German *Volk* emerging, like Oskar, from the Nazi years as both victim and perpetrator. In much of his work Grass insists on the Germans' collective guilt. While in *Die Blechtrommel* and *Die Rättin* we see him adopt an ironic stance towards any theory that may imply that the Germans were also victims of National Socialism, Grass's most recent work, *Im Krebsgang* (Crabwalk, 2002), distances itself from this one-sided view. Although *Die Blechtrommel* is indeed a story about German victims, as this study has shown, it is not until *Im Krebsgang* that Grass ventures to write about a theme that has been taboo since 1945: the suffering of ordinary Germans during and after the war. While in most of his earlier writing Grass used Auschwitz and the Nazi atrocities as a formula to warn against nationalism and reunification, his interest in the topic of ordinary Germans as victims of the cruelty of the Allied Forces seems at first glance to counteract his insistence on Germany's position as the perpetrator and the notion of collective guilt. Yet it becomes clear that Grass's new stance is ultimately also in the interest of fighting racism and neo-Nazism in contemporary Germany, and therefore supports his earlier warnings to remember Auschwitz. Grass understands that the suppression of any aspect of this fateful chapter in German history may ultimately have pernicious consequences. Suppress the memory of the Holocaust victims, and nationalism and neo-Nazism may easily rise again, but if you suppress the memory and mourning of German victims, the same might happen, as *Im Krebsgang* makes abundantly clear.

The narrator in this novel is Paul Pokriefke, an undistinguished journalist born on the sinking *Wilhelm Gustloff,* which at the height of Nazi power functioned as a *Kraft durch Freude* cruise ship, and at the end of the war was transformed into a hospital ship. The Russians torpedoed it as they were moving into Poland. In what was the worst naval disaster in history, close to nine thousand civilians died, most of them women and children. While the narrator Paul defects to West Germany just before the wall goes up, his mother Tulla Pokriefke settles in Schwerin, the hometown of the Swiss politician and Nazi supporter Wilhelm Gustloff. Tulla is a character with whom Grass's readers are familiar from the other two volumes of his Danzig trilogy, *Katz und Maus* (Cat and Mouse, 1961) and *Die Hundejahre* (The Dog Years, 1963). Haunted by her memory of the sinking ship, she persistently exhorts her son Paul to tell this other story of the German past, one in which the Germans were the victims, not the perpetrators. But Paul does not want to hear about the past. When the wall comes down, his son Konrad at last meets his grandmother, who keeps telling him of the sinking of the ship. Having become obsessed with the story of the *Wilhelm Gustloff,* Konrad writes a paper about it for school, but his teachers ban him from reading it because of its pro-fascist content. As a consequence of their attempt to silence him, he withdraws to the Internet where he creates a neo-Nazi Web site devoted to the tragedy of the *Gustloff* and defending the cause of innocent Germans as victims of Allied cruelty. In the chat room of his Web site Konrad engages in an ideological duel with someone who challenges him under the name of "David," a reference to David Frankfurter, a Jewish refugee who assassinated Wilhelm Gustloff in 1936. As the narration of the tragic sinking of the *Wilhelm Gustloff* reaches its climax, on a second narrative level the controversy between Konrad and David culminates in Konrad's killing the purported Jew. In an ironic twist meant to reveal the futility of racism it turns out that David's real name was Wolfgang Stremplin and that he was not Jewish.

This study's discussion of *Die Blechtrommel* has made clear how racial thinking and racism are inseparable from a set of paradigms of identity formation. These paradigms are 1) class, the connection between subhumans and the lower classes in Nazi biopolitics, 2) the body, the persecution of disabled bodies and minds, 3) gender, and 4) way of life. Racial states are always sexist states in that they practice coercive control over women's bodies. Agnes and Greff are good examples for the ways in which overly patriarchal societies treat women and homosexual men, for how their sexuality is policed and how they try to elude such control, either through promiscuity (Agnes), or assimilation (Greff), and ultimately through their suicide. Racist societies like Nazi Germany are patriarchal and view themselves as rational as opposed to the purported irrationality of women. In such societies the female body is ultimately seen as grotesque in the Bakhtinian sense, as unfinished and needy, like the body of a physically disabled person. Such societies tend to try and discipline the body into the classical body, a war that is also carried out on the female body, which is expected to bear racially pure offspring.

Even the choice of a way of life, sedentary or nomadic, becomes a racial marker in such societies, if one thinks of the Nazis' persecution of Gypsies and other vagrants whom they saw as a threat to the health of the *Volkskörper*. Nomadism is the thorn in the side of state construction. As Zygmunt Bauman has pointed out, the likes of Ghengis Khan came to be discredited by our modern society, whose rationalism paved the way "for the practitioners of cool, thorough and systematic genocide."[5] Ultimately, the Nazis' racist ideology came to an end through its own destructiveness, in sacrificing the German *Volk*. In his lectures delivered at the Collège de France from 1975 to 1976, Michel Foucault pointed out that the destruction of other races was only one aspect of the Nazi project, "the other being to expose its own race to the absolute and universal threat of death. Risking one's own life, being exposed to total destruction, was one of the principles inscribed in the basic duties of the obedient Nazi, and it was one of the essential objectives of Nazism's policies (the so-called *Kadavergehorsam,* obedience of the corpse). It had to reach the point at which the entire population was exposed to death. Exposing the entire population to universal death was the only way it could truly constitute itself as a superior race and bring about its definitive regeneration once other races had been either exterminated or enslaved forever."[6] What Mikhail Bulgakov said in *The Master and Margarita* in reference to the terror of Stalinism, that witchcraft once started becomes impossible to contain, is the perfect metaphor for all racial thinking: once unleashed it cannot be stopped. Grass refers to this notion of racism as a bottomless pit with the potential of swallowing also those who are not its original targets in the scene in which, instead of killing a Jew, Konrad kills a non-Jewish German.

The theme of racism has shifted from *Die Blechtrommel,* where in the form of Nazi eugenics one encounters the old state racism, to a different kind of racism in *Im Krebsgang,* racism as a social phenomenon begotten by a past that, according to Grass, is not sufficiently remembered. This new racism presented in Grass's latest novel, the neo-Nazism in contemporary Germany, nourishes itself on suppressed memories, the incapacity to mourn, and the silence and taboos surrounding topics like the sinking of the *Wilhelm Gustloff* and the massive loss of civilian life during the air raids. Grass's new book even sparked a debate in Germany as to whether there has been sufficient memory and mourning of the German victims of the Second World War, or whether silence has surrounded the atrocities committed on refugees escaping from the east, the terror of the bombing of all major German cities, and the so-called collateral damage caused by these bombings. Celebrated not only in Germany but also in the English-speaking world, this book's success is no doubt due to its theme, the loss of innocent lives during war, a timely topic in view of the hundreds of innocent civilians who died in Iraq in 2003.

Grass is not alone among German writers in arguing that Germans have repressed the collective memory of their own victimization. W. G. Sebald (1944–2001) has addressed this theme in his writings, particularly in *Luftkrieg und Literatur* (Aerial Warfare and Literature, 1999), a book based on his 1997 *Poetikvorlesungen* (writer-in-residence lectures) at the University of Zürich. During the air raids and the fire bombings, he says, Germans were so traumatized that at first they looked away and in the midst of all the rubble went about their daily business of cleaning up and tending to their gardens rather than mourning their losses: "Die Fähigkeit der Menschen, zu vergessen, was sie nicht wollen, hinwegzusehen über das, was vor ihren Augen liegt, wurde selten auf eine bessere Probe gestellt als damals in Deutschland." (The ability of people to forget what they do not wish to remember, to look away from what is happening directly before them, was rarely more challenged than in Germany at that time).[7] He argues that with only a few exceptions — Heinrich Böll, Hermann Kasak, Hans Erich Nossack and Peter de Mendelssohn — German literature that appeared immediately after the war reflected this general amnesia that surrounded the Allied bombings of German cities.[8] Even later on, German literature tended to ignore this theme. Once again there were exceptions like Alexander Kluge and Hubert Fichte, but overall German writers cloaked themselves in complete silence or at best employed a language that does not do justice to the traumatic experiences that Germans lived through.[9]

Yet Sebald and Grass differ in their discussion of German victims. While Sebald talks about the victims of the saturation bombings, a theme that may indeed have received little attention in public memory, Grass's book goes beyond this not only in making thematic the sinking of the ship but also by picking up where *Die Blechtrommel* left off; for another central theme that ties *Im Krebsgang* to *Die Blechtrommel*, in addition to the theme of racism, is that of migration, both books' representation of the exodus of German refugees from the lost homelands in Eastern Europe. Salman Rushdie suggested that Grass is a figure of central importance in the literature of migration, and that the migrant is quite possibly the defining figure of the twentieth century.[10] In his provocative article Robert Moeller then pointed out that not only could the Danzig trilogy and *Im Krebsgang* be seen as a forming a thematic quartet, but also that Grass's novella illuminates the suffering of fourteen million East Prussians, Pomeranians and Silesians who lost their homes between 1944 and 1947, and of whom perhaps up to two million died.[11] Moeller argues, however, that Grass's view of the history of Germany's remembrance of the war crimes and its victims is not complete and says that "if anything, West Germany was filled with too many memories, not too few."[12] Moeller insists that the victims of Germans and the German victims have always competed for space in public memory and that postwar Germany did indeed publicly remember the German war victims in the form of historical and sociological accounts, and primarily through initiatives coming from the Adenauer government. Especially in East Germany, the Germans' expulsion from the regions east of the Oder-Neisse line never faded from people's memory.

The question is not whether these events were remembered but how they were remembered. The theme of German suffering during and after the war, Moeller demonstrates, can be found in an abundance of film material, including the sinking of the *Gustloff* in Frank Wisbar's 1959 movie *Nacht fiel über Gotenhafen* (Night Fell over Gotenhafen), various films in which the expulsion from the east became thematic, like Hans Deppe's *Grün ist die Heide* (The Heath is Green, 1951), and Helma Sanders-Brahms's *Deutschland, Bleiche Mutter* (Germany, Pale Mother, 1979), a movie about the plight of German women raped by Russian soldiers and suffering from their traumatized husbands returning from the war. In the *belles lettres*, however, there has until recently been the sort of silence about German victims that also surrounds the Holocaust. While stories of the suffering of German expellees like Hans-Ulrich Treichel's *Der Verlorene* (The Lost Son, 1998) may be less risky,[13] only Walter Kempowski in *Das Echolot: Fuga furiosa* (The Echo Sound, 1999) dares to undertake what Grass does in *Im Krebsgang*, namely to make Jews and Germans appear as the victims of one drama, for in Wolfgang Stremplin the positions of Germans as victims and Jews as victims are ultimately merged.

Ernestine Schlant's comments regarding a language of silence employed by West German authors addressing the Holocaust thus also have their validity for the fictionalization of other chapters of the German past. Critical minds might even argue that its form of representation — Grass's use of popular culture as metaphorical language — turns *Die Blechtrommel* into a work of fiction that engages in a language of silence. They might also argue that because of its direct and nonmetaphorical engagement with the German past *Im Krebsgang* breaks this silence more radically than Grass's grotesque first novel and therefore contributes more effectively to Germany's *Vergangenheitsbewältigung*. Grass himself keeps insisting that the past cannot be mastered, but that German novelists have the responsibility to work with this past. The difference between working *with* rather than *through* the past is not a subtle one, since working *through* it, a term used in trauma studies, would be reminiscent of the unfortunately termed process of *Vergangenheitsbewältigung*. Mastering the German past would entail that the Nazi crimes can be worked through to the point that they dissolve in everyone's consciousness, truly a monstrous thought. The young Grass of *Die Blechtrommel* already seems to understand this when he says "nichts ist vorbei, alles kommt wieder"(*B*, 392; "nothing is ended, everything returns": *TD*, 473). Possibly a more suitable term than *Vergangenheitsbewältigung* — which one might associate with *Gewalt*, that is, with violently wanting to make the past disappear — would be *Vergangenheitsbeschäftigung*, dealing with the past. This *Vergangenheitsbeschäftigung* ought to make room also for irrational reactions to traumatic "final solutions" like euthanasia or the Holocaust. Allowing for humor in representations of such events is a concession to the healing quality of the grotesque. As a carnivalesque attempt to act out the German past, *Die Blechtrommel* may indeed have a healing function for the author and its readers in helping them deal with their own trauma induced by this past. Chapter 5 of this study has shown that one of the many functions of the trickster is to challenge his society into rethinking its accepted ways. For German society in the 1950s and 1960s, which was in need of accepting its irrational past rather than burying it under the guise of rationalism, *Vergangenheitsbeschäftigung* by means of Grass's first novel had the potential of a kind of carnivalesque renewal.

Im Krebsgang suggests that mastering the German past would also imply the danger of its reoccurrence and that German novelists have the responsibility to continue writing the fictional historiography of the Third Reich, for as long as all of its stories are not told, the danger of repression impends and may result in renewed racial violence. The racism now, the book implies, is largely the result of untold stories, of a limited remembrance of the Nazi past, and a lack of mourning. What the Mitscherlichs once described as the Germans' inability to mourn[14] is already a theme in *Die Blechtrommel*, where Germans are shown as incapable of crying other than with the help of onions. Ironically, it is Oskar, the potential euthanasia victim, who helps the Germans mourn. Mourning in *Die Blechtrommel* is, however, never free from the notion of collective guilt. *Im Krebsgang* expands on this *Trauerarbeit* by suggesting that mourning the past is not complete until all its victims have been mourned, and that the uncritical left-wing appropriation of Auschwitz as a formula that makes the memory of German victims taboo ultimately results in the extremism of the new generations. What is repressed or not remembered by the parent generation returns in the form of an over-reaction in the children, as either Konrad's neo-Nazism or Wolfgang's philo-Semitism. Stephan Braese has argued convincingly that the principal theme of Grass's book is ultimately the trans-generational conflict and not the sinking of the ship. The parents' repression of history, their neglected trauma, results in their children's acting out history. The final line of this book "[das] hört nicht auf. Nie hört das auf"[15] (this will never end. It will never end) seems to echo the Freudian notion of the "return of the repressed" invoked in the above-quoted line from *Die Blechtrommel*, "nichts ist vorbei, alles kommt wieder." In the turn-of-the-millennium context that *Im Krebsgang* addresses, however, this ending transcends the earlier message and carries an additional meaning. Not only does it express a sigh of relief that working with the past should never end, but it also implies a sigh of grief that racism and Nazism do not end, for when Konrad is incarcerated for the murder of David/Wolfgang, he is celebrated in yet another, newly created neo-Nazi Web site.

Almost fifty years lie between Grass's first and latest novel. In fictionalizing the tragedy of the *Wilhelm Gustloff* and the fate of German expellees from the east, *Im Krebsgang* triggers memories more forcefully than any other of Grass's previous books. And yet the two books conjoin in their attempt to effect honesty and wholeheartedness in the responses of Germans to the Nazi years. As much as *Die Blechtrommel* pointed to the danger of an uncritical embrace of rationalism while suppressing irrationalism, *Im Krebsgang* now warns against a one-sidedness of memory and mourning. While Oskar's deformed body was a metaphor for Germany's emergence from the Nazi years as a nation crippled by collective guilt, and the thirty-two-year-old Grass offered us ample parody and irony concerning the German past, in *Im Krebsgang* the seventy-five-year-old Grass now points to further remedies that will ultimately help Germany, crippled by its own past, to grow up.

Notes

[1] Hannah Arendt, ed., *Walter Benjamin: Illuminations* (New York: Schocken, 1968), 6.

[2] Irving Wohlfahrt, "Männer aus der Fremde: Walter Benjamin and the German-Jewish Parnassus," *New German Critique,* Winter 97 (v. 70): 60.

[3] Wohlfahrt, "Männer aus der Fremde," 65.

[4] Günter Grass, *The Rat,* trans. Ralph Manheim (Orlando: Harcourt Brace & Company, 1987), 41.

[5] Zygmunt Bauman, *Modernity and the Holocaust* (Ithaca NY: Cornell UP, 1989), 90.

[6] Michel Foucault, *Society must be defended: Lectures at the Collège de France 1975–1976* (New York: Picador, 2003), 259–60.

[7] W. G. Sebald, *Luftkrieg und Literatur* (Frankfurt am Main: Fischer, 2001), 47.

[8] Sebald, *Luftkrieg und Literatur,* 52. The bombing war is also a central theme in recent historiography, as in Jörg Friedrich's *Der Brand: Deutschland im Bombenkrieg 1940–1945* (Munich: Propyläen, 2002).

[9] One of the authors whom Sebald mentions in connection with this nonrepresentational language is Arno Schmidt, who in approaching the topic of German trauma hides behind his characteristic "linguistische Laubsägearbeit" (linguistic fretsaw work): Sebald, *Luftkrieg und Literatur,* 64.

[10] Salman Rushdie, *Imaginary Homelands: Essays and Criticism 1981–1991* (London: Penguin, 1991), 277.

[11] Robert Moeller, "Sinking Ships, the Lost Heimat, and Broken Taboos: Günter Grass and the Politics of Memory in Contemporary Germany," *Contemporary European History* 12.2 (2003): 150 and 151.

[12] Moeller, "Sinking Ships," 159.

[13] Cf. Stephan Braese's article on Treichel and Grass: "'Tote zahlen keine Steuern': Flucht und Vertreibung in Günter Grass' *Im Krebsgang* und Hans-Ulrich Treichels *Der Verlorene,*" in *Gegenwartsliteratur* 2 (2003), ed. Paul Michael Lützeler, 171–97.

[14] Alexander Mitscherlich und Margarete Mitscherlich, *The Inability to Mourn: Principles of Collective Behavior,* trans. Beverley R. Placzek (New York: Grove, 1975).

[15] Günter Grass, *Im Krebsgang* (Göttingen: Steidl, 2002), 216.

Works Cited

Primary Sources

Benjamin, Walter. *Illuminations: Essays and Reflections.* Edited by Hannah Arendt. New York: Schocken, 1969.

Goethe, Johann Wolfgang von. *The Auto-Biography of Goethe: Truth and Poetry: From My Own Life.* Translated by John Oxenford. London: Bell & Daldy, 1867.

———.*Dichtung und Wahrheit.* Frankfurt am Main: Insel, 1975.

Grass, Günter. *Die Blechtrommel.* Darmstadt: Luchterhand, 1986.

———. *Essays und Reden* I. Göttingen: Steidl, 1997.

———. *Im Krebsgang.* Göttingen: Steidl, 2002.

———. *The Rat.* Translated by Ralph Manheim. Orlando: Harcourt Brace & Company, 1987.

———. *The Tin Drum.* Translated by Ralph Manheim. New York: Vintage, 1990.

Grass, Günter, and Harro Zimmermann. *Vom Abenteuer der Aufklärung: Werkstattgespräche.* Göttingen: Steidl, 1999.

Grimm, Jacob, and Wilhelm Grimm. *The Complete Fairy Tales of the Brothers Grimm.* Edited by Jack Zipes. New York: Bantam, 1987.

———. *Kinder- und Hausmärchen.* Vol. 1 and 2. Edited by Heinz Rölleke. Stuttgart: Reclam, 1980.

Grimmelshausen, Johann Jakob. *Der abenteuerliche Simplicissimus.* Frankfurt am Main: Fischer, 1962.

———. *Simplicissimus.* Translated by Mike Mitchell. Sawtry: Dedalus, 1999.

Hauff, Wilhelm. *Sämtliche Märchen.* Edited by Hans-Heino Ewers. Stuttgart: Reclam, 1986.

———. *Tales.* Translated by S. Mendel. Freeport, New York: Books for Library Press, 1970.

Heine, Heinrich. *Heines Werke.* Herausgegeben von den Nationalen Forschungs- und Gedenkstätten der Klassischen Deutschen Literatur in Weimar. Berlin/Weimar: Aufbau Verlag, 1986.

Hilsenrath, Edgar. *Der Nazi und der Friseur.* Munich: Piper, 1990.

Lagerqvist, Pär. *The Dwarf.* Translated by Alexandra Dick. New York: Hill and Wang, 1973.

Mann, Thomas. *Confessions of Felix Krull: Confidence Man.* Translated by Denver Lindley. New York: Alfred A. Knopf, 1955.

———. *Der Zauberberg.* Frankfurt am Main: Fischer, 1952.

Mawer, Simon. *Mendel's Dwarf.* New York: Harmony Books, 1998.

Nietzsche, Friedrich. *Beyond Good and Evil: Prelude to a Philosophy of the Future.* Translated by Walter Kaufman. New York: Random House, 1966.

———. *The Birth of the Tragedy.* Edited by Raymond Geuss and Ronald Speirs. Cambridge: Cambridge UP, 1999.

Raabe, Wilhelm. *Der Hungerpastor.* Göttingen: Vandenhoeck & Ruprecht, 1966.

Rabelais, François. *Gargantua and Pantagruel.* Translated by J. M. Cohen. Harmondsworth: Penguin, 1955.

Rushdie, Salman. *Imaginary Homelands: Essays and Criticism 1981–1991.* London: Penguin, 1991.

———. *Midnight's Children.* New York: Alfred A. Knopf, 1995.

Schmidt, Arno. *Das steinerne Herz.* Zürich: Haffmans Verlag, 1986.

Sebald, W. G. *Luftkrieg und Literatur.* Frankfurt am Main: Fischer, 2001.

Tournier, Michel. *The Ogre.* Translated by Barbara Bray. Baltimore: The Johns Hopkins UP, 1997.

Walser, Martin. *Über Deutschland reden.* Frankfurt: Suhrkamp, 1988.

Secondary Sources

Aarne, Antii, and Stith Thompson. "The Types of the Folktale: A Classification and Bibliography." In: *The Classic Fairy Tales.* Edited by Maria Tatar. New York: Norton & Company, 1999. 373–378.

Aley, Peter. *Jugendliteratur im Dritten Reich: Dokumente und Kommentare.* Hamburg: Verlag für Buchmarktforschung, 1967.

Arker, Dieter. *Nichts ist vorbei, alles kommt wieder: Untersuchungen zu Günter Grass' Die Blechtrommel.* Heidelberg: Winter, 1989.

Bader, Rudolf. "Indian Tin Drum." *The International Fiction Review.* 11.2 (1984): 75–83.

Bagioli, Mario. "Science, Modernity, and the 'Final Solution.'" *Probing the Limits of Representation: Nazism and the "Final Solution."* Edited by Saul Friedlander. Cambridge, MA: Harvard UP, 1992.

Baigent, Michael, and Richard Leigh. *Secret Germany: Stauffenberg and the Mystical Crusade against Hitler.* London: Penguin, 1994.

Bakhtin, Mikhail. "The *Bildungsroman* and its Significance in the History of Realism (Toward a Historical Typology of the Novel)." *Speech Genres and Other Late Essays.* Edited by Caryl Emerson and Michael Holquist. Austin: U of Texas P, 1986.

———. *The Dialogic Imagination: Four Essays by M. M. Bakhtin.* Edited by Caryl Emerson and Michael Holquist. Austin: U of Texas P, 1981.

———. *Problems of Dostoevsky's Poetics.* Edited and translated by Caryl Emerson. Minneapolis: U of Minnesota P, 1984.

———. *Rabelais and his World.* Translated by Hélène Iswolsky. Bloomington: Indiana UP, 1984.

Bastian, Ulrike. *Die "Kinder- und Hausmärchen" der Brüder Grimm in der literaturpädagogischen Diskussion des 19. und 20. Jahrhunderts.* Frankfurt am Main: Haag & Herchen, 1981.

Bauman, Zygmunt. *Modernity and the Holocaust.* Ithaca NY: Cornell UP, 1989.

Berrong, Richard. *Rabelais and Bakhtin: Popular Culture in* Gargantua and Pantagruel. Lincoln: U of Nebraska P, 1986.

Bollenbeck, Georg. "German 'Kultur,' the 'Bildungsbürgertum,' and its Susceptibility to National Socialism." *The German Quarterly.* 73.1 (Winter 2000): 67–83.

Boym, Svetlana. "Paradoxes of Unified Culture: From Stalin's Fairy Tale to Molotov's Lacquer Box." *The South Atlantic Quarterly.* 94:3 (Summer 1995): 821–36.

Braese, Stephan. "Tote zahlen keine Steuern": Flucht und Vertreibung in Günter Grass' *Im Krebsgang* und Hans-Ulrich Treichels *Der Verlorene.* In *Gegenwartsliteratur* 2 (2003): 171–97.

Brode, Hanspeter. *Günter Grass.* Munich: C. H. Beck, 1979.

Broszat, Martin. "Rotkäppchen vor vierzig Jahren: Zur politischen Satire im dritten Reich." *Süddeutsche Zeitung.* 20 February 1977. 79.

Burke, Peter. *Popular Culture in Early Modern Europe.* New York: NYU P, 1978.

Clark, Katerina, and Michael Holquist. *Mikhail Bakhtin.* Cambridge, MA: Harvard UP, 1984.

Couto, Mario. "'Midnight's Children' and Parents. The Search for Indo-British Identity" *Encounter.* Vol. 58.2 (1982). 61–66.

Denkler, Horst. "Das 'wirckliche Juda' und der 'Renegat': Moses Freudenstein als Kronzeuge für Wilhelm Raabes Verhältnis zu Juden und Judentum." *The German Quarterly.* 60.1 (Winter 1987): 5–18.

Dentith, Simon. *Bakhtinian Thought: An Introductory Reader.* New York: Routledge, 1995.

Des Pres, Terrence. *Writing into the World: Essays, 1973–1987.* New York: Viking Penguin, 1991. Esp. 161–174 and 277–286.

Diederichs, Rainer. *Strukturen des Schelmischen im modernen deutschen Roman: Eine Untersuchung an den Romanen von Thomas Mann 'Bekenntnisse des Hochstaplers Felix Krull' und Günter Grass 'Die Blechtrommel.'* Jena: Eugen Diederichs, 1971.

Donahue, Bruce. "The Alternative to Goethe: Markus and Fajngold in 'Die Blechtrommel.'" *The Germanic Review.* 58, 3 (1983): 115–120.

Durzak, Manfred. "Es war einmal. Zur Märchen-Struktur des Erzählens bei Günter Grass." Ed. Manfred Durzak. *Zu Günter Grass. Geschichte auf dem poetischen Prüfstand.* Stuttgart: Metzler, 1985. 166–77.

Emrich, Wilhelm. *Deutsche Literatur der Barockzeit.* Königstein: Athenäum, 1981. 227–256.

Engel, Henrik D. K. *Die Prosa von Günter Grass in Beziehung zur englischsprachigen Literatur: Rezeption, Wirkungen und Rückwirkungen bei Salmon Rushdie, John Irving, Bernard Malamud u.a.* New York: Peter Lang, 1997.

Erdoes, Richard, and Alfonso Ortiz. *American Indian Trickster Tales.* London: Penguin, 1998.

Feingold, Michael. "A different drummer." *Village Voice.* 42.32 (1997): 83.

Foucault, Michel. *Discipline and Punish: The Birth of the Prison.* Translated by Alan Sheridan. New York: Random House, 1995.

———. *Madness and Civilization.* Translated by Richard Howard. New York: Random House, 1988.

———. *Society Must Be Defended: Lectures at the Collège de France 1975–1976.* Ed. Mauro Bertani and Alessandro Fontana. Translated by David Macey. New York: Picador, 2003.

Franke, Reinhold. "Das Märchen vom Däumling in deutscher und französischer Sprache." *Jugendschriftenwarte.* 43.11 (1938): 21–25.

Friedlander, Henry. *The Origins of Nazi Genocide: From Euthanasia to the Final Solution.* Chapel Hill: U of North Carolina P, 1995.

Friedlander, Saul, ed. *Probing the Limits of Representation: Nazism and the "Final Solution."* Cambridge, MA: Harvard UP, 1992.

Frizen, W. "Matzeraths Wohnung. Raum und Weltraum in Günter Grass' 'Die Blechtrommel.' *Text & Kontext.* 15 (1987): 145–74.

Führer, Maria. *Nordgermanische Götterüberlieferung und deutsches Volksmärchen: 80 Märchen der Brüder Grimm vom Mythus her beleuchtet.* Munich: Neuer Filser-Verlag, 1938.

Gaede, Friedrich. "Grimmelshausen, Brecht, Grass. Zur Tradition des literarischen Realismus in Deutschland." *Simpliciana. Schriften der Grimmelshausen-Gesellschaft* 1 (1979): 367–382.

Gandhi, Leela. *Postcolonial Theory: A Critical Introduction.* New York: Columbia UP, 1998.

Gerber, Hans Erhard. *Nietzsche und Goethe: Studien zu einem Vergleich.* Bern: Paul Haupt, 1970.

Glass, James M. *Life Unworthy of Life: Racial Phobia and Mass Murder in Hitler's Germany.* New York: Harper Collins, 1997.

Gopal, Raj. "Saleem Snotnose und Oskar der Blechtrommler. Zum Vergleich von Günter Grass und Salmon Rushdie." *German Studies in India.* Trivandrum: University of Kerala, 1983.

Grau, Günter, ed. *Homosexualität in der NS-Zeit: Dokumente einer Diskriminierung und Verfolgung.* Frankfurt am Main: Fischer, 1993.

Green, Martin, and John Swan, *The Triumph of Pierrot.* University Park: Pennsylvania State UP, 1986.

Greenway, John. *The Primitive Reader: An Anthology of Myths, Tales, Songs, Riddles and Proverbs of Aboriginal Peoples around the World.* Hatboro: Folklore Associates, 1965.

Guidry, Glenn. "Theoretical Reflections on the Ideological and Social Implications of Mythic Form in Grass' *Die Blechtrommel.*" *Monatshefte.* 83.2 (1991): 127–146.

Guillén, Claudio. "Toward a Definition of the Picaresque." *Literature as System.* Princeton: Princeton UP, 1971.

Hamelmann, Berthold. *Helau und Heil Hitler: Alltagsgeschichte der Fasnacht 1919–1939 am Beispiel der Stadt Freiburg.* Eggingen: Edition Isele, 1989.

Haug, Wolfgang Fritz. *Die Faschisierung des bürgerlichen Subjekts, Die Ideologie der gesunden Normalität und die Ausrottungspolitiken im deutschen Faschismus.* Hamburg: Materialienanalysen, 1987.

Hausmann, Frank-Rutger. *François Rabelais.* Stuttgart: Metzler, 1979.

Hegel, Georg Wilhelm Friedrich. *Phänomenoligie des Geistes.* Frankfurt am Main: Suhrkamp, 1970.

———. *Vorlesungen über die Ästhetik.* Ed. Rüdiger Bubner. Stuttgart: Reclam, 1971.

Herd, E. W. "Tin Drum and Snake-Charmer's Flute: Salmon Rushdie's Debt to Günter Grass." *New Comparison.* 6 (1989): 205–18.

Herf, Jeffrey. "Multiple Restorations: German Political Traditions and the Interpretation of Nazism, 1945–1946." *Central European History* 26.1 (1993): 21–55.

———. *Reactionary Modernism: Technology, Culture, and Politics in Weimar and the Third Reich.* Cambridge: Cambridge UP, 1984.

Hitler, Adolf. *Mein Kampf.* Translated by Ralph Manheim. Boston: Houghton Mifflin, 1943.

Höhn, Maria. "Frau im Haus und Girl im Discourse on Women in the Interregnum Period of 1945–1949 and the Question of German Identity." *Central European History.* 26.1 (1993): 57–90.

Höppner, Wolfgang. "'Der Kampf um das neue Goethe-Bild.' Zur Goethe-Rezeption in der Berliner Germanistik des Dritten Reiches." *Goethe: Vorgaben. Zugänge. Wirkungen.* Ed. by Wolfgang Stellmacher and László Tarnói. Frankfurt am Main: Peter Lang, 2000.

Hoffmeister, Gerhardt, ed. *Der moderne deutsche Schelmenroman. Interpretationen.* Amsterdam: Rodopi, 1985/86.

Howell, Dana Prescott. *The Development of Soviet Folkloristics.* New York: Garland, 1992.

Hyde, Lewis. *Trickster Makes this World.* New York: North Point Press, 1998.

Hynes, William J., and William G. Doty, eds. *Mythical Trickster Figures: Contours, Contexts, and Criticisms.* Tuscaloosa: The U of Alabama P, 1992.

Jacobs, Jürgen. *Der deutsche Schelmenroman: Eine Einführung.* Munich/Zürich: Artemis, 1983.

Jahnke, Walter, and Klaus Lindemann. *Günter Grass: Die Blechtrommel.* Paderborn, Munich, Vienna, Zürich: Schöningh, 1993.

Janik, Vicki K., ed. *Fools and Jesters in Literature, Art, and History. A Bio-Bibliographical Sourcebook.* Westport: Greenwood Press, 1998. Esp. 33–40, 146–168, 336–342, and 370–375.

Jung, C. G. *The Archetypes and the Collective Unconscious.* Translated by R. F. C. Hull. Princeton: Princeton UP, 1969.

———. *Psychology and Alchemy.* Translated by R. F. C. Hull. Princeton: Princeton UP, 1968.

Kade-Luthra, Veena, ed. *Sehnsucht nach Indien: Ein Lesebuch von Goethe bis Grass.* Munich: C.H. Beck, 1993.

Kaltenecker, Siegfried. "Weil aber die vergessenste Fremde unser Körper ist: Über Männer-Körper Repräsentationen und Faschismus." *The Body of Gender, Körper, Geschlechter, Identitäten.* Ed. Marie-Luise Angerer. Vienna: Passagen Verlag, 1995. 91–109.

Kamenetsky, Christa. *The Brothers Grimm and their Critics: Folktales and the Quest for Meaning.* Athens: Ohio UP, 1992.

———. *Children's Literature in Hitler's Germany: The Cultural Policy of National Socialism.* Athens: Ohio UP, 1984.

———. "Folklore as a Political Tool in Nazi Germany." *Journal of American Folklore.* 85 (1972): 221–35.

———. "Folktale and Ideology in the Third Reich." *Journal of American Folklore.* 90 (1977): 168–78.

Klee, Ernst, ed. *'Euthanasie' im NS-Staat: Die 'Vernichtung unwerten Lebens.'* Frankfurt/Main: Fischer, 1989.

Klein, Alan M. *Little Big Men: Bodybuilding Subculture and Gender Construction.* Albany: State U of New York P, 1993.

Köttgen, Gerhard. *Wilhelm Raabes Ringen um die Aufgabe des Erziehungsromans,* Berlin: Verlag Dr. Emil Ebering, 1939.

Kristeva, Julia. *Strangers to Ourselves.* Translated by Leon S. Roudiez. New York: Columbia UP 1991.

Krumme, Detlef. *Günter Grass: Die Blechtrommel.* Munich: Hanser, 1986.

Lawner, Lynne. *Harlequin on the Moon: Commedia dell'Arte and the Visual Arts.* New York: Harry N. Abrams, Inc., 1998.

Leblans, Anne. "Grimmelshausen and the Carnivalesque: The Polarization of Courtly and Popular Carnival in *Der abenteuerliche Simplicissimus.*" *Modern Language Notes* 105/3 (April 1990): 500.

Lewy, Guenter. *The Catholic Church and Nazi Germany.* New York: Da Capo Press, 2000, originally published in 1964.

Lifton, Robert Jay. *The Nazi Doctors: Medical Killing and the Psychology of Genocide.* New York: Basic Books, 1986.

Lixfeld, Hannjost. *Folklore and Fascism: The Reich Institute for German Volkskunde.* Ed. and trans. James R. Dow. Bloomington: Indiana UP, 1994.

Loewenstern, Otto von. "Der Blechtrommler in der Käsestadt: Wie ein Vollstreckungsrichter die Bekanntschaft von Oskar Matzerath machte." *Die Zeit.* 23, 7 June 1963, 49–50.

Lütjens, August. *Der Zwerg in der deutschen Heldendichtung des Mittelalters.* Breslau: M.& H. Marcus, 1911.

Lukács, Georg. *Theorie des Romans.* Neuwied am Rhein: Luchterhand, 1963.

———. *Theory of the Novel.* Translated by Anna Bostosck. Cambridge, MA: M.I.T. Press, 1971.

Mayer, Gerhard. "Zum deutschen Antibildungsroman." *Jahrbuch der Raabe-Gesellschaft.* Braunschweig, Germany, 1974. 55–64.

McGee, Robert W. "If dwarf-tossing is outlawed, only outlaws will toss dwarves: is dwarf tossing a victimless crime?" *The American Journal of Jurisprudence.* 38 (1993): 335–58.

Meid, Volker. *Grimmelshausen: Epoche, Werk, Wirkung.* Munich: Beck, 1984.

Merivale, Patricia. "Saleem Fathered by Oskar: Intertextual Strategies in 'Midnight's Children' and 'The Tin Drum.'" *Ariel: A Review of International English Literature.* 21.3 (1990): 5–21.

Miles, David H. "Kafka's Hapless Pilgrims and Grass's Scurrilous Dwarf: Notes on Representative Figures in the Anti-Bildungsroman." *Monatshefte.* 65 (1973): 341–50.

Miller, Frank J. *Folklore for Stalin: Russian Folklore and Pseudofolklore of the Stalin Era.* New York: M.E. Sharpe, 1990.

Mitscherlich, Alexander, and Margarete Mitscherlich. *The Inability to Mourn. Principles of Collective Behavior.* Translated by Beverly R. Placzek. New York: Grove Press, 1975.

Moeller, Robert. *Protecting Motherhood: Women and the Family in the Politics of Postwar Germany.* Berkeley: California UP, 1993.

———. "Reconstructing the Family in Reconstruction Germany: Women and Social Policy in the Federal Republic, 1949–1955." *Feminist Studies* 15 (1989): 137–169.

———. "Sinking Ships, the Lost Heimat, and Broken Taboos: Günter Grass and the Politics of Memory in Contemporary Germany." *Contemporary European History* 12.2 (2003): 147–181.

Money, John. *The Kaspar Hauser Syndrome of 'Psychosocial Dwarfism.'* Buffalo: Prometheus Books, 1992.

Morson, Gary Saul and Caryl Emerson. *Mikhael Bakhtin: Creation of a Prosaics.* Stanford: Stanford UP, 1990.

Mourey, Lilyane. *Grimm et Perrault: histoire, structure mise en texte des contes.* Paris: Lettres Modernes, 1978.

Mouton, Janice. "Gnomes, Fairy-Tale Heroes, and Oskar Matzerath." *The Germanic Review.* 56.1 (1981): 28–33.

Nairn, Tom. *The Break-Up of Britain: Crisis and Neo-Nationalism.* London: New Left Books, 1977.

Neuhaus, Volker. *Günter Grass.* Stuttgart: Metzler, 1992.

———. *Günter Grass: Die Blechtrommel.* Munich: Oldenbourg Verlag, 1982.

Nyiszli, Miklos. *Auschwitz: A Doctor's Eyewitness Account.* New York: Frederick Fell, 1960.

Oreglia, Giacomo. *The Commedia dell'Arte.* New York: Hill and Wang, 1968.

Petzel, Jörg. "E.T.A. Hoffmann und Arno Schmidt." *Mitteilungen der E. T. A. Hoffmann Gesellschaft.* 26 (1980): 88–98.

Pfister, Manfred. "Konzepte der Intertextualität." *Intertextualität. Formen, Funktionen, anglistische Fallstudien.* Ed. Ulrich Broich und Manfred Pfister. Tübingen: Niemeyer, 1985. 1–30.

Proctor, Robert N. *Racial Hygiene: Medicine under the Nazis.* Cambridge MA: Harvard UP, 1988.

Radin, Paul. *The Trickster: A Study in American Indian Mythology*. New York: Schocken Books, 1972.

Richter, Frank-Raymund. *Günter Grass: Die Vergangenheitsbewältigung in der Danzig-Trilogie*. Bonn: Bouvier, 1979.

Roberts, David. "Tom Thumb and the Imitation of Christ: Towards a Psycho-Mythological Interpretation of the 'Hero' Oskar and his Symbolic Function." *Proceedings and Papers of the Congress of the Australasian Universities Language and Literature Association*. Canberra, 1972. 160–74.

Robin, Régine. *Socialist Realism: An Impossible Aesthetic*. Stanford: Stanford UP, 1992.

Röder, Thomas, Volker Kubillus and Anthony Burwell. *Psychiatrists: The Men behind Hitler. The Architects of Horror*. Los Angeles: Freedom Publishing, 1995.

Röhrich, Lutz. *Gebärde — Metapher — Parodie: Studien zur Sprache und Volksdichtung*. Düsseldorf: Schwann, 1967.

Sammons, Jeffrey L. *The Shifting Fortunes of Wilhelm Raabe: a History of Criticism as a Cautionary Tale*. Columbia, SC: Camden House, 1992.

Sanders, Barry. *Sudden Glory: Laughter as Subversive History*. Boston: Beacon P, 1995.

Schlant, Ernestine. *The Language of Silence*. New York: Routledge, 1999.

Schleussner, Bruno. *Der neopikareske Roman: Pikareske Elemente in der Struktur moderner englischer Romane 1950–1960*. Bonn: Bouvier, 1969.

Schulz, Ulrike. *Gene mene muh raus mußt du: Eugenik von der Rassenhygiene zu den Gen- und Reproduktionstechnologien*. Munich: AG SPAK, 1992.

Schuster, Klaus Peter, ed. *Die 'Kunststadt' München 1937: Nationalsozialismus und 'Entartete Kunst.'* Munich: Prestel, 1988.

Schwartz, Jerome. *Irony and Ideology in Rabelais: Structures of Subversion*. Cambridge: Cambridge UP, 1990.

Sheppard, Richard. "Upstairs-Downstairs — Some Reflections on German Literature in the Light of Bakhtin's Theory of the Carnival." *New Ways in Germanistik*. Ed. Richard Sheppard. Oxford: Berg Publishers, 1990.

Spector, Robert D. *Pär Lagerqvist*. New York: Twayne Publishers, 1973.

Stallybrass, Peter, and Allon White. *The Politics and Poetics of Transgression*. Ithaca: Cornell UP, 1986.

Tatar, Maria, ed. *The Classic Fairy Tales*. New York: Norton & Company, 1999.

———. *The Hard Facts of the Grimms' Fairy Tales*. Princeton: Princeton UP, 1987.

Toporkov, Andrey. "'Rebaking' of Children in Eastern Slavic Rituals and Fairytales." *The Petersburg Journal of Cultural Studies*. I.3 (1993): 15–21.

Trappen, Stefan. *Grimmelshausen und die menippeische Satire: Eine Studie zu den historischen Voraussetzungen der Prosasatire im Barock.* Tübingen: Niemeyer, 1994.

Van Cleve, John Walter. *Harlequin Besieged: The Reception of Comedy in Germany during the Early Enlightenment.* Bern: Peter Lang, 1980.

Warneken, Jürgen. "Bürgerliche Emanzipation und aufrechter Gang, Zur Geschichte eines Handlungsideals." *Das Argument, Zeitschrift für Philosophie und Sozialwissenschaften.* 179 (1990): 39–52.

Welsford, Enid. *The Fool: His Social and Literary History.* New York: Farrar & Rinehart, 1935.

Weyrather, Irmgard. *Muttertag und Mutterkreuz: Der Kult um die deutsche Mutter im Nationalsozialismus.* Frankfurt am Main: Fischer, 1993.

Wildmann, Daniel. *Begehrte Körper: Konstruktion und Inszenierung des 'arischen' Männerkörpers im 'Dritten Reich.'* Würzburg: Königshausen & Neumann, 1998.

Williams, Paul, ed. *The Fool and the Trickster: Studies in Honor of Enid Welsford.* Totowa: Rowman and Littlefield, 1979.

Wohlfahrt, Irving. "Männer aus der Fremde: Walter Benjamin and the German-Jewish Parnassus," *New German Critique.* 70 (Winter 97): 3–85.

Wolbert, Klaus. *Die Nackten und die Toten des Dritten Reiches.* Giessen: Anabas, 1982.

Yahil, Leni. *The Holocaust: The Fate of European Jewry.* Oxford: Oxford UP, 1987.

Zimmermann, Harro, and Günter Grass. *Vom Abenteuer der Aufklärung. Werkstattgespräche.* Göttingen: Steidl, 1999.

Zimmermann, Michael. *Rassenutopie und Genozid: Die nationalsozialistische 'Lösung der Zigeunerfrage.'* Hamburg: Christians, 1996.

Zipes. Jack. "The Struggle for the Grimms' Throne: The Legacy of the Grimms' Tales in the FRG and GDR since 1945." In: *The Reception of Grimms' Fairy Tales: Responses, Reactions, Revisions.* Ed. Donald Haase. Detroit: Wayne State UP, 1993.

———, ed. and trans. *Beauty and the Beast.* New York: Signet Classics, 1989.

———, ed. and trans. *The Complete Fairy Tales of the Brothers Grimm.* New York: Bantham, 1987.

———, ed. and trans. *Fairy Tales and Fables from Weimar Days.* Hanover and London: UP of New England, 1989.

Index